A Century of Boxing Greats

A Century of Boxing Greats

Inside the Ring with the Hundred Best Boxers

Patrick Myler

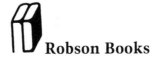
Robson Books

Published in paperback in 1999 by Robson Books,
10 Blenheim Court, Brewery Road, London N7 9WT

First published in Great Britain in 1997 by Robson Books Ltd.

British Library Cataloguing in Publication Data
A catalogue record for this title is available from the British
Library
ISBN 1 86105 258 8

Typeset in Plantin by FSH Ltd.
Printed in Great Britain by St Edmundsbury Press, Bury St
Edmunds, Suffolk.

To the memory of my parents, Patrick and Ellen, the first to indulge my passion for this crazy, wonderful, game

Contents

Introduction	xi
Muhammad Ali	1
Alexis Arguello	6
Henry Armstrong	9
Abe Attell	12
Carmen Basilio	15
Wilfred Benitez	19
Nigel Benn	22
Nino Benvenuti	27
Jack 'Kid' Berg	32
Jack Britton	35
Panama Al Brown	38
Joe Brown	41
Ken Buchanan	44
Tony Canzoneri	49
Georges Carpentier	51
Marcel Cerdan	56
Ezzard Charles	59
Julio Cesar Chavez	64
Kid Chocolate	69
John Conteh	72
Don Curry	76

Oscar De La Hoya	79
Jack Dempsey	84
Jim Driscoll	89
Johnny Dundee	92
Roberto Duran	95
Jeff Fenech	101
Bob Fitzsimmons	103
George Foreman	108
Bob Foster	112
Joe Frazier	115
Khaosai Galaxy	120
Joe Gans	122
Wilfredo Gomez	125
Harry Greb	128
Emile Griffith	131
Marvin Hagler	135
Naseem Hamed	139
Len Harvey	145
Thomas Hearns	150
Larry Holmes	154
Evander Holyfield	159
Julian Jackson	164
James J. Jeffries	168
Eder Jofre	173
Jack Johnson	176
Roy Jones Junior	181
Peter Kane	185
Stanley Ketchell	189
Jake LaMotta	194
Sam Langford	200
Benny Leonard	204
Sugar Ray Leonard	207
Ted 'Kid' Lewis	214
Sonny Liston	221
Dulio Loi	227
Ricardo Lopez	230

Tommy Loughran	233
Joe Louis	236
Benny Lynch	243
Rocky Marciano	246
Jock McAvoy	252
Mike McCallum	256
Terry McGovern	259
Barry McGuigan	262
Jimmy McLarnin	267
Freddie Miller	271
Carlos Monzon	274
Archie Moore	277
Jose Napoles	281
Azumah Nelson	284
Battling Nelson	287
Ruben Olivares	290
Carlos Ortiz	292
Manuel Ortiz	294
Floyd Patterson	297
Eusebio Pedroza	301
Willie Pep	303
Pascual Perez	307
Aaron Pryor	309
Sugar Ray Robinson	312
Barney Ross	318
Sandy Saddler	321
Vicente Saldivar	324
Salvador Sanchez	327
Max Schmeling	330
Michael Spinks	335
Dick Tiger	338
Gene Tunney	342
Randolph Turpin	347
Mike Tyson	353
Pancho Villa	359
Joe Walcott	361

Jersey Joe Walcott   364
Mickey Walker   369
Pernell Whitaker   373
Jimmy Wilde   378
Ike Williams   383
Ad Wolgast   386
Carlos Zarate   389
Author's Top Ten   392
Acknowledgements and Bibliography   393

Introduction

Boxing fans, let us suspend reality for a moment.

Imagine a place where all the great fighters since the sport's inception would reside. In this mythical land, the best match-ups imaginable could be made, without the bother of negotiating purses or the interference of worthless, self-styled governing bodies. John L. Sullivan could square up to Joe Louis (the first fight could be bare-knuckles and the return with gloves). Benny Leonard could match skills with his namesake Sugar Ray Leonard. Jack Johnson could find out if his defence was still impregnable against a rampaging Mike Tyson. Sam Langford could at last win a title. And best of all – the legends would enjoy an eternal prime.

Muhammad Ali wouldn't have got sick. Sugar Ray Robinson would still be dancing on his toes, ready to unleash those brilliant combinations. Marcel Cerdan wouldn't bear any of the scars of that horrific plane crash. George Foreman could go on fighting forever (well, this part of the dream might come true!).

The late Nat Fleischer, founder and first editor of *The Ring*, was a little man with a huge imagination. He envisaged such a boxing utopia. He called it Valhalla. In Norse mythology, this was a palace in which the souls of slain heroes feasted. If Fleischer's dream came true, he is now sitting ringside at this distant arena, savouring every blow and every delicate manoeuvre, and jotting down his impressions of the true Battles of the Centuries. Any chance of a copy of your celestial journal, Nat?

Until Fleischer moves over and gives us a seat at his precious Valhalla, we fight fans must rely on the evidence of what we have seen, read or been told, if we are to come to conclusions as to who would have won the great encounters. Often, we cannot – or perhaps don't want to – decide. It's fun trying, but the reality might be the shattering of our long-held beliefs. Dream on, brothers!

In boxing terms, what is greatness? It has been my task, in compiling this personal selection (it is no more than that) of the top one hundred fighters of the twentieth century, to try to define the term. My conclusions will please some and infuriate others, I don't doubt.

Name your top one hundred anything and you'll get one hundred arguments. Choosing the greatest fighters from 1900 to the present is like saying a glass of wine is better than a pint of beer. It's a matter of personal preference. One man's ring idol is another man's not-much-better-than-average performer. No one will dispute the rights of legends like Muhammad Ali, Sugar Ray Robinson, Jack Dempsey, Marvin Hagler, Jimmy Wilde or Roberto Duran to be included in this book. Perhaps two-thirds of those selected will earn their place in anybody's list of boxing greats. It's the last one-third that will start the arguments. But sure, healthy debate is part of the excitement of boxing. Just as long as it doesn't come to blows!

Back at the beginning of the century, boxing was a more simple game than it is today. In 1900, there were just six weight divisions. Although there were often disputes about who should be regarded as world champions, no one had to answer to the myriad of current 'governing bodies' whose only real achievement has been to cause the fragmentation of world titles. Now there are seventeen weight sections, with four main organisations recognising a grand total of sixty-eight titleholders. Try memorising that lot!

Many great fighters of the past who were shamefully denied a title chance, often because they were simply too good, would have no trouble picking up one, or several, of the ten-a-penny 'world championships' up for grabs today. So it doesn't necessarily mean that Thomas 'Hit Man' Hearns, who captured championship belts at five different weights between 1980 and 1991, was any better than Sam Langford, who fought the very best from lightweight to heavyweight during a twenty-year career, but never got a crack at a world title.

What can be said in favour of the modern system is that many more ringmen get their names in the record books as champions. It also increases their bargaining power, so they are paid better than most of their predecessors. Unfortunately, because of the various organisations' vested interests, unification fights are rare. So the term 'world champion' has become cheapened. Promoters and managers are tied to rival organisations and television networks, so the reluctance to step on toes often prevents the public seeing what they want – a showdown between claimants for a particular world title. Boxers, too, are frightened off by the stipulation that, whatever organisation's title is at stake, that body must be paid a substantial sanctioning fee. For instance, in the rare event of all four leading associations' belts being on the line, each body will claim payment. It takes a very confident – and very rich – fighter to go for broke.

World champion is supposed to mean simply that – 'best in the world' at a particular endeavour. In boxing today, the term is becoming increasingly difficult to define. There is a logical suggestion that top ringmen should just fight each other, and forget about championship labels. But that wouldn't suit the TV companies, who feel a title tag is essential to sell a big fight to their viewers. It is these same viewers, however, who are becoming more and more cynical about the manipulation of boxing by the various self-interested groups. All the fans ask for are the fights that matter – and the means to see them. In Britain, it is growing more difficult all the time to watch the modern greats in action. Outside of the big heavyweight fights, which are out of bounds anyway unless the viewer coughs up extra for the iniquitous pay-per-view service, BBC, ITV and Sky have rarely taken American shows. As a result, outstanding champions like Oscar De La Hoya, Roy Jones Junior, Julio Cesar Chavez and Ricardo Lopez are virtually unknown to all but the most dedicated fans.

The newspapers, too, give scant coverage to current boxing. Unless it's a main heavyweight fight, or a domestic contest involving someone whose 'personality' more than his talent has made him a household name, it might just merit a paragraph or the bare result – if that – in the national press. Unless one takes the 'trade' magazines, it's impossible to keep track of events.

In the long term, if boxing is to survive, it will have to find a way of getting back to basics. That means matching the top fighters against each other, and making it easy for the fans to see the fights. Otherwise, it won't be necessary for the moralists and the medical profession to keep up their campaign for the abolition of the sport. The greedy people within boxing will have done it for them.

Note: The four main bodies governing boxing today are the World Boxing Council (WBC), World Boxing Association (WBA), International Boxing Federation (IBF) and World Boxing Organisation (WBO). There are several other organisations staking claims for recognition, but they are given scant credence by genuine boxing people.

Organisations differ in the names of weight divisions. In this book, the British terms are used. Therefore, it is light-middleweight (called junior middleweight by the WBA and IBF, and super welterweight by the WBC), light-welterweight (called junior welterweight by the WBA, IBF and WBO, and super lightweight by the WBC), super-featherweight (called junior lightweight by the WBA, IBF and WBO), super-bantamweight (called junior featherweight by the WBA, IBF and WBO), super-flyweight (called junior bantamweight by the WBA, IBF and WBO), light-flyweight (called junior flyweight by the WBA, IBF and WBO), and straw-weight (called mini-flyweight by the IBF and WBO, minimum-weight by the WBA).

MUHAMMAD ALI

Original name: Cassius Clay.

Nickname: The Louisville Lip.

World heavyweight champion 1964-65, 1967, 1974-78. WBC heavyweight champion 1965-67. WBA heavyweight champion 1978-79.

Born in Louisville, Kentucky, USA, 17 January 1942.

Career: 1960-81.

Total contests: 61. Won: 56 (37 KOs). Lost: 5.

A cynic might suggest that Cassius Clay changed his name to Muhammad Ali so that he always comes first in lists of boxing's all-time greats, as in this book. If alphabetical order is the rule, then Ali does come before Clay, and Henry Armstrong, Jack Britton, Joe Brown, Georges Carpentier, Julio Cesar Chavez and other all-time greats. But only the most grudging misery-guts would deny him one of the top rungs on the fistic ladder. He may, or may not, have been the most gifted ringman, pound for pound, of all time, but he's right up there with the very best.

What no one can dispute is that Ali is the best-known, best-loved athlete of the twentieth century. It might have taken some time for people to accept that his boast 'I am the Greatest' was made more in fun than a gigantic ego-trip, and for America to recognise the merits of his anti-Vietnam War stance, but he won everyone over in the end. His handsome looks, his deeds inside and outside the ring, his outlandish proclamations and his sheer magnetism enabled him to be deemed by *Time* magazine as the most instantly recognised human being in the world.

Sadly, it is the very fact that he is so well-known that may have terminally damaged the sport to which he gave so much. The image Ali presents today of a once-great ringman stricken by the debilitating effects of Parkinson's syndrome has provided a huge supply of ammunition to those who seek to have boxing banned. The suggestion that his condition is more of a motor problem than an intellectual one has not convinced everyone. What no one can dispute is that he stayed on too long at what has been aptly called 'the Hardest Game'. It was a terrible price to pay for his love for the sport and the fans' readily reciprocated affection. Seeing him today, with his permanently glazed expression, shuffling gait, trembling hands and the great voice almost silenced, is the saddest sight of all to those who remember the graceful athlete in his prime. If boxing is ballet with blood, then Muhammad Ali was the dancer who took one encore too many and fell off the stage.

In the early part of his career, Ali was truly beautiful to watch. For such a big man (six feet, three inches and around 200 pounds) he was amazingly light on his feet. Not a devastating puncher in the mould of other great heavyweights, though he had a good percentage of inside-the-distance wins, he relied mainly on his lightning reflexes and brilliant combinations. A sway from the hips or a twist of the head enabled him to make his opponent miss by inches. The other man would become discouraged at his inability to land a telling blow and would be easy prey as Ali let rip with his slashing punches.

It was his uncanny knack of predicting the exact round his opponents would fall which delighted his fans and infuriated his detractors. The sceptics believed 'the Louisville Lip' would be shown up as a bombastic impostor when he challenged the fearsome Sonny Liston for the world heavyweight title on 25 February 1964.

Ali, then known under his birth name of Cassius Clay, bamboozled the slow-moving champion with his speed. His ripping punches had Liston cut under the right eye and looking increasingly dejected. Sonny refused to answer the bell for the seventh round, claiming a damaged shoulder. In the rematch a year later, Liston was counted out in the first round after being felled by a punch that looked less than lethal. Liston denied he had taken a 'dive' but the taint attached to the fiasco has never gone away.

If the new world champion had earned grudging respect as a boxer, he soon took a nose-dive in public popularity by declaring he had changed from Cassius Clay, his former 'slave name', to Muhammad Ali. He also vowed his allegiance to the Nation of Islam. Fight fans who cared little about his name change or his religion were angered at the way he systematically tortured challengers Floyd Patterson and Ernie Terrell because they wouldn't call him by his new name. His refusal, on religious grounds, to be inducted into the US armed forces and serve in Vietnam was the last straw. There were few tears shed when he was sentenced to prison and was barred from boxing and stripped of his championship. By the time public support had swung his way, he had lost three and a half years out of his boxing career. It is generally accepted that he was never quite the same after his return.

What the slower, heavier Ali did prove in his 'second coming' was his great courage and ability to absorb a big punch. He had been floored by Sonny Banks and Henry Cooper before he became champion, but had recovered quickly to win. In a close, fiercely fought challenge for Joe Frazier's world heavyweight title in March, 1971, Muhammad was sent crashing by a mighty left hook in the fifteenth and final round. Most recipients of such a Frazier 'special' would have stayed down, but Ali scrambled to his feet and completed the course, even though he lost for the first time in his career.

He dropped a decision, too, to Ken Norton, who broke his jaw in the second round. Ali avenged that upset by twice narrowly outpointing Norton and he also beat Frazier twice, most notably in the famous 'Thrilla in Manila'. Both fighters endured fierce punishment in what is considered by many to be the most exciting fight of all time, but it was Frazier who wilted. His trainer, Eddie Futch, retired him at the end of the fourteenth round.

But it was in the so-called 'Rumble in the Jungle', his 1974 conquest of the previously unbeaten George Foreman in Zaire, that Ali gave what most people say was his greatest performance. No longer the dancing master of old, he conducted what looked like a suicidal plan of lying against the ropes, inviting the big-hitting champion to punch away at him. This was what he termed his 'rope-a-dope' technique. Ali took most of the blows on his arms and gloves, but enough got through to his body to have him passing blood for some time after the fight. Foreman eventually punched himself out and was sent spinning to the floor for the full count by a flurry of blows in the eighth round. 'Oh, my God,' exclaimed an incredulous TV commentator, the BBC's Harry Carpenter, 'he's champion again at the age of thirty-two.'

Ali's reign lasted another three and a half years until he was upset by Leon Spinks, a 1976 Olympic gold medallist, who was having only his eighth professional contest. For the rematch seven months later, Muhammad trained harder than ever and dazzled Spinks with a vintage display of speed and cunning to take a decisive points verdict. The fight was only for the WBA version of the championship, as Spinks had been stripped by the WBC for failing to meet top contender Ken Norton.

Ali announced his retirement in 1979, but, despite his estimated $70 million earnings from the ring, he was not well off. The cost of maintaining a huge personal entourage, bad investments and his renowned generosity took care of most of his fortune. But it was pride, as much as the £10 million purse offer from promoter Don King, that led him to take on WBC titleholder Larry Holmes in 1980. It was a big mistake.

Though looking slim and fit, Ali, now thirty-eight, was tired after the first round. It was later discovered that he had taken more than the prescribed dosage of pills for a thyroid condition, which left him dangerously weakened. He was certainly in no fit state to take on the talented Holmes, winner of all his thirty-five fights to date. Ali was a pathetic figure as he hardly landed a punch. Even Holmes had no real desire to punish the man who had been his idol. Ali had lost every round by the time he retired at the end of the tenth round.

Not wishing to exit the sport with the image of him slumped on his stool, he made one last ring appearance a year after the Holmes disaster. He was well outpointed by Trevor Berbick, a twenty-eight-year-old Jamaican based in Canada, who was to go on to capture the WBC title five years later. For Muhammad Ali, it was a sad end to a glorious career. Not even 'the Greatest' could turn back the clock.

In 1996, the world held its breath as Ali's shaking hands fumbled with a burning torch to ignite the Olympic flame in Atlanta, Georgia. He managed it, and the watching television millions gave a gigantic sigh of relief. The great warmth of feeling shown on that occasion towards the man who had won a gold medal in this same event thirty-six years earlier led to Lonnie, his fourth wife, commenting: 'That is when he knew the world hadn't forgotten him.'

ALEXIS ARGUELLO

Nickname: Flaco de Explosivo (The Explosive Thin Man).

WBA featherweight champion 1974-77. WBC super-featherweight champion 1978-80. WBC lightweight champion 1981-83.

Born in Managua, Nicaragua, 19 April 1952.

Career: 1968-95.

Total contests: 88. Won: 80 (64 KOs). Lost: 8.

A huge American TV favourite in the 1970s and '80s, Alexis Arguello was a technically gifted boxer who could adapt his style to exploit his opponents' weaknesses. He could hit, too. No fewer than sixty-four of his eighty victims failed to stay around to the final bell. His handsome looks didn't harm his appeal either.

Like so many fellow Nicaraguans forced to endure poverty and political strife, Arguello sought to help his family make ends meet whatever way he could. Leaving school at fourteen to work on a dairy farm, he learned how to fight on the streets and took boxing lessons from his brother-in-law in Managua. After a year of amateur boxing, he turned professional at sixteen. Over the next six years, he ran up an impressive record before venturing outside his country for the first time. His challenge to WBA featherweight champion Ernesto Marcel in Panama resulted in a narrow points loss in February 1974.

When Marcel retired and Ruben Olivares won the vacant title, Arguello was first in line for a crack at the heavy-hitting Mexican. In his first fight in the United States, Arguello edged the first five rounds at the Fabulous Forum in Inglewood, California, but then had to stave off a strong comeback by the champion. The determined Nicaraguan, however, connected with a short left hook in the thirteenth round to score a knockdown. Olivares was soon down again and this time failed to beat the count.

Arguello kept the title until increasing weight forced him to give it up in 1977. A year later, he was WBC super-featherweight champion after knocking out Alfredo Escalera in thirteen rounds in Puerto Rico. After eight successful defences, weight difficulties again made him move up.

On 20 June 1981, he ventured to London to beat Scotland's Jim Watt, now a popular TV boxing analyst, over fifteen rounds for the WBC lightweight championship. Ray 'Boom Boom' Mancini gave Arguello a tough battle in Atlantic City that same year, before the Nicaraguan forced a fourteenth round stoppage.

Arguello tried for his fourth championship belt in 1982, but, now thirty-two, he found the task beyond him. He inflicted some early damage on the aggressive WBA light-welterweight champion, Aaron Pryor, but he was taking a pounding in the fourteenth round when the referee came to his rescue. Claims that Pryor's recovery was aided by an illegal substance in his water bottle and by reduced padding in his gloves were not substantiated. They met again the following year. Pryor won by a knockout in the tenth round.

After a two-year layoff, Arguello, faced with huge tax problems, returned to record two quick wins. But he was diagnosed as having a heart problem and the comeback was abandoned. He earned money from TV commercials, a part in an action movie and some TV boxing commentary for a Spanish language network.

For years, Arguello had expressed bitterness towards Nicaragua's

Sandinista regime after the left wing government, which he had originally supported, confiscated his property and bank account. By 1992, a new government was in power and he was able to negotiate the return of his two homes and gymnasium. Yet the old boxing bug continued to bite. He passed stringent medical tests in 1994 and returned to action with a points win over Mexican Jorge Palomares. But his comeback success was at the expense of a broken hand. He hung up his gloves for good the following year after being outscored by Scott Walker.

Arguello opened a sports bar in Managua, the Nicaraguan capital, which has a closed circuit TV system that shows films of his fights. He spends much of his time working with amateur boxers.

HENRY ARMSTRONG

Real name: Henry Jackson.

Nicknames: Hurricane Hank, Hammerin' Hank, Homicide Hank.

World featherweight champion 1937-38. World lightweight champion 1938-39. World welterweight champion 1938-40.

Born in Columbus, Mississippi, USA, 12 December, 1912. Died in Los Angeles, California, USA, 24 October 1988.

Career: 1931-45.

Total contests: 181. Won: 151 (101 KOs). Lost: 21. Drew: 9.

In this modern age, when so-called world titles are as plentiful as friends of a lottery millionaire, the feat of picking up championship belts at three different weights does not seem all that remarkable. But Henry Armstrong's capture of the undisputed world featherweight, lightweight and welterweight titles during the 1930s – and for eight months holding all three at the same time – was a unique and marvellous achievement. In 1940, Armstrong only just failed to add a fourth world title to his tally. Weighing just ten stone, two pounds (142 pounds), he held middleweight champion Ceferino Garcia, eleven and a half pounds heavier, to a draw.

Armstrong's favoured style was to bob and weave his way into close range, bury his head on his opponent's chest and whip in damaging hooks and uppercuts. Normally, the other man would collapse under the sheer volume of punches. Henry's abnormally slow heartbeat was responsible for his terrific workrate. He was also extraordinarily resistant to hard punches. In 151 fights, he was only twice beaten inside the distance, in his first contest and when he tried to regain the welterweight belt from Fritzie Zivic.

Born into poverty in Mississippi, Armstrong moved to St Louis with his family when he was four. Like so many youngsters of his era, he learned how to use his fists in neighbourhood scraps. After a brief amateur spell, boxing as Melody Jackson, he turned professional in 1931. He didn't get off to the most promising start, losing three of his first four bouts. But he then got his act together and lost only one of the next thirty-five.

A remarkably busy fighter, Armstrong's ring appearances were often just days apart. In 1937, he boxed twenty-seven times. He won all of them, all but one by the short route. One of those victories, a sixth round knockout of Petey Sarron, earned Henry his first world championship, at featherweight.

When weight-making became a problem, Armstrong, instead of trying for the lightweight crown, as might be expected, made a giant leap up to welterweight. The contract for the encounter at Madison Square Garden Bowl, Long Island, on 31 May 1938, stipulated that the champion, Barney Ross, should weigh no more than 142 pounds and Armstrong no less than 138 pounds. Henry gave the defending champion a severe beating, but eased off in the last few rounds to let the brave Ross end his career by lasting the distance.

Now he was holder of the featherweight and welterweight belts, it might have been thought that Armstrong's capture of the lightweight title from Lou Ambers was a mere formality. It was nothing of the sort. Though he successfully completed the hat-trick in August 1938, 'Hammering Hank' had to battle all the way. He floored Ambers in the fifth and sixth rounds, but had to weather a great fight-back by the New Yorker. Armstrong's eyes and mouth bled so badly that the referee considered stopping the fight. To conceal the extent of his mouth injury, Henry discarded his gumshield and swallowed the blood. Armstrong won a split decision.

Accepting that he would never make the nine stone limit again, he gave up the featherweight title later that year. He defended his welterweight belt seven times in five months, including a points win over gutsy British champion Ernie Roderick in London, before putting his lightweight title at stake in a return with Lou Ambers in August 1939. Fights were at that time scored on the number of rounds won by either boxer. Armstrong fought so recklessly that he was penalised five rounds for low blows. The unanimous verdict went to Ambers.

Armstrong was the most active welterweight champion in history. He defended that title nineteen times in less than two years, before finally surrendering it to Fritzie Zivic on 4 October 1940. Zivic, a vicious fighter who knew how to dish out the dirt, cut and almost closed the champion's eyes. He dropped Armstrong with the last blow of the fight and took a unanimous decision.

In a rematch with Zivic the following year, Armstrong absorbed a brutal beating. Unable to see out of his badly swollen eyes, he was led back to his corner in the twelfth round by referee Arthur Donovan. Armstrong announced his retirement, but made a comeback in 1942 and had forty-nine fights over the next three years. Although he beat sometime world champions Juan Zurita, Leo Rodak, Tippy Larkin, Sammy Angott, Mike Belloise and his former two-time conqueror Fritzie Zivic, all were non-title contests. He lost a ten-round decision to Sugar Ray Robinson in 1943. He finally called it quits, aged thirty-three, after losing on points to Chester Slider on 14 February 1945.

In retirement, Armstrong overcame alcoholism and became an ordained Baptist minister.

ABE ATTELL

World featherweight champion 1904-12.

Born in San Francisco, California, USA, 22 February 1884. Died in New Paltz, New York, USA, 7 February 1970.

Career: 1900-17.

Total contests: 171. Won: 91 (53 KOs). Lost: 9. Drew: 18. No decision: 51. No contest: 2.

Renowned more for his boxing skill than his punching power, Abe Attell was world featherweight champion for nine years, although during some of that period the title was disputed. Veteran San Francisco scribe Jack Fiske rated Attell the best fighter to come out of California, ahead even of 'Gentleman Jim' Corbett.

As a Jewish boy growing up in an Irish district of San Francisco, Abe soon found his natural ability with his fists useful. He became a successful amateur boxer, then turned professional in 1900 at the age of sixteen. His paid debut was especially satisfying. He knocked out Kid Lennett, who had given him a hiding in a street scrap.

Attell twice held former world champion George Dixon to a draw before outpointing 'Little Chocolate', as Dixon was tagged, in a fifteen-rounder on 28 October 1901. Abe claimed the featherweight title as a result of his win, even though Dixon had lost the championship the previous year to Terry McGovern. Young Corbett had taken the title from McGovern and then relinquished it due to increasing weight. This led to several boxers claiming the championship.

Attell earned wider recognition as world champion by knocking out Harry Forbes in five rounds in February 1904. Further dispute arose, however, when Attell was beaten by Tommy Sullivan on a fifth round KO. Abe insisted Sullivan was over the weight limit for the fight and therefore could not claim it was a title bout. His argument was generally accepted. When he flattened Sullivan in four rounds in a return match, the issue was settled beyond doubt. Attell's ambitions led him to try for the world lightweight title in 1908, but he could only manage a draw with Battling Nelson.

Despite his long reign as featherweight champion, Attell was considered lucky to get away with drawn verdicts in two clashes with skilful Englishman Owen Moran. Fate was also on his side when he met 'the Welsh Wizard' Jim Driscoll in New York in 1909. This was the era of 'no decision' contests in New York. Under the Frawley Law, in effect from 1911 to 1920, all bouts were regarded as exhibitions. Points verdicts were prohibited. A champion could only lose his title on a knockout. It was generally left to the ringside newspapermen to decide who was the better man when a fight went the distance, although their opinions had no legitimacy. The reporters made Driscoll a clear winner, but Attell retained his title status.

Attell finally yielded all claim to the title on 22 February 1912, when he was outpointed over twenty rounds by Johnny Kilbane, an Irish-American from Cleveland, Ohio. He had beaten Kilbane in a ten-rounder two years earlier, but was outsmarted in the return. The Californian had sixteen more fights before retiring in September 1913. He came back four years later to meet Phil Virgets in New Orleans, but was halted in four rounds and hung up his gloves for good.

In retirement, Attell ran several bars. His name was back in the news in 1919, when he was involved in baseball's Black Sox Scandal. Attell, a notorious gambler, got word that eight players on the Chicago team were prepared, for the right money, to throw the World Series. It seemed crazy, but Abe thought it could be done. He took the proposal to his old pal Arnold Rothstein, whom he had known since 1905, and convinced him the fix could be carried through. And it was. Despite his part in the scandal, Attell was not convicted of any crime.

He was eighty-six when he died in 1970.

CARMEN BASILIO

Nickname: the Onion Farmer.

World welterweight champion 1955-56, 1956-57. World middleweight champion 1957-58.

Born in Canastota, New York, USA, 2 April 1927.

Career: 1948-61.

Total contests: 79. Won: 56 (27 KOs). Lost: 16. Drew: 7.

The prevailing memory of Carmen Basilio is of the deposed world middleweight champion, his left eye so grotesquely swollen and discoloured that it looked like one of the onions he harvested as a youngster, after losing a bitter fifteen-rounder to Sugar Ray Robinson. The picture perfectly captured what this man was all about – a brave fighter who never knew what it was to quit.

Basilio was no master boxer, as his battle-scarred face testified. Nor was he an explosive hitter, as his twenty-seven short-route wins in seventy-nine fights shows. Indeed, *The Ring* maintained he was over-rated because he defeated an aged Robinson in their first fight, and for his undoubted toughness. 'It's easy to forget,' said the magazine in a selection of the all-time greats in its May 1994 issue, 'that before winning the 147-pound crown, he lost to, among others, Lester Felton, Ross Virgo, Johnny Cesario, Chuck Davey, Billy Graham and Kid Gavilan.'

Fair comment, but Basilio had the grit and determination to make the most of what he had. He learned as he went along and he wasn't the first fighter to prove that self-belief and an unwillingness to buckle under can go a long way to overcoming more naturally gifted opponents.

Basilio's father, an onion farmer, was a boxing fan and he encouraged his son to take up the sport. Carmen fought some bouts in the Marine Corps before turning professional at twenty-one. He beat former world champions Lew Jenkins and Ike Williams before decisioning Billy Graham to win the New York State welterweight championship in June 1953. After being held to a draw by Graham in a return match, Basilio got a crack at Kid Gavilan's world title in September of that year. A big underdog in the betting, Carmen floored and almost knocked out Gavilan in the second round. It was the first time the Cuban had ever been downed and he barely made it to his feet in time to beat the count. Gavilan recovered to take a split decision, but most observers thought Basilio was robbed of the title.

It was two years before the New Yorker got another world title chance and this time he made the most of it. In a vicious, bloody brawl at the Syracuse War Memorial, New York, on 10 June 1955, Basilio, behind on points, dropped Tony DeMarco twice in the tenth round. The referee rescued the badly battered champion in the twelfth. In their rematch in Boston, DeMarco's home town, on 30 November of that year, Basilio took just two seconds longer than in the first fight to halt his rival.

Just like in the initial encounter, Basilio and DeMarco had gone for each other from the opening bell, with little regard for defence. Carmen was badly hurt and almost stopped in the seventh round. Recalling the incident for Pete Heller, author of *In This Corner*, Basilio said: 'I got hit on the point of the chin ... It paralysed the whole left side of my body ... My left knee buckled and I almost went down but when I got back to my corner, the bottom of my foot felt like it had needles about six inches high. I just kept stamping my foot on the floor, trying to bring it back. By the time the bell rang for the eighth round, it was all right.'

Basilio lost his welterweight title to Johnny Saxton in Chicago Stadium on 14 March 1956, on a hotly disputed decision. Saxton, managed by underworld boss Blinky Palermo, had first won the championship from Kid Gavilan on another controversial verdict in 1954, then lost it to DeMarco. Against Basilio, Saxton was in big trouble, but his cornermen gained time by getting a damaged glove replaced (the same thing happened when Britain's Henry Cooper left-hooked Cassius Clay to the canvas in London in 1963) and Saxton recovered. It was generally accepted that the unrelenting Basilio had been more effective than the stylish, but more negative, challenger.

The outcry over the decision ensured a rematch. This time Basilio made no mistake, halting Saxton in nine rounds. He underlined his superiority by knocking out Saxton in the second round five months later.

Though he was only five feet, six and a half inches, the lion-hearted Basilio fancied his chances against bigger men. On 23 September 1957, he gave the greatest performance of his career to capture the world middleweight championship from Sugar Ray Robinson at Yankee Stadium, New York. Robinson was thirty-seven, seven years older than his rival, and had already won the title four times. Though considered in the twilight of his illustrious career, Robinson was still a master boxer and lethal puncher. Only four months earlier, he had flattened rugged Gene Fullmer with a left hook, regarded as one of ring history's classic knockouts.

Basilio, bleeding from the nose and left eye from the early stages, nevertheless pressed Sugar Ray back for round after round. So ferocious was the action that, at times, each man in turn looked on the point of collapse. At the end of a classic fifteen rounds, Basilio dropped to one knee and prayed. A few moments later, the decision was announced. The judges were split, but the verdict went to Basilio.

The return match, in March 1958, was just as fiercely contested.

Basilio, unable to see from his badly swollen left eye from the sixth round, made light of his handicap as he matched Robinson's best efforts blow for blow. This time, however, the decision went to Sugar Ray.

Carmen, showing the effects of his gruelling career, was twice stopped by Gene Fullmer in attempts at the National Boxing Association version of the middleweight title. He hung up his gloves after losing on points to Paul Pender for the undisputed title on 22 April 1961. He became a physical education instructor at LeMoyne College in Syracuse and also worked as a representative for Genesee Brewery. He even put his name to 'Carmen Basilio Italian Sausages'.

In June 1997, Basilio, aged seventy, underwent six-way heart bypass surgery.

WILFRED BENITEZ

WBA light-welterweight champion 1976. WBC welterweight champion 1979. WBC light-middleweight champion 1981-82.

Born in the Bronx, New York, USA, 12 September 1958.

Career: 1973-90.

Total contests: 62. Won: 53 (31 KOs). Lost: 8. Drew: 1.

The youngest fighter ever to win a world title, at seventeen, Wilfred Benitez became a champion at three different weights. He might have made an even greater impact if he had bothered to stay in shape. A naturally gifted boxer who fought from a wide-legged stance, moving his upper body to slip his opponents' punches, he often made harder work of a fight than was necessary. Nevertheless, he was rated one of the outstanding ringmen of his era.

Born in New York to a Puerto Rican father, Benitez was not yet sixteen when he had his first professional fight. That was under the legal age limit. He used a bogus baptismal certificate to get his licence. After twenty-five straight wins over the next two years, he won the WBA light-welterweight title by outpointing Antonio Cervantes in March 1976. He defended the belt three times, but a scheduled rematch with Cervantes was postponed when Benitez was hurt in a car crash. When he failed to meet the WBA's new deadline, he was stripped of the title.

Benitez moved up to welterweight, but his lack of self-discipline was evident when he clowned around against Harold Weston and was held to a draw. He trained for just a week before meeting Bruce Curry. He was floored three times and was lucky to escape with a split decision win.

Nevertheless, Benitez was still unbeaten when he challenged Carlos Palomino for the WBC welterweight title in January 1979. Near to the fight, Wilfred's father, Goyo, who had trained his son since he turned professional, clashed over tactical plans with former welter and middleweight champion Emile Griffith, who had been brought in by managers Jim Jacobs and Bill Cayton. Griffith got his way and his stand was justified when Benitez took a majority decision and his second world title.

Unfortunately for Benitez, he was champion at a time when one of the ring's most talented and charismatic figures, Sugar Ray Leonard, was also around. Leonard, a 1976 Olympic Games gold medallist, had made such an impact on the professional scene that he was able to command one million dollars, the highest ever paid to a title challenger outside of the heavyweight division. Benitez, as champion, earned $1.2 million. In a thrilling battle at Caesars Palace, Las Vegas, in November 1979, Benitez was floored in the third round and was gashed on the forehead in a head collision three rounds later. Despite these setbacks, he survived until the dying seconds of the fifteenth and last round. His legs buckled and he dropped for an eight count. Referee Carlos Padilla leaped to his rescue as Leonard moved in to finish the job.

It was time to move up another weight division. Benitez, not noted as a one-punch finisher, produced a peach of a right to knock out Antigua-born, British-based Maurice Hope in the twelfth round in Las Vegas. The win, in May 1981, brought Benitez his third world championship, the WBC light-middleweight prize. A meritorious points win over legendary Roberto Duran was the last night of glory for Benitez. He lost the title in his third defence to Thomas 'Hit

Man' Hearns on a fifteen round decision in December 1982.

The inevitable try at a higher weight was a failure. Decline had set in and it accelerated sharply. He was outscored by Mustafa Hamsho and broke his ankle in a second round stoppage by Davey Moore. Seven more fights, two of them knockout defeats, convinced him to call it a day in November 1986. He came back four years later to win two and lose two. He finally hung up his gloves in September 1990.

His $6 million career earnings squandered on a reckless lifestyle, Benitez, then residing in Puerto Rico, was given a $600-a-month special boxer's pension by the government. It was revealed that, shortly before Benitez fought Roberto Duran in 1982, his then managers, Bill Cayton and Jim Jacobs, had invested $250,000 in a high-yield trust that would have been worth $5 million when he retired. Instead, Benitez and his father withdrew the money over a period of months and spent and gambled it away. The fighter then quit his management team to join up with promoter Bob Arum.

Benitez's sad plight was compounded when he was diagnosed as suffering from inflammation of the brain while still in his early thirties. The condition is known as chronic traumatic encephalopathy. Late in 1996, he was lucky to survive after lapsing into a coma at his home in Carolina. When he awoke after three days, the first words he said to his mother, Clara, were: 'God is good.'

NIGEL BENN

Nickname: the Dark Destroyer.

WBO middleweight champion 1990. WBC super-middleweight champion 1992-96.

Born in Ilford, Essex, England, 22 January 1964.

Career: 1987-96.

Total contests: 47. Won: 42 (35 KOs). Lost: 4. Drew: 1.

Unquestionably one of the most exciting British fighters of any era, Nigel Benn combined tremendous punching power, good skills, top-rate fitness and unshakeable self-confidence. He had his weaknesses, though. His punching often lacked accuracy and he could be tagged and hurt. Even some relatively light hitters wobbled him, but observations that he had a 'glass chin' were greatly exaggerated. It was more that his aggressive style left him open to good counter-punchers.

The second of seven brothers, Benn was a bit of a tearaway as a youngster. He got into trouble through street fights and shoplifting, but learned discipline in the British Army, which included a stint in strife-torn Northern Ireland. He won the British amateur middleweight title in 1986, but was disgusted when Rod Douglas, whom he had beaten in the London trials, was picked for the Commonwealth Games team instead of him.

Turning professional with Londoner Frank Warren, Benn was an instant hit with the fans. He ran up a string of twenty-two straight victories, all of them inside the scheduled course, nineteen inside two rounds. One unfortunate victim, Ian Chantler, lasted just sixteen seconds. Nigel's explosive punching power made him the hottest property on the British fight scene.

He picked up the vacant Commonwealth middleweight title with a second round blast-out of Abdul Umaru Sanda. But his gallop came to a sudden stop in May 1989. Londoner Michael Watson, challenging for Benn's Commonwealth belt, brilliantly fended off the champion's attacks with a tight defence, then put him down for the count in the sixth round. The effect of the final punch, nothing more lethal than a left jab, posed the first serious questions about Benn's ability to withstand heavy blows.

Undaunted, Benn packed his bags and returned to action in the United States. Three wins earned him a shot at WBO middleweight titleholder Doug DeWitt in April 1990. Though floored in the second round by the tough American, he showed his great fighting heart by climbing off the canvas to drop the champion four times before forcing an eighth round stoppage.

Never one to spurn a tough challenge, Benn faced dangerous Iran 'The Blade' Barkley in Las Vegas. Many thought he was taking an unnecessary risk. There were easier contenders. But the Englishman felt he had something to prove. He was a sensation that night. His wicked hooks chopped down Barkley three times in the opening round to force an automatic stoppage under the three knockdowns in one round rule. The quality of Benn's performance can be measured by the fact that Barkley won world titles at three different weights and twice beat Thomas 'Hit Man' Hearns.

Ironically, Benn's success in the United States won him no plaudits from the British Boxing Board of Control, which, at that time, did not recognise the WBO as a legitimate organisation. The board came round, however, in time for Benn to defend his title against fellow Briton Chris Eubank.

The bout, at Birmingham's National Exhibition Centre on 18 November 1990, generated terrific excitement in the build-up. Eubank, an eccentric character with an odd, though effective, defensive style, packed a strong punch. He was unbeaten in twenty-four contests. His bragging about what he was going to do to Benn spurred the champion to retort, 'I want to humiliate him, because I detest him.'

But it was Benn who folded. He was taking a beating against the ropes in the ninth round when referee Richard Steele cradled him in his arms and told him it was all over.

It was two years and six wins later when Benn, now a super-middleweight, took that division's WBC title from Italian Mauro Galvano. The bout took place in Marino, in the champion's home country, and the Italians tried every devious stroke to enable their man to keep his belt. Benn was in command from the start and soon had Galvano cut and badly hurt. The Italian's cornermen pulled him out at the end of the third round, claiming the cut had been caused by a butt. That would have meant the contest being declared a technical draw and Galvano would have kept his title. Referee Joe Cortez, however, ruled that a punch had caused the damage and so Benn was declared the winner and new champion.

Benn beat Galvano on points in a return match in Glasgow, but was almost sensationally stopped in the final seconds. He then attempted to unify the super-middleweight title by taking on Chris Eubank in a return. Benn was defending his WBC belt and Eubank put his WBO title at stake. It was nip and tuck for the full twelve rounds, though most observers thought Benn had nicked it. The verdict was a draw.

Such was the ferocity of Benn's title defence against Gerald McClellan at London's Docklands Arena in February 1995 that it must be listed as a true 'Battle of the Century', that much used and abused term. Unfortunately, its tragic outcome overshadowed the thrill-a-minute action. The American, ackhowledged as one of the hardest hitters in the sport, had Benn on the verge of defeat several times. McClellan, too, took a great deal of punishment, but onlookers were surprised when he went down on one knee in the tenth round and was counted out. He collapsed on returning to his corner and was taken to hospital for the removal of a blood clot on his brain. He recovered sufficiently to return home to America, but the effects of his beating left him permanently handicapped.

The brutal nature of the McClellan bout left question marks over Benn's future. Even if he did fight, would he show the scars of his mental and physical trauma?

Five months after the McClellan drama, Benn was back at the London Arena to defend his WBC title against Vincenzo Nardiello. He put the bitter memory of his last outing behind him as he stopped the reluctant Italian in the eighth round. John Jarrett, writing in the *British Boxing Board of Control Yearbook 1997*, summed it up perfectly: 'On the deck five times, only twice officially, the challenger complained about everything, but his only real beef was with Benn, who was hitting him too hard!'

Defending his title for the tenth time, in Newcastle on 2 March, 1996, Benn looked a sure thing against thirty-six-year-old Thulani 'Sugarboy' Malinga, even though the South African had given him a tough time in a non-title bout four years earlier. He should have known what to expect in the return match. Malinga's rangy style enabled him to pick off a lethargic Benn with long left leads. Nigel did score a knockdown with a big right hander in the fifth round, but he was a sorry sight at the end, his eye closed tight, as the title went to Malinga. Showing a flair for the dramatic, the deposed champion announced his retirement and then went down on his knee before millions of television viewers and asked his fiancée to marry him. She said 'Yes'.

Benn's 'retirement' proved to be a hasty decision made in the heat of the moment. He was back in action in July 1996 to challenge for Irishman Steve Collins' WBO super-middleweight title at the Nynex Arena in Manchester. Collins had taken the title from Chris Eubank and kept it in a return, so excitement was at fever pitch when he stepped into the ring against Benn.

The big issue was how would Collins' rock-like chin stand up to the challenger's renowned punching power? Unfortunately, nothing was proved. Benn did land a couple of his big rights, to little noticeable effect, but who could say what the cumulative effect might be if more Benn 'specials' landed over a lengthy distance? In the fourth round, Benn missed with a right, fell over and twisted his ankle. He tried briefly to fight on, but it was obvious he could not continue and the referee waved it off.

They met again four months later, at the same venue, but the ending left a sour taste in the mouths of Benn's fans. Cheered to the echo as he entered the ring, his efforts to explain his decision to quit after six hard rounds were drowned with loud and sustained booing. He had given the Irishman a tough enough tussle, but clearly had no heart for a long, hard slog over the scheduled twelve rounds. As he told pressmen afterwards, 'It just ain't there no more.'

NINO BENVENUTI

World light-middleweight champion 1965-66. World middleweight champion 1967, 1968-70.

Born in Trieste, Italy, 26 April 1938.

Career: 1961-71.

Total contests: 90. Won: 82 (35 KOs). Lost: 7. Drew: 1.

The flashy skills of light-heavyweight gold medallist Cassius Clay failed to impress officials at the Rome Olympics in 1960 as much as the handsome Italian who picked up the welterweight top prize. The Val Barker trophy for the Games' best stylist went to Nino Benvenuti.

Olympics success was the highlight of a brilliant amateur career for Benvenuti, who lost just once – a disputed decision in Turkey – in 120 contests while wearing a vest. Years later, looking back on his honours-laden amateur and professional career, he said: 'Winning the Olympics medal was my biggest thrill.' Benvenuti was rated the top Italian fighter of all time by *The Ring*'s European correspondent, Brian Doogan, in 1995.

Born the son of a fisherman in Trieste, Giovanni – later

shortened to Nino – followed his brother Dario to a local gym and quickly showed a natural talent for the game. He won a string of national titles as a junior, picked up European light-middleweight gold medals in 1957 and 1959, and crowned his amateur career with his Olympics triumph. He turned professional the following year.

Benvenuti showed a wide repertoire of punches, as well as speed and good defensive moves, as he ran up an impressive winning streak. Among his victims were British middleweight champions George Aldridge and Mick Leahy, Trinidad's Hector Constance, world class Cuban Isaac Logart, and Americans Teddy Wright and Denny Moyer, who had lost the world light-middleweight title only the previous year. He used his ring earnings to purchase a share in an aluminium factory, install his family in a nine-room villa and buy four cars. Despite the trappings of wealth, Nino didn't neglect his training and happily spent up to ten months of the year living in spartan accommodation provided by manager Bruno Amaduizzi for his boxers.

His biggest local rival was hard-hitting Sandro Mazzinghi, from Pontedera, near Pisa, who signed to defend his world light-middleweight title against Benvenuti in June 1965. The huge interest in the fight was underlined when 40,000 fans packed the San Siro soccer stadium in Milan to see Benvenuti score a sensational knockout with a right uppercut in the sixth round. Four months later he added the European middleweight title by stopping Luis Folledo of Spain in the sixth round. Then came a return with Mazzinghi. Nino's reliance on an accurate left jab to stave off his aggressive rival didn't go down too well with the thrill-hungry crowd at the Palazzo Dello Sport in Rome. The ring was pelted with fruit and programmes when Benvenuti was announced the winner after a close contest.

A hard-earned points win over American Don Fullmer, younger brother of former world champion Gene, after which Benvenuti required eighteen stitches in a cut over his right eye and eight on the bridge of his nose, was followed by the shock loss of his world light-middleweight title to the Korean Ki-Soo Kim.

A $35,000 guarantee from Kim's promoters was enough to lure Benvenuti to Seoul in June 1966. He didn't think he had anything to fear in his first venture outside Italy as a professional. He had already beaten Kim in the Rome Olympics. But the Korean, unbeaten in twenty-four professional contests, showed his improvement by taking a split decision over fifteen rounds. Benvenuti was very upset over his first loss in sixty-six fights and what he considered an unfair verdict.

From then on, Benvenuti concentrated on the middleweight division and secured a shot at Emile Griffith's world title at Madison Square Garden, New York, on 17 April 1967. He floored the American in the second round with a right uppercut and, though dropped himself in the fourth, outboxed and outfought Griffith to earn a unanimous decision. He returned home a hero for an audience with Pope Paul VI and dinner with the Mayor of Rome. There was a police strike in his native Trieste, but the local officers interrupted their protest to provide a motorcade escort for the 'welcome home' celebrations.

A $150,000 guarantee took Benvenuti to New York for a return with Griffith, five months after their initial encounter. The American, though smaller and outreached by the champion, concentrated on a body attack and regained the title on a majority verdict. The third contest between the well-matched pair took place on the opening night of the new Madison Square Garden, 4 March 1968. Main feature on the sell-out bill saw Joe Frazier beat Buster Mathis for the New York version of the world heavyweight title.

Griffith, the betting favourite, employed the same brawling tactics that had brought him success last time. But Benvenuti's solid left jab had him ahead going into the ninth round. He then landed a terrific right to put Griffith flat on his back for a count of nine. The American was badly hurt, but his great experience enabled him to survive the round. After fifteen keenly contested rounds, Benvenuti was once again champion of the world.

The three tough battles with Griffith seemed to take something out of the Italian. He was held to a draw by unsung American Doyle Baird, then had to climb off the floor to outpoint Don Fullmer in a world title defence. He was decisively beaten on points in a non-title bout with forty-year-old Nigerian Dick Tiger.

His next championship challenger, Luis Rodriguez, looked a genuine threat. The Cuban had won and lost the world welterweight title in an epic four-fight series with Emile Griffith and, since moving up to middleweight, he had accounted for the likes of Rubin 'Hurricane' Carter, George Benton, Bennie Briscoe (twice) and Vincente Rondon, who later won the WBA light-heavyweight title. Though suffering a bad cut on the bridge of his nose that later needed twenty-two stitches and constantly complaining of being butted, Benvenuti produced a peach of a left hook in the eleventh round to leave the challenger stretched out on his back for the full count.

A shock eighth round stoppage by American Tom Bethea in a non-title bout in Melbourne, Australia, led to a return match for the Italian's world championship belt in Umag, Yugoslavia, fifteen miles from Trieste. Benvenuti was in top form as he sent Bethea crashing for the full count in the eighth round.

Nino accepted a $100,000 offer to defend his title in Rome on 7 November 1970. His challenger, the Argentinian Carlos Monzon, had lost only three times in eighty-one contests, but this was his first fight outside his own country. The champion was an overwhelming favourite.

Right from the outset, Benvenuti had problems coping with the swarming challenger. He was dropped to his knees in the twelfth round, then pitched onto his face to be counted out. The Italian got a chance to regain his title in Monte Carlo the following year, but his manager threw in the towel in the third round as Benvenuti sagged to the floor following a flurry of punches. He never fought again.

Nino prospered when his fighting days were over. He ran a smart restaurant in Rome and his suave manner and good looks got him roles in Italian movies. He also became a city councillor for the Italian Socialist Party in his home town of Trieste. When one of his sons wanted to learn to box, he sent him to New York to be coached by his great rival Emile Griffith, now a close friend.

In 1995 came the surprise news that Benvenuti had turned his back on the material world and become a volunteer in Mother Teresa's hospice in Calcutta.

JACK 'KID' BERG

Real name: Judah Bergman.

Nickname: the Whitechapel Whirlwind.

World junior welterweight champion 1930-31.

Born in London, England, 28 June 1909. Died in London, 22 April 1991.

Career: 1924-45.

Total contests: 192. Won: 157 (57 KOs). Lost: 26. Drew: 9.

When the ring announcer introduced Jack 'Kid' Berg and Mushy Callahan as contestants for the world junior welterweight title at the Royal Albert Hall, London, on 18 February 1930, there was an immediate angry reaction from Lord Lonsdale, president of the British Boxing Board of Control. 'Don't be absurd,' protested his lordship, waving his programme in the air, 'there is no such thing as a junior championship.'

There was a fair deal of support for Lonsdale's contention. The junior welterweight division (limit 140 pounds) had been introduced in America in 1922, but was recognised in some states and not in others. In Britain, even after Berg forced Callahan to retire at the end of the tenth round in a fine performance, many failed to take their own countryman's championship claim seriously.

This seems grossly unfair. If he was around today, with the myriad of 'world' titles up for grabs, there would not be the slightest doubt about his champion status. He was unlucky in that he boxed when only eight weight divisions got universal approval. (Junior welterweight was only introduced in Britain in 1968. After three contests for the British title, it was abolished, then re-introduced in 1973 as light-welterweight.)

Berg, an incredibly busy fighter throughout his twenty-one year career, defended the title twelve times in fourteen months. All the bouts took place in the United States. He was knocked out in the third round by Tony Canzoneri in 1931, but the Englishman insisted that it was just a world lightweight title defence by Canzoneri and the junior welterweight prize was not at stake. He continued to advertise himself as junior welterweight champion, until he lost all claim when outpointed by Sammy Fuller in 1932.

Born into an East London Jewish family, Jack took up the sport at fourteen. His energetic, all-action style soon won him a large local following. All of his first fifty-nine fights, of which he won fifty-three and drew three, took place in London. He then decided to try his luck in America and quickly became a favourite at New York's Madison Square Garden.

'The Whitechapel Whirlwind', as he was billed, took his first major scalp when he beat Tony Canzoneri in 1930. The American was a former world featherweight champion and would go on to win the lightweight title ten months after the Berg setback. Jack had opened the bout in a stand-up style, typical of his fellow countrymen of the period, but had more success when he changed to his more natural attacking approach. Berg was a good points winner of the non-title bout.

After winning the junior welterweight title from Callahan, Berg won further acclaim by outpointing the previously unbeaten Kid Chocolate. The Englishman, ten pounds heavier than Chocolate, who was never more than a featherweight, survived a rocky third round to tire 'the Cuban Bon Bon' with his relentless attacks. Berg took a split verdict. In 1932, the year he lost all claim to the world title, Berg repeated his win over Chocolate, then turned his back on American rings to return to England. With no junior welterweight division operating there, he moved down to lightweight and relieved Harry Mizler of his British title on a tenth round retirement.

Signs that his hectic career was beginning to catch up on him surfaced in 1936. Unusually for him, he had only three bouts that year. All ended in defeat. He journeyed to South Africa to drop a fifteen-round decision to Laurie Stevens for the British Empire title. He was then stopped in nine rounds by Jimmy Walsh to forfeit his British championship. The disastrous year was completed when Aldo Spoldi halted him in the second round on a one-off trip to New York.

Berg fought on for another nine years without getting another crack at a title. He was still good enough in 1941, at the age of thirty-two, to beat highly regarded Britishers Arthur Danaher and Eric Boon, but he lost to Ernie Roderick and was stopped in five rounds of a return with Danaher. He hung up his gloves for good after winning his three fights in 1945 and earned regular work as a movie stuntman. He was still a familiar figure around the fight circuit up to his death in 1991, aged eighty-two.

The Ring, in June 1994, rated Berg fifth best junior welterweight of all time, behind Julio Cesar Chavez, Aaron Pryor, Barney Ross and Antonio Cervantes. 'His style was simple,' said the magazine, 'the "Whitechapel Whirlwind" threw more punches than any fighter of his era.'

JACK BRITTON

Real name: William J. Breslin.

World welterweight champion 1915, 1916-17, 1919-22.

Born in Clinton, New York, USA, 14 October 1885. Died in Miami, Florida, USA, 27 March 1962.

Career: 1905-30.

Total contests: 344. Won: 104 (28 KOs). Lost: 27. Drew: 21. No decision: 190. No contest: 2.

The statistics alone tell a remarkable tale of Jack Britton's career. He began boxing at small clubs around Milwaukee and Chicago as a twenty-year-old and had his last fight at almost forty-five. Into that twenty-five year career, the Irish-American packed in no fewer than 344 contests.

The fact that he only scored twenty-eight wins inside the distance shows that he relied on skill rather than punching power to defeat his opponents. Further testimony to his brilliant defensive style and his punch resistance is that only one man, Steve McKinney, ever knocked him out. That happened in Britton's first year as a professional. Over half of his bouts ended in 'no decision'. Britton polished his skills in his busy early days, but it was not until he teamed up with legendary manager 'Dumb' Dan Morgan that he began to get noticed. Three meetings with gifted Chicago lightweight Packey McFarland were applauded for the fine scientific boxing exhibited by both men. The first bout was a draw and the others 'no decision' affairs.

In June 1915, Britton earned a claim to the world welterweight championship when he outpointed Mike Glover in Boston. Englishman Ted 'Kid' Lewis also billed himself as world champion, so the pair were matched for the undisputed title on 31 August of that year, again in Boston. There was no love lost between the pair. Insults were exchanged and they refused to shake hands at the start of the bout. Britton boxed well, but found himself outspeeded by Lewis, who abandoned his usual whirlwind style to beat the American at his own game. Jack went to the victor's corner at the end and said, 'I guess you knew too much for me tonight, Kid, but maybe we'll meet some other time.'

How right he was. Britton and Lewis were to swap punches a remarkable twenty times in all over four years. It was one of the fiercest rivalries in ring history. The final score ended up as four wins for Britton, three victories for Lewis, and one draw. The rest were 'no decision' bouts.

After the initial win for Lewis, the pair fought two 'no decision' bouts, then clashed again for the title, in April 1916 in New Orleans. This time the American emerged the winner on points over twenty rounds. Britton won again when the pair met in a twelve-rounder six months later, but it was Lewis' turn to take the championship belt in June 1917. That was over twenty rounds. They finished playing ping-pong with the championship in 1919, when Britton celebrated Saint Patrick's Day by knocking out his great rival in the ninth round in Dayton, Ohio. The last of the great series was in 1921, when Britton retained his title by outpointing Lewis over fifteen rounds.

The most controversial contest of Britton's career was when he defended his title against world lightweight champion Benny

Leonard in June 1922. Leonard, a master craftsman, was ahead on points when he floored Britton in the thirteenth round. Inexplicably, he lashed out with a punch that landed while Britton was still down. The referee immediately disqualified the lightweight titleholder. Leonard gave no satisfactory explanation for throwing the fight away. Some ring historians have suggested that he deliberately fouled Britton so that he would not be relieved of his lightweight title. This seems scarcely credible. Could he not merely have beaten Britton, then relinquished the newly won welterweight title to continue as a lightweight?

Britton, then thirty-seven, lost his title to Mickey Walker, sixteen years his junior, on 1 November 1922. He continued to box for another seven years, but never got another title chance. He had lost most of his ring earnings in failed land investments in Florida and fought long past his prime as the only way he knew how to make ends meet. He finally quit the ring to become a boxing instructor and mentor to young sportsmen in New York City.

PANAMA AL BROWN

Nickname: the Elongated Panamanian.

World bantamweight champion 1929-35.

Born in Colon, Panama, 5 July 1902. Died in New York, USA, 11 April 1951.

Career: 1919-42.

Total contests: 155. Won: 123 (55 KOs). Lost: 18. Drew: 10. No decision: 4.

For a bantamweight, Panama Al Brown was an odd sight indeed. At five feet, eleven inches, he was taller than most middleweights. He had an incredible seventy-six inch reach, which enabled him to keep opponents speared on the end of his long jab while setting them up for his potent right hand.

Brown was very much at odds with the popular view of the average pugilist. He spoke seven languages and his sophisticated tastes led to a friendship with writer Ernest Hemingway. Brown was a homosexual, a rare enough orientation among boxers, and not readily disclosed in the easily shocked society of the 'twenties and 'thirties. He was an inveterate traveller, spending much of his career in Europe, where he was extremely popular.

Alphonso Teofilio Brown, as he was named at birth, first got interested in boxing while working as a clerk with the United States Shipping Board in Panama's Canal Zone. He watched US servicemen in the ring and fancied his chances at the sport. Turning professional at twenty, he won the Isthmus flyweight title by defeating Sailor Patchett.

This good win got the attention of American fight manager Dave Lumianski, who took the youngster to New York. By 1926, Brown had reached a number six spot in the world bantamweight ratings. He then took off for Paris for a year. He won six, lost two and drew one of his European outings before returning to the United States to win the vacant world title by easily outscoring Vidal Gregorio in June 1929.

Continuing his globe-trotting, Brown defended his title in New York, Paris, Montreal, Marseilles, Toronto, Milan, London and Tunis. He also fought many non-title bouts in various countries. Here was a world champion in its true sense. It was not all plain sailing, however. British featherweight champion Nel Tarleton held him to a draw in Liverpool and a riot followed the split decision awarded to him in a title defence against Kid Francis in Marseilles.

The merry-go-round stopped in Valencia, Spain, on 1 June 1935, when Baltazar Sangchilli relieved him of his world title on a fifteen-round decision. America's National Boxing Association (forerunner of the WBA) had already ceased to recognise Brown as champion due to his failure to meet leading contender Baby Casanova. So only the New York and European commissions' versions of the title passed to Sangchilli.

Brown avenged his defeat by Sangchilli three years later, but the Spaniard was by then no longer a champion. The Panamanian returned to New York, but was knocked out in seven rounds by Harry Jeffra and returned to the land of his birth to round off his career. He finally called it a day after outpointing Kid Fortune in 1942.

Brown had earned well during his world travels, but he was broke when he died in New York after contracting tuberculosis in 1951. His body was taken back to Panama for burial in Amador Guerrero Cemetery.

JOE BROWN

Nickname: Old Bones.

World lightweight champion 1956-62.

Born in New Orleans, Louisiana, USA, 18 May 1926. Died in New Orleans, 21 November 1997.

Career: 1946-70.

Total contests: 161. Won: 104 (47 KOs). Lost: 42. Drew: 13. No contest: 2.

Joe Brown was one of those talented ringmen who, common for his time, spent years fighting for peanuts in far-flung venues, before he got the world title shot he long deserved when seemingly past his prime. Although he was thirty by then, the skills he had polished in a thirteen-year apprenticeship stood to him. After winning the world lightweight title from Wallace 'Bud' Smith in August 1956, he defended it successfully eleven times. 'Old Bones,' as he became known, was thirty-six when he lost the title to Carlos Ortiz and he went on boxing for another eight years.

Born in New Orleans and brought up in Baton Rouge, Louisiana, Brown followed his father into the carpentry trade. He learned to box with the US Navy in the Pacific during World War Two. His first professional bout, a win over Leonard Caesar in New Orleans, took place in September 1943. His second was not for another three years, after he was discharged from the Navy, and his opponent was again Leonard Caesar. This time Brown was on the losing end. He later drew with and outpointed Caesar.

Joe's early record was patchy, with occasional losses and draws hindering his progress. He did notch up a useful scalp when decisioning a future world lightweight champion, Jimmy Carter, in 1947, but he suffered knockout defeats against Sandy Saddler and Johnny Bratton. It was not until he teamed up with influential manager Lou Viscusi, who had handled Willie Pep, and top trainer Bill Gore, that Brown's career took a definite upturn. To his fine defensive skills, he added power. He scored knockouts in consecutive bouts with Ray Rioja, Ray Portilla and Arthur Persley. This impressive run earned him a shot at world lightweight champion Wallace 'Bud' Smith, although Smith's title was not at stake. Brown won on points to earn a return match, this time for the title.

Brown got off to a good start in the championship fight, scoring well with his snappy left and following rights. But there was consternation in his corner at the end of the second round, when it was discovered he had broken his right hand. He picked up a cut eye shortly afterwards to add to his troubles. But Joe made light of his handicaps by using his skills to keep slightly ahead.

Nevertheless, Brown knew it was close coming up for the fourteenth round and decided he should try something spectacular. Ignoring his damaged hand, he battered the champion to the canvas with a brilliant combination. Smith rose at 'seven' but he was back on his knees from another attack when the bell came to his rescue. Brown's cornermen advised him that his big round was enough to ensure victory and that he should box his way through the final round. Joe won all right, but only on a majority verdict. He gave Smith a chance to regain the title six months later and this time he left nothing to chance. Brown won on an eleventh round stoppage.

Joe proved himself a worthy champion with successful defences against Orlando Zulueta, Joey Lopes, Ralph Dupas, Kenny Lane, Johnny Busso, Paolo Rosi, Dave Charnley (twice), Cisco Andrade and Bert Somodio before being outsmarted by a younger, quicker Carlos Ortiz in Las Vegas on 21 April 1962. 'I got tricked by Ortiz,' said Brown in 1996, still bitter after all those years. 'He'd run out of his corner and grab me. I couldn't use any of my boxing skills. Then he would flurry. It finally dawned on me that I was losing the fight. He wasn't doing nothin' to me, wasn't causing any damage. He just made me look bad.'

What Joe did not realise at the time he lost to Ortiz was that the 'old bones' were creaking more and more. Any hopes of another bid for his former title were dashed when England's Dave Charnley finally beat him at the third try, on a sixth round knockout. Brown tested his waning skills against other top ten contenders, but was outpointed by Alfredo Urbina, Nicolino Locche, Manuel Gonzalez and Paul Armstead. He was halted in three rounds by Carlos Hernandez. His career dragged on, with appearances in Argentina, Brazil, Venezuela, Mexico, Jamaica, South Africa, Colombia, Spain, Finland and England as well as various parts of the United States, until he finally called it quits in 1970. Aged forty-four, he still had enough left to outpoint Ramon Flores in Tucson, Arizona.

Joe had opened a business in Baton Rouge which included a hotel, nightclub and barber shop, but while he was away fighting, the guy who was supposed to be running it didn't do such a good job. When the business folded, Brown also lost his house in Houston, Texas. He moved back to his birthplace, New Orleans, where he drove a cab and also worked as a security guard and bartender. In his old age, he suffered from failing eyesight and was penniless when taken in by his half-sister, Geraldine. He died of prostate cancer in 1997. Of his ring career, he once said: 'To me, boxing was a job. I think I did my job pretty good.' No one will argue with him on that.

KEN BUCHANAN

WBA world lightweight champion 1970. World lightweight champion 1971-72.

Born in Edinburgh, Scotland, 28 January 1945.

Career: 1965-82.

Total contests: 69. Won: 61 (27 KOs). Lost: 8.

In 1971, Ken Buchanan was voted Sportsman of the Year by the British Sportswriters' Association, and was acclaimed in the United States as Fighter of the Year. Yet the Scot was never truly recognised for his talents by the British sporting public and was more appreciated in America, where he had his most important victories.

One of the reasons for his low profile in his home country was that most of his early career was spent behind the closed doors of private sporting clubs, thus preventing ordinary fans from seeing him in action. Buchanan's abrasive personality, his rocky relationship with his manager, Eddie Thomas, and his return of the Lonsdale Belt to the British Boxing Board of Control in a fit of pique, didn't help to expand his sparse British fan club. It is only in retrospect, years after his retirement, that the British have come to recognise Buchanan, a stylish boxer with a solid punch and sound chin, for the great sporting ambassador he was abroad during the 1970s. For this, he was honoured by the Queen, who presented him with an MBE.

Buchanan, who got his first pair of boxing gloves from his aunt when he was seven, joined one of Scotland's best amateur clubs, Sparta, and won his first medal in the boys' forty-nine pounds (three stone, seven pounds) division.

In 1965, he won the Scottish and British ABA titles and signed up as a professional with Welshman Eddie Thomas, a former British, British Empire and European welterweight champion, who also managed Howard Winstone, a future WBC featherweight champion. Right from the start, Buchanan's relationship with Thomas was uneasy. The Welshman's training methods were criticised by the boxer's father Tommy, who had a strong influence on his son. And the fact that the manager lived in Wales, 400 miles from Ken's home, didn't make things any better.

Boxing politics was a major part of the problem. Thomas had close connections with Britain's leading post-war promoter, Jack Solomons. By the mid-1960s Solomons' power was waning and a partnership of Harry Levene, Mike Barrett, Jarvis Astaire and Mickey Duff more or less controlled big-time boxing in Britain. As a result, Buchanan was unable to get fights on shows presented by Solomons' rivals. He had his first ten bouts at the exclusive National Sporting Club, located at the Café Royal in London's Regent Street. Here, members combined the boxing with dinner and were required to watch the contests in silence. If members got carried away during an exciting fight and started cheering, they would be admonished by a booming voice over the loudspeaker system: 'Gentlemen, remember where you are!'

It was at another members-only London club, the Anglo-American, that Buchanan got his first big chance in February 1968. He challenged veteran Maurice Cullen for the British lightweight title. The Scot, though he had won all his twenty-three fights to date, was the underdog against the highly skilled champion. Buchanan, however, was much too strong. He floored Cullen four times before putting him down for the full count in the eleventh round.

The new British champion now expected to earn some decent money. But a series of low-key contests, plus the falling-through of a scheduled final eliminator for the world title, fuelled his frustration. He had got married and taken out a mortgage on a smart home in the expectation of a profitable boxing career. With his manager unable to do business with the London promotional cartel, he made the shock decision to quit boxing at the age of twenty-four. He sent his licence and his Lonsdale Belt back to the British Boxing Board of Control and went back to work at his old trade, carpentry.

His new sense of freedom from the hassle and the rigours of training didn't last long. After a heart-to-heart chat with Eddie Thomas, he decided to give boxing another go. He was rewarded with a match against Miguel Velazquez for the vacant European lightweight title. Buchanan had to travel to Madrid for the bout. He started well, but was floored in the ninth round and lost a hotly disputed decision.

Lady Luck at last smiled on the Scot in September 1970. When Mando Ramos pulled out of a challenge to WBA champion Ismael Laguna in San Juan, Puerto Rico, Buchanan was called in as a replacement. Despite the energy-sapping sun that beamed down on the open-air Hiram Bithorn Stadium, Ken got his jab working well. Though staggered in the twelfth round and practically exhausted, he put on a strong finish to win on a split decision.

The first Britisher to win the world lightweight title since Freddie Welsh in 1917, Buchanan was astonished to hear that he would not be accepted as champion in his own country. The British Board only recognised the WBC and had already decided that the world title was vacant. If that wasn't enough of a body blow, Buchanan was even more depressed when he arrived home in Edinburgh. Wearing a sombrero to meet the expected crowd, he found only six people there to greet him – and that included his wife Carol, son Mark and his parents-in-law.

Things brightened up when he outscored Ruben Navarro in Los Angeles to win WBC appproval as champion. The BBBC announced it would now recognise him as world champion. Now it was the WBC's turn to twist the knife. When Buchanan signed for a return with Laguna, the WBC took back its belt because he failed to meet Pedro Carrasco, its designated main contender. Still holder of the WBA version, the Scot picked up a hefty $100,000 for meeting Laguna at Madison Square Garden, New York. In a thrilling battle, Buchanan survived a badly cut left eye to emerge with a unanimous decision.

His contract with Eddie Thomas was up for renewal, but Buchanan insisted there were things that needed to be sorted out. An angry Thomas said he was no longer interested in managing a 'back-stabbing, ungrateful' boxer. The champion's father, who had been granted a manager's licence, took over the job.

Buchanan's world came tumbling down at Madison Square Garden on 26 June 1972. Roberto Duran, an arrogant, unbeaten Panamanian who had been a professional fighter since he was fifteen, swarmed all over the Scot with his unrelenting, no-holds-barred style. Buchanan, repeatedly fouled, went down from a low right-hander at the end of the thirteenth round. The referee, seeing the champion's agony, decided he would not be able to continue. He declared Duran the winner on a technical knockout. Duran refused to give his badly abused victim a rematch. A decade later, the Panamanian great described Buchanan as the toughest and most difficult opponent he had ever faced.

Buchanan won his next thirteen fights, including a sixth round stoppage of former world champion Carlos Ortiz and a points verdict over fellow-Scot Jim Watt to regain the British title. Another try for a world title, this time the WBC version, ended in defeat against Ishimatsu Suzuki (who later changed his name to Guts Ishimatsu) in Tokyo. He had to duck a hail of bricks and bottles when he went to Cagliari, Italy, to defend his European title and stopped local favourite Giancarlo Usai in twelve rounds. His father wasn't so lucky. He needed seven stitches in a head wound.

Now aged thirty, Buchanan decided it was time to call it a day and devote more time to his hotel in Edinburgh. However, his wife sued for divorce and went to live elsewhere with their two children. The hotel business fell away and he was forced to sell up. In 1979, he returned to the ring to win two fights in Denmark, but he lost on points to Irishman Charlie Nash when he challenged for the European title in Copenhagen. Clearly, his best fighting days were behind him, but he fought six more times up to January 1982, losing the last four, before retiring again. He returned to work as a joiner, but yielded to the temptation of pulling on the gloves on unlicensed 'pirate' shows. It was the final ignominious fling of a once-great champion.

In December 1996, it was reported that Buchanan was living off state handouts in a dingy flat near Glasgow. It was a far cry from the customised Mercedes-Benz with its personalised 123 KB number plate; dancing with Princess Anne; dining with racing hero Jackie Stewart, and mixing with singer Andy Williams and ring greats, Floyd Patterson and Muhammad Ali. Now the best occasions are being asked to guest amateur boxing shows in Scotland. But Ken is philosophical about his fall from grace. 'There are plenty of poor souls out there worse off than me,' he has said.

Sky TV broadcast a discussion in 1997 involving former *Boxing News* editor Harry Mullan, promoter Frank Warren and ex-boxer and commentator Glenn McCrory to choose the best British fighter of all time. Their final choice came down to three men – Jimmy Wilde, Ted 'Kid' Lewis and Ken Buchanan.

TONY CANZONERI

New York-recognised world featherweight champion 1927. World featherweight champion 1928. World lightweight champion 1930-33, 1935-36. World junior welterweight champion 1931-32, 1933.

Born in Slidell, Louisiana, USA, 6 November 1908. Died in New York, USA, 9 December 1959.

Career: 1925-39.

Total contests: 175. Won: 137 (44 KOs). Lost: 24. Drew: 10. No decision: 4.

A strong pressure fighter with a high degree of skill, Tony Canzoneri was one of the outstanding ringmen in an era of great talent. He mixed with the best in three weight divisions and fought in twenty-two championship contests in the ten years he was at his peak. His only knockout defeat was in the last bout of his career.

Canzoneri started boxing as an amateur in New Orleans and picked it up again when his family moved to New York. After winning the New York State amateur bantamweight title, he turned professional in 1924 at the age of sixteen. Within two years he had only lost once in thirty-nine bouts when he met Bud Taylor for the vacant NBA bantamweight title. The ten-rounder ended in a draw. Taylor won the re-match on points. Canzoneri finally got the better of Taylor in their third meeting, but it was a non-title affair.

Tony moved up to featherweight and earned New York State Athletic Commission recognition as world champion by beating veteran Johnny Dundee in October 1927. A points win over Benny Bass the following year made him undisputed champion. He lost the title in his first defence, to Frenchman Andre Routis, and again stepped up a weight. His first attempt at the world lightweight title ended in defeat against Sammy Mandell. But, in November 1930, he smashed Al Singer, who had beaten Mandell, to the canvas for a sensational knockout in sixty-six seconds of the first round.

Canzoneri had three memorable fights with Englishman Jack 'Kid' Berg in 1930 and '31. Tony lost the first, a non-title bout, then won on a third round knockout to lay claim to Berg's world junior welterweight title. The Londoner insisted that only Canzoneri's lightweight title had been at stake, while the American claimed that, as both boxers were inside the junior welterweight limit, that division's title automatically passed to him. Their third meeting resulted in a points win for Canzoneri, cementing his claim as the legitimate titleholder. Tony risked both titles against the highly talented Cuban Kid Chocolate and was acclaimed for a fine points victory. He lost his junior welterweight title to Jackie Jadick in January 1932, but regained it the following year by beating Battling Shaw, who had dethroned Jadick.

Canzoneri then lost both his world titles to brilliant New Yorker Barney Ross in June 1933. He failed to avenge his defeat in a return three months later. But Tony had not finished collecting championship belts yet. When Ross relinquished the title on winning the welterweight crown, Canzoneri was in the wings ready to regain the lightweight prize with a points win over Lou Ambers in May 1935. He lost it to Ambers the following year and was again on the losing end when they met in May 1937.

Canzoneri fought on for another two years, until Al 'Bummy' Davis knocked him out in the third round. He retired to open a restaurant, perform a nightclub act and provide backing for Broadway shows.

GEORGES CARPENTIER

Nickname: the Orchid Man.

World light-heavyweight champion 1920-22.

Born in Lens, Pas de Calais, France, 12 January 1894. Died in Paris, France, 28 October 1975.

Career: 1908-26.

Total contests: 109. Won: 88 (56 KOs). Lost: 14. Drew: 6. No decision: 1.

One of the most popular boxers in history, Georges Carpentier might have been invented for Hollywood. Strikingly handsome, with a charming manner, he was an exciting fighter with a dynamite right hand. Known as 'the Orchid Man' for his habit of wearing the flower in his buttonhole, he took part in the first million dollar gate, a world heavyweight title challenge to Jack Dempsey. When his career was interrupted by World War One, the Frenchman became a national hero while serving in his country's army air corps. He was as well liked in America as he was in Europe. Even the English forgave him for consistently bowling over their best heavyweights.

Amazingly, Carpentier fought at every weight from flyweight to heavyweight. He was French lightweight champion at fifteen and won European titles at welterweight, middleweight, light-heavyweight and heavyweight. Though he won a world title at light-heavyweight, his lack of size proved too much of a handicap when he tried for the premier prize against Dempsey.

Originally a participant in the French sport of *savette*, in which feet were used, he converted to orthodox boxing under the tutelage of François Descamps, who discovered him as a boy and stayed with him throughout his career. Georges became a professional boxer in 1908 at the age of fourteen. In 1911, Carpentier won the French, and then the European, welterweight titles. He came through a stiff test by outpointing American Harry Lewis, a former world champion, then took the European middleweight title by knocking Englishman Jim Sullivan cold in the second round.

Manager Descamps, however, got carried away with the teenager's success by pitting him against two of the toughest American middleweights of the period. Frank Klaus, who was on the way to winning the world title, gave the Frenchman a bad body pounding and split his lip. Descamps saved him from further punishment by jumping into the ring during the nineteenth round, earning his man's disqualification. He took the same course of action when Billy Papke, the current world champion and a rough, tough fighter, gave Carpentier a going-over.

His struggles to make middleweight were blamed for Carpentier's setbacks and he stamped his authority among the light-heavyweights by taking the European title with a second round knockout of England's Bandsman Rice. It looked like his ambitions were again being over-stretched when he challenged another Englishman, Bombardier Billy Wells, for the European heavyweight title in Ghent, Belgium, in June 1913. Carpentier, outweighed and outreached, was dropped twice by accurate right-handers in the opening round. By the fourth round, however, Georges had discovered Wells' weakness to body punches. A smashing blow to the heart sank the Englishman to the canvas to be counted out.

Carpentier was invited to London to meet Wells in a return and this time the confident Frenchman gunned down the bombardier in little over a minute. Now a favourite with the English, he was brought back in July 1914 to meet American Gunboat Smith. The bout was billed, ludicrously, for the 'white heavyweight championship of the world'. That was because the genuine world champion, Jack Johnson, the first black man to win the world heavyweight title, was currently out of favour with boxing authorities across the globe. Carpentier won when Smith was disqualified for hitting him while he was down in the sixth round.

Boxing took a back seat for Georges while he served his country as an observation pilot in the Great War. His exploits earned him the *Croix De Guerre* and the *Medaille Militaire*. When his ring career resumed at the end of the war, Carpentier continued his humiliation of British heavyweights by flattening Joe Beckett in seventy-three seconds in London. Having conquered Europe, it was time to set his sights on America and the big prizes. On 12 October 1920, the Frenchman knocked out Battling Levinsky in the fourth round in Jersey City to become world light-heavyweight champion.

Legendary US promoter Tex Rickard pulled off a master stroke when he matched Carpentier with Jack Dempsey for the world heavyweight title on 2 July 1921. Over 80,000 people paid $1,789,238 to watch the fight at Boyle's Thirty Acres in Jersey City. It was the first time the million-dollar barrier had been broken. Old photographs taken from the back of the arena show the ring as a tiny white dot, but those seat-holders were happy just to be there when history was made. Even most Americans hoped for a French win. While Carpentier had been a war hero, Dempsey had been accused of being a draft-dodger. The heavyweight champion had further upset his fellow countrymen by carelessly allowing himself to be photographed, supposedly working for the war effort in an American shipyard, but wearing expensive patent leather shoes.

The film of the fight shows the contrast between the boxers. Dempsey was twenty-five pounds the heavier man, while the challenger looked exactly what he was, a light-heavyweight. Carpentier looked even smaller, in fact, as he fought out of a crouch, his left arm appearing to rest on his left thigh, as he sought the opening for his deadly right hand. The Frenchman found his target in the second round. A straight overhand right landed on Dempsey's cheek and staggered 'the Manassa Mauler'. Had it been a couple of inches lower, it might have caused the championship to change hands. But the punch had a more damaging effect on Carpentier. He broke his thumb in two places and sprained his wrist. At this early stage, the European champion had lost his most effective weapon. Dempsey, relentless, poured punches into the challenger's body, then concentrated his attack on the head in the fourth round. A right to the jaw floored Carpentier. He looked to be out, but he suddenly sprang to his feet at 'nine'. Dempsey moved in for the kill. A right to the heart doubled up the Frenchman, then a right to the jaw finished the job.

Still king of the light-heavyweights, Carpentier defended his title against Ted 'Kid' Lewis in London. He scored a first round knockout in controversial circumstances. Lewis turned to the referee to complain about his opponent's holding, leaving his chin exposed to Carpentier's trusty right.

Disaster struck in Carpentier's next defence. 'Gorgeous Georges' put his world light-heavyweight and European heavyweight titles at stake against Battling Siki, a Senegalese brawler with little skill, but a heavy punch. Carpentier had secured the film rights to the contest, in Paris on 24 September 1922, and sought to 'carry' Siki for several rounds to ensure the film's value.

His plan went all right for about a round and a half, but he was disturbed at the fury with which Siki fought back after being floored in the second round. A wild swing put the champion on the canvas for 'two'. A Carpentier right forced another count in the third round, but again the challenger bounced up and charged in. The champion, trying to get away, slipped and fell. It was all Siki from the bell for round four. He smashed Carpentier's nose, closed one of his eyes and gashed the other, then knocked him out in the sixth round. If that was not enough sensation, it was then announced that the referee had disqualified Siki for tripping the champion. The crowd kicked up such a fuss at the blatant injustice that the decision was reversed. Siki was the new champion.

Carpentier was obviously nearing the end of his distinguished career. He had enough left to stretch out British heavyweight champion Joe Beckett for the second time inside a round. A return trip to America resulted in a match with Gene Tunney, who was later to beat Dempsey for the heavyweight title. Carpentier was taking stiff punishment against 'the Fighting Marine' when his seconds threw in the towel in the fifteenth round. A draw with little-known Eddie Huffman and a points defeat by Tommy Loughran, a future light-heavyweight champion, convinced him it was time to call it a day. He signed off after knocking out Rocco Stragmalia in three rounds at Alan, Indiana, on 15 September 1926.

For a good many years after his retirement, Georges operated a high class bar and restaurant in Paris and spent most Sundays enjoying his favourite sport, fishing. He retained his good looks and his slim figure and would take delight in meeting fans who visited him on trips to the French capital. He was eighty-one when he died in 1975.

MARCEL CERDAN

Nickname: the Casablanca Clouter.

World middleweight champion 1948-49.

Born in Sidi Bel-Abbes, Algeria, 22 July 1916. Died in Azores, mid-Atlantic, 27 October 1949.

Career: 1934-49.

Total contests: 110. Won: 106 (61 by KO). Lost: 4.

The shocking news that an Air France Constellation FBA-ZL had crashed in the Azores, on the night of 27 October 1949, plunged France and the boxing world into mourning. All forty-eight people on board died. Among them was Marcel Cerdan. He had been on his way from Paris to New York in a bid to regain the world middleweight title he had lost to Jake LaMotta four months earlier.

In New York, the singer Edith Piaf, Cerdan's lover, collapsed when she was told of the tragedy. The concert she was to give the following evening was about to be cancelled when she insisted it should go ahead. 'This evening is for Marcel,' she said. She was supposed to sing eight songs. She had only begun the fourth, *Hymne a L'amour* (a Hymn to Love), when she fainted. The curtain came down on her performance – and on a great love affair.

No French sportsman, with the possible exception of Georges Carpentier, was more idolised by his fellow countrymen than the handsome, cheerful Cerdan. And no wonder. He was an exceptional fighter who lost only four times, each time in questionable circumstances, in 110 contests. Two of his defeats were on disqualifications. In another, he was the victim of an outrageous points decision. The fourth loss, to LaMotta, occurred when he had to retire due to the intense pain from a dislocated shoulder. So it can be safely stated that he never met his master in the ring.

Cerdan was born into a boxing family in Algeria, then a French possession. His father, a pork butcher, promoted amateur tournaments. Marcel, at the age of eighteen, followed his two elder brothers into the professional game. His record stood at 34-0 when he took the French welterweight title from Omar Kouidri in Casablanca. Within a few months he was also European champion.

When World War Two broke out, Marcel served in the French navy before his artillery unit was disbanded by the Germans. After boxing several times in Nazi-occupied Paris, Cerdan used forged travel permits to flee the capital. He joined the Free French Navy. During this period, he impressed Americans by winning two major Inter-Allied boxing tournaments.

When the war ended, Cerdan picked up the threads of his career. He had now blossomed into a middleweight and won the French title with a third round knockout of Assane Diouf. He knew he would have to travel to America to pursue his world title ambitions. His US debut, in December 1946, saw him notch up a good points win over Georgie Abrams, although he was given a difficult time by the balding American.

Cerdan returned to Paris to pick up the European middleweight title with a first round knockout of Leon Foquet. Winning appearances in London, New York, Montreal, Chicago and Paris followed, but he suffered a shock defeat by Belgium's Cyrille Delannoit in Brussels to lose his European championship. Almost everyone who saw the fight, even the partial Belgians, regarded the points verdict as a travesty. Cerdan was back in Brussels two months later to regain the title from Delannoit.

Such was the Frenchman's appeal that 20,000 fans paid almost $250,000 to watch him challenge Tony Zale for the world middleweight title at Roosevelt Stadium, Jersey City on 21 September 1948. Zale, the renowned 'Man of Steel' from Gary, Indiana, was two to one favourite, but, apart from hurting Cerdan with a hard right in the fourth round, it was the challenger's fight all the way. One of the most dramatic fight photos of all is that showing Zale, his head slumped on his chest, sagging against the ropes at the end of the eleventh round. He had just risen after being floored. The gallant champion, who had been unable to cope with the Frenchman's speed and punching power, was through. He could not leave his corner for the twelfth round.

Marcel was given a surprise boxing lesson for seven rounds by Englishman Dick Turpin before he caught the British champion with a payoff left hook in a non-title bout in London. He won another bout in Casablanca as a warm-up for his first world title defence, against the Bronx Bull, Jake LaMotta, in Detroit on 16 June 1949.

LaMotta was not a great puncher, but he was a rough, tough brawler who boasted never to have been floored. He wrestled Cerdan to the floor in the opening round, causing damage to the champion's shoulder. Marcel fought on as best as he could, though in pain. LaMotta, realising he was fighting a virtual one-armed opponent, piled on the pressure. By the end of the tenth round, Cerdan accepted it would be foolish to go on taking punishment without the chance of turning the tide.

The loss of his world title hit Cerdan hard. But there was a guaranteed return with LaMotta and he would show what a fully fit Frenchman would do. Tragically, he never got the chance.

EZZARD CHARLES

Nicknames: the Cincinnati Cobra, the Cincinnati Flash.

NBA heavyweight champion 1949-50. World heavyweight champion 1950-51.

Born in Lawrenceville, Georgia, USA, 7 July 1921. Died in Chicago, Illinois, USA, 27 May 1975.

Career: 1940-59.

Total contests: 122. Won 96 (58 KOs). Lost: 25. Drew: 1.

Strangely, Ezzard Charles, though he won his only world title at heavyweight, is honoured more as a great light-heavyweight. *The Ring* rates him best of all in that division, ahead of Archie Moore, Bob Foster, Gene Tunney (also heavyweight champion) and Tommy Loughran. This grading is based on Charles' excellent record against the top light-heavies of the 1940s. He beat Joey Maxim three times (and twice more when Ezzard was heavyweight king), Jimmy Bivins, Lloyd Marshall and Anton Christoforidis. But his greatest feat was to beat the great Archie Moore three times, twice on points and the last time by an eighth round knockout.

Though he never weighed more than ten pounds over the light-heavyweight limit, Charles knew his best chance of earning big money lay in the heavyweight division. He was no great crowd-pleaser, as he used his skills more than punching power to secure victory. He put himself in further bad odour with the public by defeating the much-loved Joe Louis, then a slow, old fighter. In an odd twist of fate, Charles finally earned acclaim as a true warrior in two fights he lost, against Rocky Marciano.

Born in Georgia, Charles moved with his family to Cincinnati as a child. He used to hang around a local gym and was lured into the game by listening to the old pros talking. As an amateur, Ezzard won all his forty-two contests, including the 1939 National Amateur Athletic Union middleweight title.

Turning professional at eighteen, he lost only twice in his first thirty-six bouts. But 1943 was a bad year for him. He was outpointed by Jimmy Bivins and knocked out by Lloyd Marshall, defeats he later avenged. He took off for Europe as a GI during World War Two and collected a string of inter-services titles.

It was 1946 before Charles resumed his career in the United States. He ran up an impressive winning streak against top light-heavyweights before he met Sam Baroudi in February 1948. The outcome of the fight was to have a significant effect on Ezzard's approach to boxing from then on. In the tenth round, Charles launched an all-out attack and put his opponent down for the full count. Baroudi, carried from the ring in a coma, died a few days later.

Although he decided to carry on boxing, Charles was never again the aggressive fighter who had earned the nickname 'the Cincinnati Cobra'. Indeed, he was often criticised for failing to apply the finishing blow when he had an opponent at his mercy. Yet, such was his ability, he was able to beat most of those he faced, even when he moved up to heavyweight. Wins over top-rated big men like Elmer Ray, Jimmy Bivins, Joe Baksi and Joey Maxim made him an automatic choice to contest the vacant world heavyweight title on the retirement of Joe Louis. Though it was recognised only by the National Boxing Association as a world title fight, Charles' points win over veteran Jersey Joe Walcott on 22 June 1949 was enough to convince most people that he was the best heavyweight around. The British Boxing Board of Control, ludicrously, gave its blessing to American Lee Savold as world champion on the strength of his win over British titleholder Bruce Woodcock in London.

When Joe Louis made a comeback and ran up a string of wins, including a knockout of Savold, the way was clear for the old 'Brown Bomber' to meet Charles for the undisputed world title. On 27 September 1950, Charles had little trouble outpointing the man who had been his idol. He even seemed to ease off in the late rounds, not wanting to see the once great champion lying unconscious at his feet. Like James J. Corbett, who toppled the hugely popular John L. Sullivan, or Gene Tunney, who finished the career of Jack Dempsey, or Larry Holmes, who beat the shell of what was once Muhammad Ali, Charles was not universally loved for daring to reveal that Joe Louis was a mere mortal who could not go on for ever. Ezzard's cautious style did not help his appeal. The fans prefer a heavyweight champion who goes for the spectacular finish.

Charles repeated his points win over Jersey Joe Walcott and there seemed to be little point in them meeting for the third time. Walcott, aged thirty-seven, had also lost twice to Joe Louis in title fights and few gave him a ghost of a chance of succeeding at the fifth attempt. Maybe Charles was complacent, but he walked into one of the sweetest left hooks in ring history to suffer an astonishing seventh round knockout on 18 July 1951. When Ezzard failed to regain the title the following year, suffering a points loss to Walcott, and was outpointed by Rex Layne in his next fight, his career seemed to be hitting the skids.

Charles, however, determinedly put together a nine-fight winning streak that included victories over title contenders Cesar Brion, Jimmy Bivins, Tommy Harrison and a revenge win over Rex Layne. His resurgence was halted when Cuban Nino Valdes and skilful Harold Johnson, a future world light-heavyweight champion, beat him on points. Back he bounced again with knockouts over Coley Wallace and Bob Satterfield. These good performances earned him a crack at his old title, now in the lethal hands of Rocky Marciano, who had taken over from Walcott.

In fact, Charles, now thirty-three, was looked upon as an easy opponent for the unbeaten Marciano. He turned out to give 'the Rock' one of the hardest fights of his career. Ezzard's stinging punches opened a cut over the champion's left eye in the fourth round and he stubbornly resisted Marciano's best efforts to club him to the canvas. By the half-way stage of the fifteen-rounder, however, Marciano's great strength and aggressiveness began to take effect and, in the eighth, it was the challenger's turn to bleed, from a cut on his right eyelid. Charles had trouble surviving through rounds nine to thirteen, but he somehow found the heart to fight back and share the fourteenth. The effort took away the last of his strength and he was driven around the ring throughout the last round by the ferocity of Marciano's onslaught. Charles was still there at the final bell, but the decision for the champion was beyond any doubt.

Charles' game showing was undoubtedly worth a rematch. It took place in September 1954, three months after their first encounter. This time it looked bad for the challenger as early as the second round, when he was dropped by a booming right. He somehow managed to maul and clinch his way through the next few rounds. Then, in the sixth, the fight took a dramatic turn. Charles' elbow caught the titleholder on the nose, splitting it wide open. Blood flowed like a fully turned-on tap. Marciano's cornermen pleaded with the New York Commission doctor not to stop the contest. He reluctantly let it go on. Before the eighth round, Rocky's trainer, Charlie Goldman, told the champion: 'Go after him now or you'll bleed to death.'

A desperate Marciano went for the kill, but ran into a countering right that opened a cut by his left eye. Ignoring his severe handicaps, he smashed a right to Charles's head that floored him. On his feet at 'four' but badly hurt, Ezzard staggered along one side of the ring. Marciano landed a long, looping left and a right that grazed the challenger's head as he fell. Charles could only rise onto one knee as the referee counted him out.

The two title defeats ended Charles' title aspirations. He had another twenty-three contests over the next five years, but lost thirteen of them. He suffered the ultimate humiliation when he was disqualified for persistent holding against Dick Richardson in London and was booed out of the ring.

After nineteen years in the ring and thirteen world championship contests, it came as a shock to the boxing world in 1961 when Charles disclosed that he had nothing left of the $2 million he had earned. Asked where it all went, he said with a shrug: 'Beats me. I guess I put too much into rebuilding my house, and I dropped a lot of dough in an athletic club venture that went sour on me. I could handle boxing but not money. It just kind of melted away.' With a wife and three children to support, he took the same sad road that so many other ex-champions had followed when their money ran out. He became a professional wrestler. He also worked as a 'greeter' at a nightclub in Newport, Kentucky.

Fate dealt him an even bigger blow in 1966 when he lost the use of his legs, then his power of speech. He was diagnosed as suffering from a form of multiple sclerosis. The once proud champion ended his days confined to a wheelchair. He was unable to pay his huge medical bills and his fellow boxers, among them Rocky Marciano, Archie Moore and Muhammad Ali, rallied round to raise money at a benefit night. Charles was six days short of his fifty-fourth birthday when he died in the Veterans' Hospital in Chicago in 1975.

Marciano, on the occasion of his own retirement from boxing, probably gave the most accurate summary of Charles' stature: 'Ezzard was never given enough credit. He beat Joe Louis fair and square, but by the treatment he got from the press and the public you would have thought he lost. I'll tell you this – he gave me the two hardest fights of my life. I had to reach down into my boots to find the strength to overcome him. He was a smart boxer and could hit harder than people think. He was just unlucky to come to the top in an era when the fans were hungry for blood and guts. They just didn't appreciate Ezzard's finer points.'

JULIO CESAR CHAVEZ

Nickname: J.C. Superstar.

WBC super-featherweight champion 1984-87. WBA lightweight champion 1987-89. WBC lightweight champion 1988-89 . WBC light-welterweight champion 1989-94, 1995-96. IBF light-welterweight champion 1990-91.

Born in Sonora, Mexico, 12 July 1962.

Career: 1980–present.

Total contests: 107. Won: 102 (85 KOs). Lost: 3. Drew: 2.

One of the most remarkable records in ring history was close to achievement when Julio Cesar Chavez took his tally to eighty-seven straight wins in 1993. The brilliant Mexican looked odds on to rack up a magical one hundred. But the bubble burst when he was held to a draw by WBC welterweight champion Pernell Whitaker, a decision that should have gone against Chavez, according to most fair-minded observers.

He then lost for the first time when Frankie Randall took his WBC light-welterweight title. Although Chavez regained the championship in controversial circumstances in a return with Randall, he had clearly shown the first signs of vulnerability. Like so many renowned champions of the past, 'J.C. Superstar' learned that even greatness has its limits.

Ring historians have expressed doubt as to the veracity of Chavez's long winning streak. He was, apparently, disqualified in the first round of his twelfth fight, when he struck Miguel Ruiz after the bell. Both *The Ring Record Book* and *Pugilato* for several years listed the bout as a loss for Chavez. But it was discovered that the local boxing commission in Culiacan officially changed the result the day after the fight. It now appears in the record books as a first round win for Chavez.

What is not in doubt is Chavez's right to be recognised as a ring great. With his fine craftsmanship, unwavering determination, solid chin and hard, accurate punching, he would have stood out in any era. There was no weakness in his fighting make-up. He was especially adept at cutting down the ring and forcing his opponent to fight his fight. He was deadly at close range, whipping in vicious hooks and uppercuts. No one threw a better left hook to the ribs than Julio. *The Ring* rates him the top junior welterweight of all time and second in its junior lightweight category behind Alexis Arguello. At his peak, he was considered the best pound-for-pound boxer in the world at the time.

Unlike most fighters who won world titles in several weight divisions, Chavez seemed to get even better as he moved up in weight. His finest single performance came at light-welterweight when he came from behind to snatch victory in the dying seconds against Meldrick Taylor in March 1990. Referee Richard Steele caused a major controversy when he threw his arms around Taylor as he sagged against the ropes following a desperate onslaught by Chavez. There were only two seconds to go to the end of the twelfth and last round. The referee explained that the time of the stoppage was immaterial. Taylor was out on his feet and in danger of getting badly hurt.

'In boxing,' commented *The Ring* in its report of the fight, 'one measure of greatness is how a champion rebounds from defeat.

Chavez rebounded before being defeated. This is not to suggest that he'll win for as long as he chooses to fight ... but, his future battles aside, Chavez left an indelible mark on the fight game with his thrilling victory.'

Though he was idolised in his native Mexico, Chavez never quite earned the same warm respect from Americans, although he fought the majority of his thirty-three world title fights in the United States. One of the marks against him was that he spoke only Spanish. Another was his association with two of the most controversial men in boxing – WBC president Jose Sulaiman and American promoter Don King.

One of a family of ten children born and brought up in Ciudad, Chavez followed three elder brothers into boxing. He was just seventeen when he had his first fight for pay. His manager, Ramon Felix, guided him carefully up to his first world title chance in September 1984. He took the vacant WBC super-featherweight title with an eighth round stoppage of Mario Martinez.

Julio was called upon to show what his chin was made of in his second title defence, when Roger Mayweather connected with a right in the first round that *The Ring* said 'would have levelled a skyscraper'. He not only stood up, but he halted Mayweather in the next round. Chavez defended his championship belt nine times before stepping up to lightweight in November 1987, when he dispatched Edwin Rosario in ten rounds to capture the WBA title. He added the WBC version of the world championship the following year by beating Jose Luis Ramirez on a technical decision. An accidental clash of heads in the eleventh round left Ramirez with a bad cut and unable to continue. Chavez, ahead on all three judges' scorecards, was declared the winner.

Another move up the scales in 1989 saw Julio take over as WBC light-welterweight champion by stopping his old rival, Roger Mayweather, in the tenth round. He added the IBF version in his dramatic last round victory over Meldrick Taylor, but gave it up after one defence. During that year, reports surfaced about Julio's bad living habits. The Mexican City *Excelsior* alleged that Chavez had a drink problem, that he was 'overweight and confused by fame, money, vanity and bad friends' .

The Mexican marvel's winning run finally came to an end in September 1993, when he tried for Pernell Whitaker's WBC welterweight title in San Antonio, Texas. Chavez, weighing just two pounds over the light-welterweight limit, fought well but was unable to cope with the heavier man's slippery southpaw skills and looked to have been beaten for the first time in his career at the end of the twelve rounds. One judge made Whitaker the winner by 115 points to 113, but the two others made it even at 115-115. So it was a majority draw. Neutral observers said Chavez was mighty lucky to keep his unbeaten record.

In his own division, Chavez was considered well-nigh unbeatable. He was a fifteen-to-one favourite going into his twelfth defence of the WBC light-welterweight title against Frankie Randall in January 1994. The champion's record stood at eighty-nine wins and a draw. Seventy-four of his victims had failed to stay the course. There had been a lot of talk, however, about Julio's lack of motivation and of over-indulgence in the good life. He had lost his drive, the hardness and concentration of purpose that had made him one of the most formidable fighters of recent years, it was said.

If Chavez was not fired up for the fight, Randall certainly was. The challenger stuck to a perfect fight plan, boxing and moving, but standing still and fighting when he needed to. Chavez was floored for the first time in his career in the eleventh round and he might have been stopped had Randall not been over-cautious at that point.

The split verdict went to Randall. Had Chavez not been deducted two points for low blows, he would have got away with a draw and kept his title.

Chavez won the title back in a rematch, but he earned little credit for the way it was achieved. He seemed to be behind on points when there was a bad clash of heads in the eighth round. Chavez, his right eye cut, turned away and seemed to have surrendered. Confusion reigned until it was announced that Chavez had won on a technical decision. The WBC had ruled that if a fighter was unable to continue after an accidental butt, the opponent should have one point deducted and the round in which the fight ended should be scored, even though it was incomplete. Two judges gave the fight to Chavez 76-75, while the third official made Randall the winner by 77-74.

It was clear that Chavez was no longer the force he had been. He held onto his title until he came up against the new kid on the block, the unbeaten former Olympic Games gold medallist Oscar De La Hoya, on 7 June 1996. Julio earned the biggest purse of his career – $9 million – for the Las Vegas fight that attracted huge interest, especially in Mexico. While Chavez was an authentic son of Old Mexico, De La Hoya was born in Los Angeles of Mexican parentage. There was no doubt, however, that Chavez was the one the Mexicans wanted to win.

The eagerly awaited clash came to an abrupt end before the end of the fourth round. Chavez, having his 100th fight, suffered a horrific gash over his left eye from a long right-hander. His face was a mask of blood when the ringside doctor decided there was no way he could continue. It was an unsatisfactory ending, but De La Hoya had shown in the short time the bout lasted that his youth and speed would have been too much for the thirty-three-year-old champion. The cut might have saved Chavez from a more humiliating defeat.

In June 1997, Chavez enjoyed the satisfaction of scoring his 100th victory. But he was beset with problems outside the ring. Though cleared of $1.3 million tax evasion charges, he was caught up in a row with Bob Arum over money owed to the promoter. When a Mexico City newspaper linked him to drug-traffic cartels, he threatened to sue, and took out full-page ads alleging a conspiracy against him. He went on Mexican television to deny stories that he had kidnapped and threatened a friend in order to make him talk about the supposed unfaithfulness of Julio Cesar's wife, Amalia, who was suing him for divorce.

Chavez underwent plastic surgery on his suspect eyebrows, and put up a gallant effort in a return match with De La Hoya in September 1998. But he new his best wasn't good enough and quit on his stool at the end of the eighth round.

KID CHOCOLATE

Real name: Eligio Sardinias Montalbo.

Nickname: the Cuban Bon Bon.

World junior lightweight champion 1931-33. New York-recognised world featherweight champion 1932-34.

Born in Cerro, Cuba, 6 January 1910. Died in Cuba, August 8, 1988.

Career: 1928-38.

Contests: 146. Won: 131 (50 KOs). Lost: 9. Drew: 6.

A hugely popular fighter on the New York circuit during the late 1920s and 1930s, Kid Chocolate combined dazzling speed with good two-fisted punching ability. Although sometimes criticised for being too fond of the good life and neglecting his training, he was only beaten nine times in 146 fights. Who knows what he might have achieved if he had always been in top condition?

Born Eligio Sardinias Montalbo, it was no surprise that he changed to 'Kid Chocolate' when he went to the United States to further his fighting career. Like many poor kids of his time, he learned to box while selling newspapers on the street. He was frequently called upon to defend his sales pitch against intruders. After winning an amateur boxing tournament sponsored by the Cuban newspaper *La Noche*, Chocolate was guided by the paper's sports editor, Luis Gutierrez. Part of the youngster's development was credited to his watching films of great fighters. He was unbeaten throughout his amateur career and won his first twenty-one professional bouts by knockout. In 1928, aged eighteen, he took off for New York.

Quickly establishing himself as a class performer, Chocolate was ranked number one featherweight contender a year after his arrival in the United States. He outscored one-time world champions Fidel LaBarba and Al Singer, but then lost his unbeaten record to tearaway Englishman Jack 'Kid' Berg. Chocolate, outweighed by ten pounds, had his best round in the third, when he scored with several strong uppercuts. But Berg's unrelenting attacks earned him a close decision. When Chocolate lost a return with LaBarba and was also decisioned by world featherweight king Battling Battalino, it looked as if he might not fulfil his early promise. But he shot back to form in 1931, when he halted Benny Bass in seven rounds to take over as world junior lightweight champion.

A bid for Tony Canzoneri's world lightweight belt, however, ended in failure. He found Canzoneri's aggression a bit too much to handle and was beaten on points. Chocolate lost again to Jack 'Kid' Berg in a non-title bout, but picked up New York Commission recognition as world featherweight champion by stopping Lew Feldman in the twelfth round. He defended this title against Fidel LaBarba and England's Seaman Tommy Watson before his struggles to make the nine-stone limit forced him to relinquish it.

It was evident that Chocolate's best days were behind him in 1933, when Canzoneri knocked him out in the second round. He assured himself of a miserable Christmas that year by dropping his junior lightweight title to Frankie Klick on a seventh round stoppage on 25 December. The Kid fought on for another five years and only lost three of his last fifty fights, but few of his opponents were top-class. His ring earnings mostly spent on New York's night life, he returned to Cuba to open a gym. He was awarded a pension by the Cuban government in recognition of his services to his country and to sport.

JOHN CONTEH

WBC light-heavyweight champion 1974-77.

Born in Liverpool, England, 27 May 1951.

Career 1971-80.

Total contests: 39. Won: 34 (24 KOs). Lost: 4. Drew: 1.

John Conteh was one of those fighters who have the potential to reach great heights, but fall short for a combination of reasons that have little or nothing to do with their ring talents. While he must rate as one of Britain's top ringmen, he could have made a much more significant impact on the game had it not been for brittle hands, an uncertain temperament and a myriad of problems outside the ring.

At his peak in the mid-1970s, Conteh was a class act. Blessed with movie star good looks and an impressively sculptured body, he boxed brilliantly behind an accurate left jab and scored with lightning-fast combination punches. There were doubts expressed about his level of commitment, however, and he showed a stubborn streak that got him involved in several promotional and managerial disputes.

Conteh, born to a Sierra Leone father and an Irish mother in the tough Toxteth district of Liverpool, proved his natural ability early in his amateur days. He crowned his unpaid career by taking the Commonwealth Games middleweight gold medal in 1970, but doubts over his mental toughness surfaced when he seemed to freeze in the European championships.

Turning professional in 1971, Conteh showed the style, the punching power and the charisma to quickly build up a large following. The only temporary setback, a points loss to cagey American Eddie Duncan in his eighteenth outing, was soon forgotten when he captured the European light-heavyweight title with a twelfth round stoppage of West Germany's Rudiger Schmidtke.

The stage was set for an all-British showdown with Chris Finnegan, the 1968 Olympic Games gold medallist, who was now the British and Commonwealth titleholder. In a bitterly contested fifteen-rounder in May 1973, Conteh earned a close decision to become a triple champion. The British weekly paper, *Boxing News*, said that Conteh's classy moves and punching power had reminded ringsiders of Sugar Ray Robinson and Jose Napoles. The return match exactly a year later ended in strong controversy when a butt, ruled to be accidental, left Finnegan with a badly cut left eye and unable to continue in the sixth round.

The reward for the Liverpudlian was a crack at the WBC light-heavyweight title, which had been stripped from Bob Foster for failing to defend it against Conteh or Jorge Ahumada, of Argentina. Conteh was matched with Ahumada in London on 1 October 1974. Conteh boxed brilliantly to frustrate and outscore the head-down, hard-hitting Argentinean. Spearing Ahumada with left jabs, he continually rocked his opponent with accurate combinations. Any doubts about his ability to mix it with the best were dispelled in the later rounds, when the Englishman was forced to stand toe-to-toe with the bustling Ahumada.

Boxing News commented: 'There were fears that Ahumada might prove too strong and purposeful in the closing rounds, but Conteh fought with icy professionalism. It was probably British boxing's greatest night since Randolph Turpin whipped Sugar Ray Robinson at Earls Court in July 1951 to win the world middleweight title. Conteh gave one of the best all-round displays of fighting seen from a British boxer in the last twenty years.' The future promised nothing but further glory and riches for twenty-three-year-old Conteh. But he wasn't the first boxer to discover on reaching the pinnacle that there was a very steep, slippery slope on the other side.

Having achieved his goal to have a world championship belt fastened around his waist, Conteh began to take stock of other aspects of his newly acquired status. Money was the principal consideration. His working class instincts were that the men who ruled boxing were in the meat business and people like him were the meat in the sandwich. He wanted a bigger bite of what was on the menu. Conteh's stubborn refusal to play the game the way others decreed led to him sacking his long-time trainer, George Francis, and getting into legal wrangles with matchmaker Mickey Duff, the British Boxing Board of Control and the World Boxing Council. He discovered that legal advisers' fees don't come any lower than managers' and promoters' percentages.

A broken hand suffered in a non-title fight with Willie Taylor in Scranton, Pennsylvania, proved especially costly. Though he managed to win the fight on points, he was out of action for fourteen months. On his return, he defended his title successfully twice before the WBC stripped him for failing to go through with a contracted title fight with Miguel Cuello, of Mexico, in Monte Carlo. Conteh felt the fight should have taken place in England, but the British Board refused to allow a live telecast. By staging the bout in Monte Carlo, which was outside the British Board's jurisdiction, it could be beamed live into Britain. But Conteh, still bristling at what he saw as the British Board's intransigence, pulled out of the Cuello match two days before it was due to go on. The result: he was no longer WBC champion.

Conteh managed to gain three cracks at his former world title, but ended up on the losing end each time. Awkward southpaw Mate Parlov outpointed him in Belgrade, Yugoslavia, and Matthew Saad Muhammad (formerly Matt Franklin) twice beat him in Atlantic City. The second match with Muhammad, in March 1980, was a total humiliation for the once-proud Liverpudlian. He later admitted he was beaten before he went into the ring. His concentration was so lacking that, when he was knocked down in the fourth round, he found himself staring at the audience and picking out Frank Sinatra and Faye Dunaway. He was down five times inside two minutes in that round before the referee led him to his corner. He later took out his frustration by going on a drinking binge and smashing up his hotel bedroom.

There were many more 'smashing' nights as cocaine was added to his high drinks intake. He cheated on his wife, Veronica, by having an affair with Jake LaMotta's daughter, Stefanie, and he was fined £100 for assaulting a waiter at Conteh's own restaurant. Considering its owner's reckless lifestyle, it was no surprise when the restaurant went into liquidation.

Conteh had just one more fight after the Muhammad débâcle, a fifth round win over American journeyman James Dixon in Liverpool on 31 May 1980, four days after his twenty-ninth birthday. A later attempt to pick up the threads of his career failed when an irregularity was discovered at the base of his skull and the brain specialist said he could not agree to his continuing to box. Conteh reckoned that he earned more than three-quarters of a million pounds in the ring and another £150,000 from advertising and personal appearances. What he didn't spend on legal bills, a stay at a psychiatric clinic and bad investments, mostly went down the drain on drink.

He showed the fighting spirit that was absent from the latter end of his career to overcome the worst of his demons. He earned minor acting roles and proved himself an informative and entertaining television analyst on big fight nights. But one cannot reflect on Conteh's boxing career without wondering how much more he might have achieved.

DON CURRY

Nickname: the Lone Star Cobra.

WBA welterweight champion 1983-85. World welterweight champion 1985-86. WBC light-middleweight champion 1988-89.

Born in Fort Worth, Texas, 9 September 1961.

Career: 1980-97.

Total contests: 40. Won 34 (25 KOs). Lost: 6.

In the mid-1980s, Don Curry was rightly regarded as the best fighter, pound for pound, in the world. He excelled as both boxer and puncher. He was undisputed welterweight champion of the world and looked unbeatable.

But, as so often happens in this most unpredictable of sports, he came crashing down to earth in a huge upset by Britain's Lloyd Honeyghan. Not only did he lose his unbeaten record and his WBA, WBC and IBF championship belts to the unheralded London-based Jamaican, but Curry needed twenty stitches in a cut over his left eye. He was also cut in the lower lip and his nose was broken.

Up to that disastrous night in Atlantic City on 27 September

1986, Curry had looked set for a long and honours-laden career. He blamed the struggle to make the weight had left him weak against Honeyghan. Moving up to light-middleweight, he won the WBC title, but lost it on the first defence. He was never the same brilliant ringman he had been in the lower division.

Curry came from a strong boxing background. His brother Bruce was WBC light-welterweight champion from May 1983 to January 1984 and another brother, Graylin, was a useful professional. But Don was always the hottest of the Currys. A national Golden Gloves champion in 1980, Don was strongly tipped to take home a gold medal from that year's Olympic Games in Moscow. President Jimmy Carter dashed that particular dream by ordering an American boycott of the competition. Curry won the 'alternative' Games, then turned professional with a record of only half a dozen defeats in over 300 amateur contests.

Within three years the sleek Texan was WBA welterweight titleholder after outpointing Korean Jun-Sok Hwang over fifteen rounds in his home town, Fort Worth, although he had to climb off the floor to win. Only Marlon Starling, who was later to beat Honeyghan for the WBC belt and also became WBA champion, took Curry the distance in a WBA title defence. It was Don's second win over Starling, whose unbroken run he had snapped before either became a champion. Curry took his title on the road, belting out fellow American Roger Stafford in the first round in Italy, Elio Diaz, of Venezuela, in Texas, Italy's Nino LaRocca in Monte Carlo and Welshman Colin Jones in Birmingham, England.

The WBC version of the welterweight championship was held by Milton McCrory and the eagerly awaited showdown between the two unbeaten titleholders was staged in Las Vegas on 6 December 1985. Curry had won all his twenty-two fights, all but four by the short route. McCrory's record stood at twenty-seven victories and a draw. He had stopped twenty-two opponents. What looked like being a good, competitive match was over inside two rounds, with McCrory down for the second time and counted out after one minute, fifty-three seconds of the round.

Another second round success, at the expense of Eduardo

Rodriguez, suggested Curry was set for a long reign as world champion. But persistent rumours about his difficulties in making the ten stone, seven pounds limit were proved conclusively when Honeyghan dumped him off the throne in one of the best ever performances by a British-based boxer. It was one of the biggest upsets of the decade.

Curry moved up to light-middleweight and earned a crack at Mike McCallum's WBA title. The Texan was doing nicely until McCallum connected with a perfect left hook to lay the challenger out cold in the fifth round. It looked like Curry had gone from great champion to has-been in less than a year. But he showed strong resolution by capturing the WBA belt from Italian Gianfranco Rosi at San Remo on 8 July 1988. Rosi was forced to retire after taking a hiding for nine rounds.

Curry's reign at light-middleweight lasted just seven months. His power was missing and his timing way off as he lost a decision to little-known Frenchman, Rene Jacquot in Grenoble, France. He retired in 1991 to manage and train fighters.

His estimated $5 million earnings disappeared, Curry got into a couple of scrapes with the law. Though acquitted of a drug conspiracy charge, he spent six weeks in jail for failing to pay child support. He made the inevitable return to the ring in 1997.

Aged thirty-five, he won his first comeback fight, but quit after losing in seven rounds to Emmet Linton, a fighter he had formerly trained.

OSCAR DE LA HOYA

Nickname: Golden Boy.

WBO super-featherweight champion 1994. WBO lightweight champion 1994-96. IBF lightweight champion 1995. WBC light-welterweight champion 1996-97. WBC welterweight champion 1997.

Born in Montebello, California, 4 February 1973.

Career: 1992–present.

Total contests: 30. Won: 30 (24 KOs).

The 'Golden Boy' tag stuck after Oscar De La Hoya arrived home from Barcelona in 1992 as the only member of the American boxing team to take an Olympic Games gold medal. But he continued to show the Midas touch as he piled up the millions after only a handful of professional fights.

The Californian, of Mexican parentage, has proved to be a winner in all areas. Not only is he a highly talented fighter, who can box as well as punch, but he is exciting to watch and is marketable with his clean-cut image, charm and good looks. By April 1997, after decisioning Pernell Whitaker to pick up his fifth world title in just twenty-four bouts, De La Hoya's personal fortune was worth a staggering $40 million – and there was lots more to come.

Oscar's style is super efficient. He keeps good concentration, uses a lightning left jab and hits extremely hard with both hands. At five feet, ten inches, he's taller than many middleweights. He has fine judgement of distance, good timing and a tight defence. If there is a weakness, it could be his chin. He was floored twice in his super-featherweight days and he took a count in the last round against Whitaker, although most observers considered it a combination of a slip and a shove. Nevertheless, he has shown excellent recuperative powers whenever he has been hurt. The first two boxers to knock him down, Narciso Valenzuela and Giorgio Campanella, were dispatched in one and three rounds respectively. Like a true professional, he worked hard on his defence and is now much more difficult to hit.

Growing up in tough East Los Angeles, Oscar tried his best to avoid getting into fights with other boys. So many times did he run home crying that his father, Joel De La Hoya, a former professional boxer from Durango, Mexico, took him to a gym to learn how to deal with bullies. After all, Don Joel had received the same medicine from his father, who had boxed as an amateur in Mexico in the 1930s. 'Oscar hated physical confrontations,' recalled his brother, Joel Junior. 'He never had a street fight. He preferred to play with skateboards near the house and baseball in the park. Nothing violent.'

Once he started going to the gym, De La Hoya decided: 'I have to be tough. No more crying.' His natural ability soon developed and he went on to a fine amateur career, picking up trophies galore. Every time he won a fight, his uncles and cousins would give him a dollar, or a quarter, so he learned early on that this was a game that could bring him good rewards.

After his Olympic triumph, De La Hoya could almost name his own price for his signature on a professional contract. He was expected to go with New York manager Shelley Finkel, who had heavily subsidised him as an amateur on the way to Olympic gold.

Instead, he signed with Bob Mittleman and Steve Nelson in return for a large bonus. This calculating trait in his character would surface several more times as he sought to have the best people around him, regardless of assumed loyalties.

After just eleven fights (all wins, ten inside the distance) De La Hoya captured his first prize, the WBO super-featherweight belt, by halting Jimmi Bredahl in the tenth round, in March 1994. He was a natural lightweight, however, and moved up to that division to take his second WBO trophy by knocking out Jorge Paez in two rounds. Critics who dismissed the Californian as a coddled Olympic hero got their answer when he came through a rough, tough battle with Puerto Rican John-John Molina. De La Hoya put his opponent down in the first round, but had to survive butts, kidney punches and mauls before emerging with a unanimous decision.

The WBO belt didn't have much status in America, so it was a step up for Oscar when he challenged Rafael Ruelas for the IBF lightweight title in May 1995. It was a strange experience for him, meeting a fighter taller than himself (by one inch) and with a longer reach. But he made light of his apparent disadvantages by dropping Ruelas twice and forcing a stoppage in the second round.

Challengers were set up and dispatched with ruthless efficiency. A smashing left hook shattered Genaro Hernandez's nose and forced the retirement after six rounds of his previously unbeaten East Los Angeles rival. Jesse James Leija was gunned down inside two rounds and said afterwards: 'De La Hoya has a lot of power. He should be a middleweight.'

Maybe not a middleweight, but Oscar thought he would try light-welterweight. His challenge to Julio Cesar Chavez for the WBC title on 7 June 1996 was a sure-fire box office success. Tickets, priced from $100 to $700, sold out within sixteen days. The paid attendance at Caesars Palace, Las Vegas, was 14,738. The live gate was $7,579,100. More than 1,500 press credentials were issued, a record for the arena.

Despite his Mexican background, De La Hoya knew he was on a loser with the Mexican fans, who always support their native-born son. Chavez was an icon, the pre-eminent Mexican fighter of his era.

De La Hoya, in an attempt to show his dual allegiances, entered the ring wearing a robe that was divided into half Mexican flag and half stars and stripes. He couldn't win, however. An over-zealous Mexican resident of Mexico City later brought a suit against him for defaming the Mexican flag.

Chavez came into the fight with a marvellous record of ninety-six wins, one loss and a draw, against De La Hoya's twenty-one straight victories. But the thirty-four-year-old WBC champion was nowhere near the force he once was. Badly cut over the left eye after just one minute, he found De La Hoya too big, too fast and too young. By the fifth round, Chavez's face was covered in blood. There was no way he could continue. Referee Richard Steele led him to his corner.

In less than a year, De La Hoya was looking for new and even bigger game. A measure of his elevated status was his installation as 7/2 favourite to whip WBC welterweight champion Pernell Whitaker on 12 April 1997. Whitaker, with only one loss and a draw, both hotly disputed, in forty-two fights, had his younger (by nine years) and taller (by five inches) opponent confused at times with his flashy southpaw skills and there were many observers who thought the unanimous verdict for De La Hoya was unjust. But Oscar was the stronger puncher and always came back well whenever Whitaker looked like outsmarting him. For De La Hoya, it was victory number twenty-four and he had his fifth world championship belt.

Sadly for British fight fans one of the best match-ups of the 'nineties was shunned by the television networks. The fight broke American pay-for-view records with receipts of almost $40 million, but Sky, ITV and the BBC refused to pay a paltry £40,000 for the British rights.

De La Hoya, unhappy with the 'too defensive' strategy adopted for the Whitaker fight, ditched his trainer, Jesus 'The Professor' Rivero, and brought in legendary Emanuel Steward. Oscar told his new man: 'I want to be the greatest prize-fighter who ever lived. I know that's a large order. But to be the very best, a champion has to fight the best out there. I'm ready for any sacrifice to achieve my goal.'

That goal was a record of six world championships in different divisions, then retirement to a life of golf – he has a handicap of five – and furthering his education towards a career in architecture and as an actor.

Allegations that he was a protected fighter hurt De La Hoya. In early 1999, he announced he was ready to take on any welterweight to prove he was the world's best pound-for-pound boxer. Ike Quartey, a former WBA champion and unbeaten in thirty-five fights, gave Oscar plenty of trouble, flooring him, but being dropped twice himself. De La Hoya won a split decision to bring his record to 30–0 and his total earnings to date to a staggering $98 million.

His angelic image suffered a blow when his drinking, partying, gambling and womanising habits became public knowledge, but in the ring he could do nothing wrong.

JACK DEMPSEY

Real name: William Harrison Dempsey.

Nickname: the Manassa Mauler.

World heavyweight champion 1919-26.

Born in Manassa, Colorado, USA, 24 June 1895. Died in New York, USA, 31 May 1983.

Career: 1914-27.

Total contests: 80. Won: 60 (50 KOs). Lost: 6. Drew: 8. No decision: 6.

Truly one of the outstanding ring champions who transcended the sport, Jack Dempsey, during 'the Roaring Twenties', epitomised the ability of the fighting spirit to beat the odds. The former miner and fruit-picker who 'rode the rods' from town to town, picking up a few dollars a fight and lots of useful experience, rose to become one of the world's most instantly recognised and best loved personalities. Right up to the day he died, aged eighty-eight, he was never called anything but 'Champ'.

Existing photographs and movies of his fights show Dempsey, his unshaven chin and habitual scowl serving to enhance his image as a ferocious fighter, raring to rip into his opponents as soon as the opening bell sounds. There were no frills to Jack's style. He waded in, throwing bombs that were aimed at causing utmost havoc. He did develop a useful ability to bob and weave as he advanced, but his prime object was to seek and destroy in the shortest possible time.

Nowhere was that vicious approach better epitomised than in his slaughter of the giant Jess Willard to capture the world heavyweight title at Toledo, Ohio, on 4 July 1919. Seven times in the opening round Willard was pounded to the canvas by the merciless challenger, who was five inches shorter and fifty-six pounds lighter. Only Willard's incredible gameness kept him going until the end of the third round, when his cornermen finally conceded that he could not carry on.

Dempsey's manager, Jack 'Doc' Kearns, had bet his entire purse of $27,500 on Jack winning in the first round, at odds of ten to one. It looked like he had made a shrewd gamble when the referee counted to ten, but the crowd's roars had drowned out the bell that 'saved' Willard. Dempsey had actually left the ring and was on his way back to his dressing room when a frantic Kearns called him back to tell him the fight was not yet over.

The loss of his big pay-day did not matter to Dempsey in the long run. He went on to amass a fortune by taking part in boxing's first match that took in over a million dollars at the gate. He made promoter Tex Rickard a very happy man by ensuring four further million dollar gates, one of them a non-title fight, when he knocked out Jack Sharkey.

One of nine children of parents whose blood was a mixture of Irish, Scottish and Native American, William Harrison Dempsey took the name 'Jack' after the Irish-born world middleweight champion of the late nineteenth century, Jack 'the Nonpareil' Dempsey. His two older brothers, who boxed professionally, also called themselves Jack Dempsey. As each retired, he passed on the name and it was the youngest of the three brothers who eventually made the name even more famous than had 'the Nonpareil', actually named John Kelly.

At the start of his career, Dempsey fought mostly in saloons, where he challenged any man to beat him, in the manner of John L. Sullivan's great boast that he could 'lick any son-of-a-bitch in the house'. He took greater risks stowing away on the underside of rail carriages, known as 'riding the rods', to travel from one location to another in search of work. Like so many of his desperate compatriots, he slept rough in hobo camps alongside the tracks. Sometimes he would pick up temporary jobs in mining and timber camps. The tough life served to harden him for the boxing career which formally began in 1914, when he earned $3.50 for his first fight. He was billed in those early days as 'Kid Blackie'. It was not until he teamed up with 'Doc' Kearns, however, that he began to attract notice as a lean, mean fighting machine.

Kearns guided him shrewdly and Dempsey ran up an impressive string of quick knockouts, with just a few hiccups along the way. He was twice held to a draw and twice outpointed by 'Fat' Willie Meehan, whom he managed to beat only once in their five encounters. He was knocked out in the first round by 'Fireman' Jim Flynn, but he avenged the only stoppage loss of his career by flattening Flynn in a return, also in the opening round.

After capturing the world heavyweight title from Willard in 'the Slaughter in the Sun' at Toledo, Dempsey knocked out challengers Billy Miske and Bill Brennan before making history by participating in the first fight to take over a million dollars at the gate. The challenger was the handsome Frenchman Georges Carpentier and the venue was Boyle's Thirty Acres in Jersey City, New Jersey. The date was 2 July 1921.

Although Carpentier was the fans' favourite, he had little chance of upsetting the champion, who was twenty-five pounds the heavier man. The Frenchman's pet right-hander, which had laid low the best of European heavyweights, staggered Dempsey momentarily in the second round, but the 'Manassa Mauler' duly dispatched the challenger in the fourth round.

Dempsey's next title defence, against Tommy Gibbons, put Shelby, Montana, on the map – but it also bankrupted the town. The townspeople had put up the money to finance the fight, which was a commercial flop. The fight itself was a fifteen-round bore. Dempsey was unable to floor the clever challenger and had to settle for a points decision.

If the Gibbons bout failed to ignite, the same could not be said of Jack's next fight, against Argentina's Luis Angel Firpo, at New York's Polo Grounds on 14 September 1923. In many experts' opinion, it ranks as the most exciting fight of all time.

In a sensational first round, Dempsey knocked down Firpo seven times and was floored twice himself. Only the assistance of ringside reporters enabled the champion to climb back into the ring in time after he had been sent flying through the ropes by the onrushing 'Wild Bull of the Pampas'. Dempsey finally finished off the brave challenger in the second round.

It was three years before Dempsey again put his title on the line. He had a falling out with manager Kearns, who disapproved of Jack's choice of movie star Estelle Taylor as his wife. There followed a bitter war of words and a legal battle before the profitable partnership of Dempsey and Kearns was finally ended. While married to Estelle, Dempsey had his nose straightened and appeared in minor movie roles.

Worried about ongoing legal and domestic problems, Dempsey returned to ring action on 23 September 1926, for the third million dollar gate. He faced the rugged, clever Gene Tunney, in driving rain at Philadelphia, Pennsylvania. Tunney, beaten just once, by Harry Greb, in his eleven years career, was the complete opposite in style to the swarming, heavy-hitting champion. New Yorker Gene was a stylish, upright boxer with a fast, accurate jab and a strong right and he made brilliant use of the ring. He proved too smart for a ring-rusty Dempsey and took a deserved points verdict over ten rounds.

The inevitable return was fixed for Soldier Field in Chicago on 22 September 1927, just one day short of a year since their first encounter. It attracted a crowd of 102,000, making it the first $2 million fight. The fight is remembered for probably the most enduring controversy in boxing history, the famous 'Long Count' . Dempsey, again unable to fathom Tunney's slick skills, finally got his big chance in the seventh round, but threw it away by his stubborn refusal to obey the referee's instructions. Dempsey caught the champion against the ropes and floored him with a barrage of punches. Instead of retreating to a neutral corner, he attempted to stand over the fallen Tunney, as he had been allowed to do in his earlier contests. Referee Dave Barry refused to start the count until Jack took up a position in a neutral corner, as the rules now specified.

By the time Dempsey obeyed the referee's command, Tunney had begun to regain his senses. He wisely stayed on the canvas until the count reached nine, although movies of the fight show he was down for fourteen seconds. Gene got to his feet and promptly 'got on his bike' until his head cleared completely. Dempsey's one and only chance to become the first boxer to regain the heavyweight title was well and truly gone. Tunney retained his title with another ten rounds points win.

Dempsey never fought seriously again, although he took part in scores of exhibition matches, many of which ended in Jack knocking out his opponents. In a five-months-period in 1931, he engaged in thirty-four exhibitions before a total attendance of 230,155 who paid $477,260 to see him perform. No other fighter in history matched these figures. Jack also acted as a referee in boxing and wrestling bouts. In the latter, it would sometimes be arranged that a supposedly angry wrestler would turn on the referee, giving Jack a chance to settle the argument with one of his famous right-handers.

He enlisted in the US Coast Guard in 1942 and was commissioned a lieutenant commander. He also managed and promoted fighters.

Dempsey fronted a popular bar and restaurant on New York's Broadway until the 1970s, when the owner of the site wanted to redevelop it and took out a compulsory purchase order. Gone forever was the place where thousands of fans shook the hand of the man who shook the world. The late Nat Fleischer aptly described Dempsey as 'a champion among champions'.

JIM DRISCOLL

Nickname: Peerless Jim.

European-recognised world featherweight champion 1912-13.

Born in Cardiff, Wales, 15 December 1881. Died in Cardiff, 31 January 1925.

Career: 1901-19.

Total contests: 69. Won: 52 (35 KOs). Lost: 3. Drew: 6. No decision: 8.

If Jim Driscoll was such a master boxer, how come he sported such a beautiful pair of cauliflower ears? Well, apart from his sixty-nine recorded fights, he took part in hundreds of bouts in boxing booths, where he would face all-comers, many of them much bigger and stronger than the skinny Welshman. No matter how skilful he became, he couldn't duck all the punches aimed at him!

Driscoll learned to box while working as a copy boy for his local newspaper in Cardiff, Wales. He used to wrap pages around his fists and spar with anyone willing to take him on. His favourite trick was to stand on a paper with his hands down by his sides, defying his workmates to hit him. Few succeeded. A professional boxer at eighteen, Jim (sometimes called Jem) won his first ten fights inside the distance, proving he was no powder-puff puncher. Indeed, over half his total career wins were by the short route.

Driscoll won the Welsh featherweight title in 1901, his first year of boxing. Six years later he knocked out Joe Bowker in seventeen rounds to win what was billed as the vacant British championship. But the National Sporting Club, then the governing body of British boxing, refused to recognise it as a title fight due to Bowker's long absence in America. Driscoll did not gain official recognition until 1910, when he beat Seaman Hayes. He went on to win the Lonsdale Belt outright.

After adding the British Empire title to his collection, he took off for the United States in search of the world championship. A 'newspaper decision' over tough Leach Cross earned him a match with world titleholder Abe Attell at the National Athletic Club, New York, on 19 February 1909. The trouble was that this was the 'no decision' era, so Driscoll would have had to knock out Attell to take the title.

The Welshman fought brilliantly, winning every one of the ten rounds with his darting left jab and fading quickly out of range of the frustrated champion's counters. At the end, Attell had one eye closed and his nose was badly swollen. Driscoll was unmarked. While the ringside reporters unanimously made Jim the winner, the 'no decision' law saved the American's title. Driscoll later claimed that he and Attell had agreed the title would change hands on what the newsmen decided, but the champion denied any such arrangement.

Disgusted at what he considered unfair treatment in America, Driscoll returned to Britain for a showdown with his great Welsh rival, Freddie Welsh, in Cardiff. In a rare flash of temper, Jim got himself disqualified for butting in the tenth round. On 3 June 1912, 'Peerless Jim' stopped Frenchman Jean Poesy in twelve rounds in London to win recognition as world featherweight champion by the International Boxing Union (forerunner of the European Boxing Union) and in Britain. He retired as undefeated champion the following year after boxing a twenty round draw with another great British rival, Owen Moran, from Birmingham.

Driscoll served in the British Army as a physical training instructor during World War One, but he had so little means afterwards that he was compelled to make a ring comeback. Now aged thirty-nine and greying at the temples, he managed to dispose of another British veteran, Pedlar Palmer, in four rounds. He was held to a draw over twenty rounds by Francis Rossi before bidding a sad farewell to the sport after being stopped in the sixteenth round by talented Frenchman Charles Ledoux. It was clear to the audience at London's National Sporting Club on 20 October 1919, that Driscoll was not a well man. In fact, he was stricken with tuberculosis, and only went through with the fight because he needed the money.

While he still had the strength, Jim boxed rings around the Frenchman, who had earned European recognition as world bantamweight champion seven years earlier. But Driscoll was exhausted by his efforts to keep his aggressive opponent at bay and he took a succession of painful shots to the body in the fifteenth round. His seconds implored him to quit, but he insisted on giving it one more try. He was on the brink of his first knockout defeat when his cornermen threw in the towel. It was only his third loss in sixty-nine fights.

The old warrior was given a standing ovation by the club members, who passed the hat and raised a £1,500 bonus to help him in his retirement. Within five years he was dead, at the age of forty-four.

JOHNNY DUNDEE

Real name: Giuseppe Carrora.

Nickname: the Scotch Wop.

New York-recognised world featherweight champion 1922-23. World featherweight champion 1923-24. World junior lightweight champion 1921-23, 1923-24.

Born in Sciacca, Sicily, Italy, 22 November 1893. Died in East Orange, New Jersey, USA, 22 April 1965.

Career: 1910-32.

Total contests: 335. Won: 90 (22 KOs). Lost: 31. Drew: 19. No decision: 194. No contest: 1.

Publicity photos of Johnny Dundee, showing him wearing a kilt, tall hat and a monocle, were designed by his manager, Scotty Monteith, to present the fighter as a Scot. It didn't fool anybody. Dundee was as Italian as a dish of spaghetti. So he settled for a dual nationality nickname, 'the Scotch Wop'.

Giuseppe Carrora, to give him his real name, stepped into the ring an astonishing 335 times. The total could be more, for many of his bouts were 'no decision' affairs, and it was not unknown for such contests to go unrecorded. Even more remarkably, almost all of his bouts went the scheduled distance. He only stopped twenty-two opponents and was only halted twice himself. He relied on brilliant skills and nifty footwork to dazzle some of the best fighters of his era. A speciality of his style was to launch punches as he bounced off the ropes. A dangerous tactic for some, but Dundee brought it to a fine art.

Taken to America as a child, Dundee was raised in the notorious 'Hell's Kitchen' district of New York. His parents ran a fish market there and the youngster frequently got into street brawls. Spotted by Scotty Monteith, he was taken under the manager's wing and was only sixteen when he had his first professional contest, with no amateur experience.

His manager believed in making him work. In 1911 alone, Dundee fought forty-seven times, more than the entire career totals of many modern ringmen. His busy schedule kept him in peak condition and enabled him to sharpen his skills through experience of opponents with a wide variety of styles. By 1913, Dundee, aged twenty, was considered good enough to challenge Irish-American Johnny Kilbane for the world featherweight title. After twenty rounds, it was declared a draw. Between 1915 and 1920, Dundee fought the great Benny Leonard eight times in 'no decision' bouts. Though Leonard generally came out on top, the newspapermen gave the nod to Dundee in three of the encounters between classic boxers.

'Junior' world championships were unknown until 1920, when the New York State Athletic Commission introduced five junior divisions, junior flyweight, junior bantamweight, junior featherweight, junior lightweight and junior welterweight. Only two, junior lightweight and junior welterweight, were taken any way seriously. Dundee was matched with George 'KO' Chaney on 18 November 1921, for the first junior world championship. Chaney was disqualified in the fifth round and Dundee had his arm raised by announcer Joe Humphries as 'the new junior lightweight champion of the world'. He also got a $2,500 belt put up by promoter Tex Rickard.

If Johnny's status as a world champion was doubted by some, he enhanced his reputation by adding the world featherweight title to his collection in 1922, although again his claim was only recognised in New York. Dundee had got his chance when Kilbane, who had been held to a draw in their first meeting, refused to meet him in a return. The 'Scotch Wop' scored one of his rare KOs when he put Londoner Danny Frush away in the ninth round to pick up the vacant title.

Dundee fluctuated between featherweight and junior lightweight for the next few years. He briefly lost control of the junior lightweight title to Jack Bernstein in May 1923, then won it back in a rematch seven months later. In the meantime, he earned universal recognition as world featherweight champion in June 1923 by convincingly outpointing Frenchman Eugene Criqui, who fought with a steel plate inserted in his jaw, a souvenir of an encounter with a German sniper in World War One.

Increasing weight forced Dundee to relinquish the featherweight title and concentrate on the higher division. But he lost the junior lightweight belt to Steve 'Kid' Sullivan in June 1924. Signs that his long, gruelling career was beginning to tell were evidenced when he lost nine of his next eleven fights. Foolishly, Dundee starved himself for one last try at the featherweight title, knowing the effort would leave him weak. He lasted fifteen rounds with Tony Canzoneri for the vacant NBA version of the championship in October 1927, but was a clear loser.

Johnny continued to fight until 1932, when he was forty-one, without getting another crack at a title. He lost most of his ring earnings running a mediocre stable of racehorses.

Triple champ Henry Armstrong.

Bang on: Muhammad Ali belts Britain's Brian London for a third-round knockout and *(below)* Joe Frazier is guided to a neutral corner by referee Arthur Mercante after left-hooking him to the floor in the last round of their fight.

Dear old pals: Muhammad Ali, Joe Frazier and George Foreman get together in 1989 to promote the video *Champions Forever* and *(below)* Jack 'Kid' Berg poses for Cariña Fahy in the 1930s.

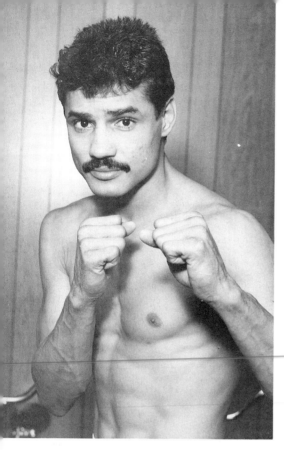

Alexis Arguello, versatile Argentinean *(left)* and 'Old Bones' Joe Brown, defender of the lightweight title twelve times *(right)*. *(Below)* Panama Al Brown, the five foot eleven inches world bantamweight champion.

AL . BROWN à l'écran

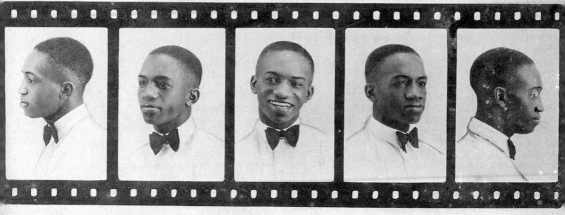

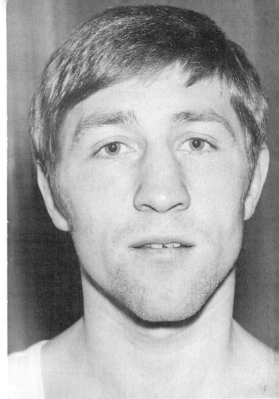

Nigel Benn, action man, and (*right*) Scot Ken Buchanan, one of the best of British.

Remembering when: Georges Carpentier (*on the left*) and Jack Dempsey meet up in 1971, fifty years after their million-dollar-gate heavyweight title fight.

John Conteh, classy but temperamental Englishman, who won the WBC light-weight title and *(right)* Marcel Cerdan, tragic victim of an air crash. *(Below)* Sugar Ray Leonard ducks a right from Roberto Duran during their third meeting, for the WBC super-middleweight title, won by Leonard on points.

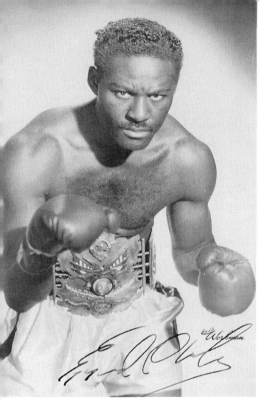 

Ezzard Charles, heavyweight champ, but rated by some as best light-heavyweight of all and (*right*) Bob Foster, deputy sheriff, who won the world light-heavyweight title in 1968 with a terrific knockout of Dick Tiger. (*Below*) Len Harvey, the master technician who won only British recognition as world light-heavyweight champion.

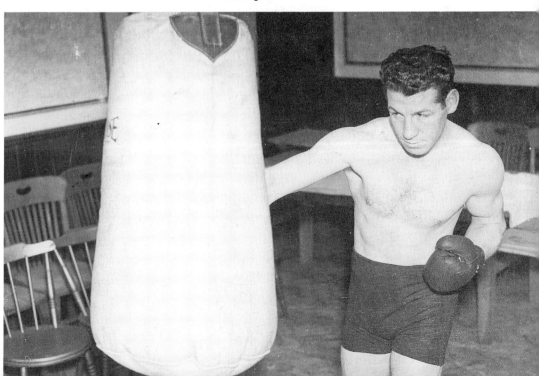

This one's a hit: WBO super-middleweight champion Thomas 'Hit Man' Hearns stuns challenger Michael Olajide with a right on the way to a unanimous points victory. *(Below)* Larry Holmes destroys Marvis Frazier, Joe's son, in the first round.

ROBERTO DURAN

Nickname: Manos de Piedra (Hands of Stone).

WBA lightweight champion 1972-78. World lightweight champion 1978-79. WBC welterweight champion 1980. WBA light-middleweight champion 1983-84. WBC middleweight champion 1989-90.

Born in Guarare, Panama, 16 June 1951.

Career: 1967–present.

Total contests: 115. Won: 101 (70 KOs). Lost: 14.

Roberto Duran would never claim to be boxing's number one 'Mr Nice Guy' . The Panamanian idol, who tested his punching power as a young man by knocking out a horse, outraged Britons by his rough treatment of Ken Buchanan in winning the WBA lightweight title. He hit the unfortunate Scot with everything but the kitchen sink – he would have used that, too, if he could find one handy! When he knocked out Ray Lampkin in a lightweight title fight, Duran watched his battered victim being carted away to hospital, then told the TV interviewer: 'I didn't hit him quite right. If I did hit him right, he would be in the morgue, not the hospital.' He once knocked out the wife of an opponent when she attacked him in a Panama City ring after he had beaten her husband.

After he won his fourth world title, a brilliant win over Iran Barkley giving him the WBC middleweight title at the age of thirty-eight, Duran demanded that a statue be erected to him in Panama City. 'I want recognition now,' he said, 'not when I'm dead.' But, whatever his lack of etiquette, no one can deny Duran his place among the ring's supermen. A professional at sixteen, a world champion at twenty-one, he was still a match for top contenders in his mid-forties.

The Ring, in May 1994, paid Duran the ultimate accolade of naming him number one lightweight of all time. It meant that, in a division of many fighting legends, he topped the likes of Benny Leonard, Joe Gans, Tony Canzoneri and Ike Williams. 'Even crusty historians who generally dismiss the modern era rate "Manos de Piedra" with the greatest fighters ever,' stated the magazine. 'He had a reputation as a coal-eyed, foam-at-the-mouth killer, but, as proved by masterful victories over arch-rival Esteban DeJesus, he came to understand pace and learned to apply strategy. He was a far more polished fighter at the end of his reign (as lightweight champion) than when he overwhelmed Ken Buchanan to win the crown.' In its June 1996 issue, ranking the top fifty fighters of the last fifty years, *The Ring* placed Duran at number three. Only Sugar Ray Robinson and Muhammad Ali were ahead of him. Justifying Duran's high rating, the magazine said: 'Who can match his mix of talent, ferocity, accomplishment and longevity?'

If there is one caveat as to his superman status, it concerns the one true blot on his record – the infamous surrender in the second of his three fights with Sugar Ray Leonard. When Duran, who had been getting the worst of the exchanges, turned his back and shouted 'No mas' ('No more'), not only did the phrase earn its place in boxing folklore, but huge questions were asked about the Panamanian's heart. It was Leonard who gave the best analysis of what happened in New Orleans on the night of 25 November 1980: 'To make any man quit is an achievement. To make Roberto Duran quit seemed impossible. It was better than knocking him out. I outclassed him, humiliated and frustrated him. He couldn't take it mentally. I didn't hurt him or make him bleed. I just made him look a fool before millions.'

In assessing Duran's career, however, one must look to his many great performances, such as the triumph over Buchanan to win his first world title in his twenty-ninth fight, the memorable points win over Leonard in their first meeting, the dramatic comeback after the Leonard return bout débâcle to blast out WBA light-middleweight champion Davey Moore, and the astonishing capture of the WBC middleweight title from Iran Barkley when supposedly finished as a top-notch fighter.

Duran was the personification of the hungry fighter who made good. Born into abject poverty in Guarare, he was raised in the slums of Chorillo, on the banks of the Panama Canal. His father had done a runner, leaving his wife to raise nine children on her own. By the age of thirteen, Roberto's irregular schooling was over and he was out on the streets hustling money whatever way he could. He even stole fruit from an orchard owned by Carlos Eleta, who later became his manager.

Boxing, for which he found he had a penchant, pointed the way to a better life. After winning all but three of his sixteen amateur fights, he turned professional and won twenty-one bouts before Eleta took over. The wealthy landowner, recognising the youngster's potential, got his contract for a bargain $300. Eleta made a shrewd investment by bringing in two of boxing's most respected trainers, Ray Arcel and Freddie Brown, to develop Duran's natural talent.

Just ten days after his twenty-first birthday, Duran battered and brutalised Ken Buchanan at Madison Square Garden, New York, on 26 June 1972, to capture the WBA lightweight title. The crafty Scot was simply overwhelmed by the challenger's ruthless attacks. As the bell rang for the end of the thirteenth round, Duran sank a left hook into Buchanan's groin area. The champion went down in agony and was unable to come out for the next round. Duran's arm was raised as 'the winner and new champion'.

Duran was unbeatable at lightweight over the next seven years. He successfully defended his title eleven times. Only one man managed to survive until the final bell. Recognition as undisputed world champion came by knocking out Esteban DeJesus, the only man to have beaten him in sixty-four bouts. Years later, when he learned that DeJesus was dying of AIDS, he visited the stricken fighter at his home and, in a rare show of compassion, shed tears as he embraced his old adversary.

His battles with the scales forced Duran to relinquish the lightweight title in January 1979. Within five months, he had earned a crack at Sugar Ray Leonard's WBC welterweight belt. The showdown between the two great ringmen took place during a Montreal rainstorm on 20 June 1980. It promised to be a classic – and it was.

Duran gave the best performance of his career to dethrone Leonard, who had won all his twenty-seven previous contests. The Panamanian knew his best chance was to knock the silky-smooth champion out of his stride and he used every psychological, as well as physical, weapon at his disposal to do so. When he wasn't taunting Sugar Ray about his boxing ability, he was snarling insults, questioning his masculinity and throwing in abusive remarks about his wife. At the end of each round, he would swagger back to his corner, waving to his supporters in the 46,317 crowd and inviting their applause, which was readily forthcoming.

Duran never gave up his attack, weaving his way in close to let rip with vicious punches, pushing his opponent into the ropes and generally roughing him up. Leonard showed his brilliant skills, whenever he was allowed, and at the end of fifteen unforgettable rounds, there was little to separate them. The three judges each made Duran the winner, two of them by a single point. The third official had the Panamanian two points in front.

The magnificence of Duran's triumph was soured by his shock retirement in the return with Leonard five months later. In Panama, he was disgraced. His house was stoned, he was called a homosexual and the Panamanian government withdrew the special tax exemption it had granted him as a national hero. But Roberto was no coward. The simple truth is that he was confused and demoralised by his failure to deal with Leonard's outstanding skills. He quit out of sheer frustration. His decision was astonishing, given his macho image, but understandable in the circumstances.

Switching his home base to Miami, Florida, Duran redeemed himself by giving Davey Moore an eight round battering to take the WBA light-middleweight title in June 1983. Five months later, he made an audacious bid for Marvin Hagler's undisputed world middleweight championship. It was the first time anyone had challenged for a world title at four different weights. Duran put up a brave showing, but lost on points over fifteen rounds. Roberto, whose love of the good life saw his weight zoom up to around thirteen stone in between fights, got himself down to the light-middleweight limit to face Thomas 'Hit Man' Hearns for the vacant WBC championship in June 1984. He suffered the most comprehensive defeat of his career when Hearns poleaxed him with a smashing right-hander in the second round.

It looked like Duran had reached the end of the road when Robbie Sims, whose only claim to public recognition was that he was Hagler's half-brother, beat him on points. But old 'Hands of Stone' still had one great performance left in his locker. On 24 February 1989, he outsmarted the much-feared Iran Barkley to take the WBC middleweight title on a split decision.

The publicity drums began beating for a showdown between Duran and Leonard. The Panamanian needed the money to pay off a $1.5 million debt to the US Internal Revenue Service. The third clash between the bitter rivals was arranged for Las Vegas on 7 December 1989. It was for Sugar Ray's WBC super-middleweight belt and gave the Panamanian a chance to erase the odour left over from the 'no mas' affair nine years before.

Alas, Duran, at thirty-eight, couldn't turn back the clock. He fought with little conviction and was well beaten on points in a dull fight. His fans implored him to hang up his gloves, but he carried on and was still good enough, in 1995, to give Vinny Pazienza, twelve years the younger man, a tough workout over twelve rounds for the IBC super-middleweight title. Still going strong in June 1997, he scored the 100th win of his career by outpointing Jorge Castro, a former WBA middleweight champion.

It was the saddest sight of all, however, on 28 August 1998, when a plainly 'shot' Duran was battered to defeat in three rounds by William Joppy in a WBA middleweight title bout. Pale and podgy, his greying hair dyed black, he hardly landed a punch on a man born after Duran had started his professional career. Referee Joe Cortez acted humanely in calling a halt to the slaughter.

Boxing News commented: 'There's something tragic about a gifted, poverty-stricken kid who can make $50 million, only to end up fighting as a sad, slow-moving grandfather because he can't pay his tax bill.'

The late Ray Arcel, who trained fighters for sixty-five years, was asked by prize-winning photographer/author Arlene Schulman for her book *The Prizefighters* what had happened to Roberto's money. 'He misused it,' said Arcel. 'He had bad advice, bad investments. But I root for him. Some of us are blessed with tremendous talent. You don't lose it. And I think he may know more about boxing than I do.'

JEFF FENECH

IBF bantamweight champion 1985-87. WBC super-bantamweight champion 1987-88. WBC featherweight champion 1988-89.

Born in Sydney, Australia, 28 May 1964.

Career 1984-96.

Total contests: 32. Won: 28 (20 KOs). Lost: 3. Drew: 1.

Australia has produced plenty of outstanding fighters, but surprisingly few world champions. Undoubtedly, were they campaigning today, the likes of Peter Jackson, Young Griffo, Frank Slavin, Les Darcy and Dave Sands would have picked up some of the wide selection of 'world titles' up for grabs. It was not until 1952, when Jimmy Carruthers scored a shock first round knockout over South African Vic Toweel, that the Aussies rejoiced in claiming a king of the ring. Another bantamweight, Lionel Rose, ruled the roost from 1968 to '69, the same year that Johnny Famechon, son of a former French champion, completed Australia's hat-trick of world titles by capturing the WBC featherweight title from Jose Legra.

Then there was Jeff Fenech. The son of Maltese immigrants, Sydney-born Fenech, judged on a record of achievement, probably qualifies as the outstanding Australian fighter of all time. He won world titles at three different weights.

A bit of a tearaway as a kid, Jeff channelled his aggression into boxing. He made such good progress that he was picked to represent his country in the 1984 Olympic Games. On his return home, he turned professional and won the Australian flyweight title in only his third contest. Amazingly, four fights later, he was a world champion. He won the IBF bantamweight title by stopping Japan's Satoshi Shingaki in nine rounds in Sydney on 26 April 1985. After knocking out Shingaki in the third round of a return, Fenech turned back the challenges of Americans Jerome Coffee and Steve McCrory before relinquishing the championship belt to try for the WBC super-bantamweight title in May 1987. Once again claiming hometown advantage, Jeff relieved Thailand's Samart Payakarun of the championship on a surprise fourth round stoppage. He beat American Greg Richardson and once-great Mexican Carlos Zarate before, yet again, handing back the belt to move up a weight. The WBC featherweight title had been vacated when Azumah Nelson stepped up to super-featherweight in January 1988. In March of that year, Fenech stopped Victor Callejas, of Puerto Rico, in the tenth round to take his third world title.

After three defences, the Australian announced his retirement, but came back in June 1991 to box a twelve-round draw with Azumah Nelson in Las Vegas for the WBC super-featherweight title. Fenech bitterly disputed the decision and was favoured to dethrone the veteran Ghanaian when they were rematched in Melbourne in March of the following year. Nelson, however, turned in a brilliant performance to halt the challenger in the eighth round. It was Fenech's first defeat.

He retired, only to make a comeback in 1995. He won twice, lost once, then quit for good the following year after being stopped in two rounds by South African Philip Holiday in an IBF lightweight title fight in Melbourne.

BOB FITZSIMMONS

Nicknames: Ruby Robert; the Fighting Blacksmith.

Born in Helston, Cornwall, England, 26 June 1863. Died in Chicago, Illinois, USA, 22 October 1917.

World middleweight champion 1891-94. World heavyweight champion 1897-99. World light-heavyweight champion 1903-05.

Career: 1883-1914.

Total contests: 62. Won: 40 (32 KOs). Lost: 11. Drew: 0. No decision: 10. No contest: 1.

What is a world heavyweight champion of the last century doing in a book of great fighters of the twentieth century? Well, though Bob Fitzsimmons had been knocked off the heavyweight throne by James J. Jeffries in 1899, he hadn't finished collecting championships as the world entered the new century. In 1903, at the age of forty, Fitz astonished the boxing world by flooring light-heavyweight champion George Gardner five times in twenty rounds to become the first man to hold world titles at three different weights. He had been middleweight champion from 1891 to 1894. It was not until Henry

Armstrong in the 1930s that another triple world champion arrived.

Legend depicts Fitzsimmons as something of a physical freak. Though standing just under six feet, his sparse red hair, freckled skin and strong upper body supported by spindly legs made him look nothing like a fighter who could topple the best heavyweights of his era. Yet, never weighing more than the light-heavyweight limit of twelve stone, seven pounds (175 pounds), his skill and punching power proved more than adequate when he faced much bigger men. When Fitzsimmons fought Ed Dunkhorst in 1900, he conceded four inches in height and a massive sixty-two pounds in weight. But he knocked 'the Human Freight Car' off the tracks inside two rounds. It is Fitz who is credited with the origin of the remark: 'The bigger they are, the harder they fall.'

Bob was such an outstanding champion that several countries claimed him as their own. He was born at Helston, in Cornwall, and though his family took him to New Zealand at the age of nine, England has always proudly acknowledged him as its first world heavyweight champion, even though he never fought in the land of his birth. His early days as a professional fighter were spent in Australia and he became an American citizen after winning the world heavyweight title. Fitzsimmons, who developed his strength working as a blacksmith, first showed promise by winning a New Zealand amateur tournament supervised by the legendary English bare-knuckle champion, Jem Mace. He was encouraged by Mace to try his luck as a professional. On moving to Australia, where he spent seven years, he ran up a record of fifteen wins and five losses, with six 'no decisions'.

Fitz emigrated to America in 1890. On the strength of three knockout victories, he secured a match with world middleweight champion Jack 'the Nonpareil' Dempsey. 'Ruby Robert' was already twenty-eight years old when he entered the ring in New Orleans to face Irish-born Dempsey on 14 January 1891. He gave the brave Dempsey a savage beating before knocking him out in the thirteenth round. Two impressive wins over Irishman Peter Maher, a top-ranking heavyweight, gained Fitzsimmons his dream match – against world heavyweight champion James J. Corbett. Bob was a

10/6 underdog when he entered the specially built arena in Carson City, Nevada, on Saint Patrick's Day, 1897. At thirty-five, he was four years older than 'Gentleman Jim' and was sixteen pounds lighter. He was dismissed by Corbett as 'an over-rated nobody'.

For six rounds, it seemed that Fitzsimmons had stepped out of his class. The heavyweight champion completely outboxed him, peppering him with stinging left jabs which had him bleeding heavily from the nose. When a hard left hook dropped the challenger for a count of nine, it looked like the end for Fitz. He showed great courage, however, by weathering the storm and fighting back with such fury that he soon wiped the smile from the arrogant champion's face. With his wife, Rose, shouting encouragement from the ringside, Fitzsimmons turned imminent defeat into victory with a blow that was to earn its place in ring history as 'the solar plexus punch'. In fact, it was nothing more than a stiff left hook to the stomach. Corbett collapsed in agony, gasping for breath, and was counted out in the fourteenth round.

Fitzsimmons enjoyed the fruits of his great victory for two years before defending his heavyweight title for the first time. His opponent at Coney Island, New York, on 9 June 1899, was James J. Jeffries, a former boiler-maker from San Francisco, and one-time sparring partner to Corbett. Though relatively inexperienced, he had won all of his eleven fights and only two opponents had lasted the distance. At twenty-three, he was twelve years younger, and sixty-four pounds heavier, than the champion. As early as the second round, Rose foresaw her husband's downfall. She left the ringside after Bob was floored by a terrific left to the mouth. Fitz had his moments of hope, especially when he split the challenger's left eyebrow with a stiff left, but Jeffries was just too big and too powerful. A long right, followed by a left to the chin, left Fitzsimmons flat out in the eleventh round.

Fitz made a brave bid to regain his title in a return with Jeffries in July 1902. He surprised the champion by outboxing him and smashing his nose, gashing him under the right eye and also drawing blood from a mouth injury. But 'Big Jeff' kept landing with heavy thumps to the body to gradually sap the strength from the veteran challenger. A smashing left hook to the jaw finished off Fitzsimmons in the eighth round.

Bob announced his retirement, but made a remarkable comeback to capture the world light-heavyweight title. The new weight division had only come into being in 1903. Irish-born George Gardner was only its second champion. It was Gardner whom Fitzsimmons challenged at San Francisco on 25 November 1903.

Fitz scored a psychological blow by going to the champion's dressing room before the fight, slapping him on the back and exclaiming, 'Hi, George, how are you? I hope you're feeling like a good fight tonight.' Such a display of confidence from the old man made Gardner apprehensive. He allowed Fitz to gain control. Though Bob tired badly towards the end of the twenty rounds, he managed to stave off Gardner's late aggression to take a well-deserved decision and his third world championship.

'Ruby Robert' fought only once, a six-round 'no decision' bout with Philadelphia Jack O'Brien, over the next two years before putting his light-heavyweight title at stake against O'Brien in San Francisco on 20 December 1905. His lengthy absence from the ring, together with his advancing years, had slowed his movements and his punches were generally off target. He was dropped three times and, totally exhausted as he slumped on his stool at the end of the twelfth round, he told referee Eddie Graney, 'Eddie, I'm all done up, I can't go on.'

Fitz laid off for two years, then stepped back into the ring to face the formidable Jack Johnson. It turned out to be a total mis-match. Bob, aged forty-four, was tied up in knots by the gifted black Texan and was knocked out in the second round. In 1909, Fitzsimmons was invited back to Australia to meet Bill Lang, the country's heavyweight champion, in Sydney. The bout was scheduled for twenty rounds, a considerable disadvantage to Fitz, who was conceding twenty years to his opponent. Yet, for six rounds, the old-timer showed such skill that the crowd cheered every move he made, while jeering their own champion's efforts. But Bob's efforts took so much out of him that he was an easy target for Lang's knockout blow in the twelfth round.

Fitzsimmons kept himself busy with personal appearances and acting in plays with his third wife, Julia. He had his two final ring outings in Pennsylvania in 1914, in six-round exhibitions with K.O. Sweeney and Jersey Bellew. The audiences were amazed at the skill shown by the fifty-year-old ex-champion.

After divorcing Julia, Bob married Russian-born Temo Ziller, a travelling evangelist. He abandoned the vaudeville circuit to join her in hot gospel tours. From fighting his fellow men, he was now concentrating on fighting the evils of the world. While appearing in Chicago in October 1917, Fitz was taken ill with lobar pneumonia. His condition deteriorated rapidly and the man who had barely known a day's illness in his life passed away at the age of fifty-four.

GEORGE FOREMAN

Nickname: the Punchin' Preacher.

World heavyweight champion 1973-74. WBA and IBF heavyweight champion 1994-95.

Born in Marshall, Texas, USA, 22 January 1949.

Career 1969–present.

Total contests: 81. Won: 76 (68 KOs). Lost: 5.

Once upon a time, there was a fierce giant called George. He devoured his victims as quickly as they were served up to him. If anyone dared ask why he was so mean to everyone, he would give them a withering scowl that suggested 'You're next!' When he had satisfied his appetite for human sacrifices and his pot of gold was safely tucked away, big bad George gave a tired sigh and went into a deep sleep.

Ten years passed. Fear spread throughout the land when it was learned that George was coming back. The pot of gold had developed a hole and much of his wealth had leaked out.

But, lo and behold, the new George was a gentle giant. His head was shaved to give him the appearance of a benign Buddhist monk. Instead of humans, his taste was for cheeseburgers. He still knocked over people who stood in his way – but he did it with a smile. All he wanted to do was help underprivileged kids. The last pages of the fairytale have yet to be written, but big George deserves to live happily ever after.

There's no doubt that the Brothers Grimm couldn't have dreamed up a more magical tale than the real-life adventures of George Foreman, Mark One and Mark Two. There really have been two George Foremans (or should that be Foremen?) The bald, blubbery, far-from-beautiful behemoth of the 'nineties, though still good enough to take the WBA and IBF heavyweight titles from Michael Moorer at the advanced age of forty-five, is unrecognisable as the beautifully sculptured athlete who destroyed Joe Frazier to win his first world title over twenty years earlier. Yet each ranks among the best single performances in heavyweight history.

Born in Marshall, Texas, George was a school bully and rebellious teenager. He was introduced to boxing as a way to keep him out of trouble. He took to the sport so well that, by 1968, he was an Olympic Games heavyweight gold medallist. These were the Games where several American athletes staged 'black power' demonstrations at the medal ceremonies. Foreman refused to fall in line and patriotically waved the Stars and Stripes on the winner's rostrum.

Turning professional the following year, Foreman won his first thirty-seven bouts, all but three by knockouts. But he still looked unready for Joe Frazier when Smokin' Joe agreed to defend his world heavyweight title on George's twenty-fourth birthday, in Kingston, Jamaica, on 22 January 1973. Foreman dealt with the previously undefeated Frazier as effortlessly as he did all the others. He sent the champion crashing to the canvas six times before referee Arthur Mercante stopped the slaughter after ninety-five seconds of the second round. One left hook lifted the champion clean off his feet.

Further quick-time dismissals of Joe Roman and Ken Norton made the six foot, four inches Texan look unbeatable. The champion's trainer, Dick Sadler, boasted: 'I've moulded a monster.

I've taken the best of Joe Louis, Jack Johnson and Rocky Marciano and rolled it into one.' But the monster was about to be destroyed. No one thought Muhammad Ali, at thirty-two and no longer the dancing master of old, would survive the phenomenal punching power of the champion. 'The Rumble in the Jungle', in Zaire on 30 October 1974, produced one of the most stunning ring upsets of all time. Foreman, a 3/1 favourite, was psyched out of the fight by Ali's 'rope a dope' tactics. Tired and demoralised at his inability to down his tormentor, Foreman was sent spinning to the canvas to be counted out in the eighth round.

George was so shattered by his defeat that he wondered if he could ever regain his self-respect. He returned to the ring for a gimmick promotion in Toronto, Canada, when he beat five opponents on the one night, three by knockout. A sensational battle with Ron Lyle, with both men on the floor repeatedly, climaxed in a fourth-round win for Foreman. He followed that by repeating his earlier win over Joe Frazier, although this time it took him five rounds.

Then, on an extraordinary night in March 1977, something happened that changed his life dramatically. A surprise loser on points to Jimmy Young, he claimed he got a vision from God as he lay on the bench in his dressing room after the fight. He quit the ring to become an ordained preacher, then set up the George Foreman Youth and Community Centre in the small town of Humble, Texas, to help poor and wayward kids. The trouble was that it took money to run and maintain such a centre, and that was something he didn't have much of. Five times married, George had lots of alimony to pay out, not to mention feeding and clothing his nine children – four of whom were called George! He saw only one way out: 'I'm going to be the heavyweight champion of the world – again.'

The flabby, middle-aged Foreman who stepped back into the ring for the first time in ten years was so unlike his former self that his comeback was looked upon as a sick joke. But it was George who had the last laugh. He notched up nineteen straight knockouts from 1987 to 1990. Sure, most of his victims were 'stiffs', but there were occasional glimpses that Foreman could still make an impact on the heavyweight scene. 'Smokin'' Bert Cooper, who was dispatched in three rounds, had given champion Evander Holyfield plenty of trouble.

Emphatic proof that George's left hook was as potent as ever came in a stunning second round knockout of 'Great White Hope' Gerry Cooney. The win earned forty-three-year-old Foreman a crack at Holyfield's undisputed world title in April 1991. Though he was clearly beaten, George had the satisfaction of still being on his feet at the final bell. Another points defeat, against Tommy Morrison for the WBO belt, suggested that the old-timer's dream of ever winning a big prize again would never come true. But the sceptics were about to be silenced. The fight game has produced its fair deal of shock results over the years, but none topped Foreman's knockout of Michael Moorer for the WBA and IBF versions of the heavyweight championship in Las Vegas, Nevada, on 5 November 1994. For eight rounds, George took a systematic boxing lesson from the southpaw champion and it looked like the referee might call a halt to save him from further punishment. But Foreman produced a beauty of a straight right that left Moorer flat on his back to be counted out.

The miracle had happened. George Foreman was a world champion again at forty-five, the oldest man in history to win a title.

His reluctance to defend against a suitable contender led to the WBA stripping him of his belt in March 1995. He vacated the IBF title four months later rather than face Germany's Axel Schulz, whom he had beaten on a hotly disputed decision, in a return. Fifty in January 1999, he still hadn't announced his retirement.

'I quit boxing in 1977 with millions of dollars,' said Foreman. 'Every day was a weekend. I didn't have to work. But the worst thing that could happen to me is to not have a reason to get up and go to work. I love boxing. I'm scared to lose it. I want to do it until I decide I don't want to do it anymore.'

BOB FOSTER

World light-heavyweight champion 1968-74.

Born in Albuquerque, New Mexico, USA, 15 December 1938.

Career: 1961-78.

Total contests: 65. Won: 56 (46 KOs). Lost: 8. Drew: 1.

Funny, isn't it, how skinny guys often make the biggest hitters? Looking at Sandy Saddler, Thomas Hearns or Bob Foster didn't suggest they could dent an egg, but they had more one-punch knockout power than most mighty-muscled specimens. Foster, a gangling six feet, three inches, never weighed much more than the light-heavyweight limit of twelve stone, seven pounds (175 pounds). Flat footed, with his left arm dangling onto his thigh, he would stalk his opponent, raking him with his long left, waiting for the opportunity to strike with the pay-off punch. His favourite was his left hook, but his right wreaked plenty of damage too.

Only when he ventured into the upper reaches of the heavyweight division was Foster found wanting. Though his oft-stated ambition was to become the first light-heavyweight to win the heavyweight crown, he could not match the strength of Joe Frazier, Muhammad

Ali, Doug Jones or Ernie Terrell, all of whom beat him inside the distance. In his own division, Foster ranks among the best in history. He won the light-heavyweight title with a terrific knockout of Dick Tiger, who had never been stopped before, then defended it successfully fourteen times before retiring as undefeated champion.

Foster boxed as an amateur in his native New Mexico and later while serving with the US Air Force. He was unbeaten in over a hundred amateur bouts and earned a place on the 1959 Pan American Games team. His hopes of being included in the 1960 Olympic side were dashed when he was offered the middleweight place. Such an effort at weight-making would have left him weak, so he declined the offer. The light-heavyweight spot went to Cassius Clay, who won gold.

Turning professional in 1961, Foster won his first nine contests before his over-ambitious handlers put him in with Doug Jones, a top-rated heavyweight who would give Clay (not yet Muhammad Ali) a tough ten-rounder five months later. Jones was too strong for Foster and stopped him in eight rounds. Undeterred, Foster took on the six foot, seven inch Ernie Terrell, a future WBA heavyweight champion. He was taking a hammering when the referee rescued him in the seventh round. The folly of conceding weight to the big men was finally recognised when he was outpointed by, appropriately, Zora Folley.

By then, however, Foster was feeling a bit disillusioned with boxing and began to look at alternative careers. He took a job in a munitions plant and fought only once in 1966. The feeling that he hadn't given the sport his best shot goaded him into making 1967 a busy year, with the world light-heavyweight title as his target. He won all his seven fights, six by knockouts.

He was rewarded with a chance at Dick Tiger's world championship on May 24, 1968. The fight drew almost 12,000 fans to Madison Square Garden, New York. Tiger, who had been twice middleweight champion before moving up to take the light-heavyweight belt from Jose Torres, hurt Foster in the opening round, but the challenger, who towered over him by seven inches, took control from the third round. A right uppercut, followed by an explosive left hook, put the Nigerian down for the full count in the fourth round.

In order to get his world title chance, Foster had to raise the financial backing himself. So he was left with little more than his training expenses for his great win.

Though now holding down a job as a deputy sheriff in Albuquerque, he set his sights on the heavyweights, where the big money was. He was given a puncher's chance against Joe Frazier in their world heavyweight title clash in Detroit on 18 November 1970, but it was Smokin' Joe's left hook that did the damage. Foster was counted out in the second round.

Back in his own division, he reigned supreme. He halted dangerous challengers Vicente Rondon and Mike Quarry in two and four rounds respectively, but was taken fourteen rounds by brave Britisher Chris Finnegan at Wembley, London, in September 1972. Finnegan, a classy southpaw and former Olympic Games gold medallist, fought his heart out until exhaustion, and Foster's pet left hook, laid him out.

Foster was stopped in eight rounds by Muhammad Ali for the North American heavyweight title. There were signs that the old left hook was losing much of its potency when he was twice taken the full fifteen rounds by South African Pierre Fourie. Held to a draw by Jorge Ahumada in his fourteenth title defence, Foster, then thirty-six, announced his retirement after the WBC said they were stripping him for failing to meet Ahumada again or the other leading contender, England's John Conteh.

He returned to win five fights over the next three years, but quit for good in June 1978 after losing twice on stoppages. He continued his long career in law enforcement in his home town of Albuquerque.

JOE FRAZIER

Nickname: Smokin' Joe.

New York-recognised world heavyweight champion 1968-70. World heavyweight champion 1970-73.

Born in Beaufort, South Carolina, USA, 12 January 1944.

Career: 1965-81.

Total contests: 37. Won: 32 (27 KOs). Lost: 4. Drew: 1.

If ever a fighter had an appropriate nickname, it was 'Smokin' Joe Frazier. You could almost see the steam coming from his nostrils as he bore down relentlessly on his foes, bobbing and weaving to get into range for his heavy bombs. And when they landed, it was 'Goodnight, baby!'

Dubbed 'the black Marciano' in his early days, he didn't manage to emulate Rocky by going through his career undefeated. That was largely because he was unlucky enough to share the same era as Muhammad Ali and George Foreman, each of whom beat him twice. Marciano had been fortunate that the quality of opposition wasn't as high in the fifties. The peak of Frazier's career was undoubtedly his great win over Ali in their first meeting. He put Muhammad on his back with a mighty left hook, his favourite punch, and won on points to inflict the first defeat on the self-styled 'Greatest'. Their two other fights were also classics.

Frazier was born, the seventh son of thirteen children, on his father's run-down vegetable plantation in Beaufort, South Carolina. School didn't hold much attraction for him and, by the age of seven, he was working on the farm. He got married at fifteen, then followed his elder brothers to Philadelphia, where he settled. He got a job, fittingly in view of his later profession, in a slaughterhouse.

Somewhat ashamed of his pudgy appearance, Joe joined a local amateur gym to lose weight. He was attracted to the boxing set-up and, once he gave it a try, made rapid progress. He only lost twice in forty amateur bouts, both times to huge Buster Mathis. He was lucky enough to make the 1964 Olympics team when Mathis, who had beaten him in the trials, had to withdraw with a broken thumb. Frazier took his place. He made the most of his opportunity by taking home the gold medal from Tokyo.

Frazier turned professional the following year. He was managed by a syndicate of mainly white businessmen who called themselves Cloverlay Inc. But Joe's training and the choice of opponents were in the more experienced hands of Yank Durham. Eddie Futch later took over this role. Though short for a heavyweight (just under six feet) Frazier's perpetual motion style enabled him to make rapid progress. In the first three years, he notched up nineteen straight wins, seventeen by the short route. Top quality victims included Eddie Machen, Doug Jones, Oscar Bonavena and Canada's 'Man of Steel', George Chuvalo. Joe was already the number one contender for the world title.

When Muhammad Ali was stripped of his title for refusing to serve with the U.S. armed forces in Vietnam, the New York State Athletic Commission matched Frazier with his old amateur rival, Buster Mathis, for its version of the heavyweight crown. The fight, at the new Madison Square Garden, New York, in March 1968, was evenly contested for the first six rounds. Then Frazier's bulldog style took over. He pounded his massive opponent unmercifully to force a stoppage in the eleventh round. After four successful defences of the New York version of the title, Smokin' Joe halted Jimmy Ellis, the WBA champion, in five rounds to become undisputed world champion on 16 February 1970.

Just over a year later, Frazier was matched with Muhammad Ali in a fascinating meeting of undefeated heavyweights. Long before the two stepped into the Madison Square Garden ring, the battleground was laid out. Ali, clearly the winner of the battle of words, stung Frazier by calling him a 'stand-in' champion and an 'Uncle Tom' black man. To this day, Joe has not forgiven his great rival for those taunts.

In the ring, where it really mattered, Frazier was the master that night. Before a worldwide audience of some 300 million, watching on closed-circuit television or via satellite, the champion bullied Ali to the ropes, never giving him a second to relax, and pounding him with vicious hooks to the body and head.

Ali played his part in making it a memorable contest. He used his speed and longer reach to spear the oncoming titleholder with stinging jabs and sharp right counters. Both men showed remarkable courage and durability as the battle entered its late stages, with neither showing a marked superiority. The fifteenth and last round proved decisive. Frazier manoeuvred his opponent onto the ropes, then launched a wide left hook with all his body weight behind it. The punch caught Ali flush on the chin and sent him crashing to the canvas, his legs in the air. Only two other boxers, Sonny Banks and Henry Cooper, had previously managed to put 'the Greatest' on the seat of his pants. Both had paid dearly for their effrontery. Not Frazier. Though he didn't manage to finish off Muhammad, the knockdown confirmed his right to the points verdict.

There had to be a rematch. But first, after two easy defences against over-matched Terry Daniels and Ron Stander, Frazier travelled to Kingston, Jamaica, to meet undefeated, but untested, George Foreman on 22 January 1973. It was intended as a 'warm up' for Joe's return with Ali. Big mistake. Frazier, who had spent as much time performing with his musical group 'Smokin' Joe and the

Knockouts' as he had in serious training, was down six times in two rounds before the referee came to his rescue.

The shock loss of his title didn't affect interest in the second match between Frazier and Ali in January 1974. It attracted 20,748 fans to Madison Square Garden and set a non-title, indoor gate record of $1,053,688. It was another keenly contested affair, with Joe landing the bigger punches, but Ali outscoring him from long range. The unanimous decision after twelve rounds went to Muhammad.

Impressive knockouts over Jerry Quarry and Jimmy Ellis set up Frazier for the third and final clash with Ali, the famous 'Thrilla in Manila' on 30 September 1975. Ali was now world heavyweight champion again, having upset Foreman the previous year. In one of the most exciting battles in ring history, Ali took the early rounds with his sharper punching. But Frazier's sheer grit and determination then took control so that, by the twelfth round, honours were about even. Muhammad then opened up with a blistering barrage to cut Frazier's mouth and bring up a huge swelling around his left eye. Although Ali himself was so exhausted and sore that he almost quit, he dredged up enough energy to subject the even more battered and weary Frazier to a further onslaught in the fourteenth round. Joe's trainer, Eddie Futch, refused to let him out for the last round.

In a final fling at regaining lost prestige, Frazier took on George Foreman for the second time. He shaved his head bald to make him look more menacing, but Foreman wasn't impressed. Joe took another hammering and was knocked out in the fifth round. At least he had lasted three rounds longer than in their first encounter.

Frazier made the startling revelation in his 1996 autobiography *Smokin' Joe* that, in the latter years of his career, a cataract had made him almost blind in his left eye. The sight of his right eye was also rapidly deteriorating. He had managed to conceal the problem from boxing commission doctors by wearing contact lenses, which were difficult to detect. 'I accepted the hurt, and damage, as the price of being the best,' he said. 'I saw myself as a warrior who was obliged to carry on through thick and thin....I was willing to make the sacrifice to be the champion I became – and to have the life I had. A small price to pay.'

Frazier wisely hung up his gloves after the second Foreman fight, but he had one more try in 1981. He looked slow and cumbersome as he struggled to draw with journeyman Floyd 'Jumbo' Cummins.

He quit the ring for good and went on the road with his musical group. He had his own gym in Philadelphia and also managed fighters. His son, Marvis, looked promising for a spell, but old Joe should never have let him into the ring with Larry Holmes and Mike Tyson. Both saw him off inside a round.

KHAOSAI GALAXY

WBA super-flyweight champion 1984-91.

Born in Petchaboon, Thailand, 15 May 1959.

Career: 1980-92.

Total contests: 50. Won: 49 (43 KOs). Lost: 1.

Outside of the Orient, Khaosai Galaxy was hardly a household name. Even to dedicated fight fans, he is best known as one of the only twins to have both won world titles. But the Thailander was a god in his own part of the world.

He boxed for eleven years and for eight of those he reigned supreme as WBA super-flyweight champion. When he retired as undefeated titleholder in 1992, he had made nineteen successful defences, scoring seventeen knockouts. *The Ring*, in 1994, rated the Thai southpaw the best super-flyweight of them all, even though the division had only been introduced fourteen years earlier. 'Gilberto Roman and Jiro Watanabe were better boxers,' stated the magazine, 'but Galaxy's incredible power and lengthy reign gave him the edge. He simply overpowered his opponents, usually finishing with a destructive left hand.'

Starting out as a kick-boxer, Galaxy switched to orthodox boxing in 1980. In only his sixth bout, he fought for the Thai bantamweight title, but was outpointed by Sakda Saksuree. It was the only time he lost in a career total of fifty fights. He avenged his defeat by stopping Saksuree in six rounds, then won the Thai title by knocking out Sak Chorsirriat in the seventh round. When Japanese Jiro Watanabe failed to defend his WBA super-flyweight title against Galaxy, the Thai was matched with Eusebio Espinal, of the Dominican Republic, for the vacant championship in Bangkok on 21 November 1984. Galaxy won on a sixth round KO.

Most of his title defences took place in Thailand, but he looked unbeatable as he disposed of quality challengers like Israel Contreras, David Griman, Rafael Orono, Elly Pical and Yong Kang Kim. When Galaxy, aged thirty-two, decided to hang up his gloves in January 1992, he got a tremendous send-off from his countrymen. Before his farewell ring appearance, a unanimous points win over Mexican Armando Castro in Bangkok, he had to stand for thirty-five minutes accepting accolades, as well as gold chains worth £50,000. The Thepsapin Stadium was packed with 11,000 Thais and the fight drew an estimated 25 million viewers throughout the Orient.

Khaosai never made a comeback, but his twin brother, Kaokor, completed a unique achievement by capturing the WBA bantamweight title in 1988. Twins had never before been world champions. Sadly, Kaokor had to retire from boxing in 1989 after being injured in a car crash as the brothers were returning from helping at a charity event in Bangkok.

JOE GANS

Real name: Joseph Gaines.

Nickname: the Old Master.

World lightweight champion 1902-08.

Born in Baltimore, Maryland, USA, 25 November 1874. Died in Baltimore, 10 August 1910.

Career: 1891-1909.

Total contests: 156. Won: 120 (85 KOs). Lost: 8. Drew: 10. No decision: 18.

The first black American to capture a world title, Joe Gans won widespread acclaim for his near-perfect boxing skill. He could make an opponent miss by inches with a mere flick of his head, then counter with deadly accurate punches. His ability to study his opponents' strengths and weaknesses, then capitalise on what he had found, made him a very difficult man to beat. *The Ring* editor, Nat Fleischer, who spent over fifty years reporting from the ringside, said Gans was the best lightweight he had ever seen.

Gans, who sold oysters and fish on the wharves around Baltimore as a youngster, got his introduction to boxing by taking part in 'battle royals'. These were free-for-alls in which six black youngsters would be pitched into a ring together. They would scrap away until only one was left standing. He would be declared the winner.

Boxing manager Al Herford spotted young Gans and took him under his wing. Joe made his professional debut in 1891, aged seventeen. He only lost three of his first seventy fights and his rare defeats were most likely due to promoters paying him extra money not to try too hard. When he fought the former world bantamweight and featherweight champion, Terry McGovern, for instance, Gans went down four times from punches which barely landed. When he took the full count in the second round, he left the ring to a shower of newspapers and cigar butts. The scandal led to boxing being outlawed in Chicago.

Like most black boxers of the period, Gans came up against the colour bar whenever his name was put forward as a world title challenger. He was twenty-six before he got his just deserts, a crack at Frank Erne's lightweight championship. Erne, the only Swiss-born boxer ever to win a world title, used his accurate left jab to open a cut over the challenger's left eye. Gans was so severely handicapped that he quit in the twelfth round. But Joe made a careful study of Erne's style and his homework paid off when they met again, in May 1902. Gans landed a smashing right to the champion's chin to score a spectacular first round knockout.

Gans made fourteen successful title defences over the next six years, but his constant struggles to make the weight started to affect his health. He tried for Joe Walcott's welterweight title in 1904 and managed to gain a draw after twenty rounds, but Walcott remained champion. Gans lost on points to another great black fighter, Sam Langford, who later took on many top heavyweights, including Jack Johnson.

In 1906, Tex Rickard, staging the first of his many spectacular promotions, offered Gans $11,000 to defend his lightweight title against Battling Nelson at the mining town of Goldfield, in Nevada. It may seem to be good money for the time, but the Danish-born challenger got over twice that amount. Besides, Gans was made to weigh in at the ringside just before the fight, giving him no time to put back precious pounds. Boxing under a fierce sun, Gans outboxed the aptly named 'Durable Dane' for thirty-two rounds, but then broke his hand. The handicap was too much and he took such a body pounding that he once had to stop to vomit over the ropes. Nevertheless, Joe still managed to frustrate Nelson with his defensive skills to such an extent that the challenger hit him low in the forty-second round and was disqualified.

Gans made four more successful defences, but his weight reducing was growing more and more difficult and he was already in the grip of tuberculosis, which would kill him. In a return match with Battling Nelson at Colma, California, on 4 July 1908, 'the Old Master' was knocked out in the seventeenth round. They met again at the same venue two months later. This time Gans was ahead going into the twenty-first round, when Nelson landed the pay-off blow.

Gans had just one more fight before retiring in 1909. A year later he was dead, aged thirty-six.

WILFREDO GOMEZ

Nickname: Bazooka.

WBC super-bantamweight champion 1977-83. WBC featherweight champion 1984. WBA super-featherweight champion 1985-86.

Born in Las Monjas, Puerto Rico, 29 October 1956.

Career: 1974-89.

Total contests: 48. Won: 44 (42 KOs). Lost: 3. Drew: 1.

A skilful boxer with devastating punching power in both hands, Wilfredo Gomez scored knockouts in every one of his eighteen world title fights at super-bantamweight and went on to pick up championships at two higher weights. In his entire career, only two of his forty-four victims survived to the final bell. The Puerto Rican idol also showed a brilliant defence. If there was a weakness, it was his suspect chin. He was stopped in the only three fights he lost and was floored on several other occasions.

Rated by *The Ring* as the best super-bantamweight since the division came into being in 1976, Gomez's promise was recognised early. He won a world amateur championship in Havana in 1974 and was considered a near certainty for a gold medal in the 1976 Olympics if he had remained in a vest.

Gomez didn't get off to the most auspicious start as a professional, being held to a draw on his debut in November 1974. However, he won the next thirty-two by knockouts, which included picking up the WBC super-bantamweight title from Korea's Dong-Kyun Yum. Though floored in the first, Gomez battled through a rough period to take control from the fourth round. In the twelfth round, Yum was knocked out for the first time in sixty-two fights. Gomez was a world champion, though still five months short of his twenty-first birthday.

Nothing excites the fans more than a match between unbeaten rivals. In October 1978, Gomez was paired with the great Mexican Carlos Zarate, the reigning WBC bantamweight champion, who had won all of his forty-seven contests, only one going the distance. Gomez, under fire for the first three rounds, blasted Zarate to the canvas three times in the fourth and once more in the fifth before the bout was stopped.

The Puerto Rican's great winning streak was finally snapped in August 1981, when he attempted to take Salvador Sanchez's WBC featherweight title. In a bout billed as 'the Battle of the Little Giants', Gomez was floored twice before being stopped in the eighth round. Wilfredo returned to the super-bantamweight division and made four more defences of his WBC belt, including a twelfth round knockout of former bantamweight champion Lupe Pintor, before relinquishing the title for another crack at the WBC featherweight championship.

This time Gomez made no mistake. He won a twelve-round decision over his compatriot Juan LaPorte in March 1984. But he only managed to hang onto it for nine months. In his first defence, he was battered to defeat in eleven rounds by the powerful Ghanaian Azumah Nelson.

Gomez showed he wasn't a spent force by bouncing back to take his third world title, victory over Rocky Lockridge in May 1985 giving him the WBA super-featherweight belt. But most neutral observers thought the decision, in San Juan, showed definite hometown bias. Less than a year later, Gomez was dethroned by Panamanian Alfredo Layne, who stopped him in the ninth round. Wilfredo had just two more fights, both wins, over the next two years before calling it a day.

The sad pattern of Puerto Rican fighters hitting bad times once their careers were over continued with Gomez. In 1994 he was accused of domestic violence, then jailed for drug-related offences.

HARRY GREB

Nickname: the Pittsburgh Windmill.

World middleweight champion 1923-26.

Born in Pittsburgh, Pennsylvania, USA, 6 June 1894. Died in Atlantic City, New Jersey, USA, 22 October 1926.

Career: 1913-26.

Total contests: 299. Won: 105 (48 KOs). Lost: 8. Drew: 3. No decision: 183.

One of the fight game's legendary characters, Harry Greb had only a passing acquaintance with the Marquis of Queensberry Rules. He was a rough, tough battler whose style was based on a high workrate, more than a single pay-off punch. He employed every dirty tactic the referee would let him away with. If the official was in a tolerant mood, that would include head, shoulders, elbows, low blows and sticking his thumb in his opponent's eyes.

Ironically, it was Greb who came off worse in the long run. He suffered a detached retina in 1921 when Kid Norfolk gave him a taste of his own medicine by thumbing him in the right eye. Though half blind, Harry fought on for another five years, until his death on the operating table.

Greb hardly ever trained. He relied on his frequent fights to keep him in shape. In 1917, he fought thirty-two times and the following year stepped between the ropes twenty-six times. In his thirteen-year career, he totalled an amazing 299 contests, more than half of them 'no decision' bouts. Though he stood only five feet, eight inches and never weighed more than 158 pounds, Greb thought nothing of taking on top heavyweights. 'The bigger they are, the slower they are and the more target I have to aim at,' he would say. A notorious womaniser, he boasted that he liked to make love in the dressing room before a fight to help him relax.

Contrary to long-held belief, Greb was not a Jew who changed his name by spelling Berg backwards. He was born Edward Henry Greb to a German-American father and an Irish mother. Pius Greb threw eighteen-year-old Harry out of his Pittsburgh home when he said he was going to be a professional boxer. The vast majority of Greb's early fights were 'no decision' affairs, but he gained invaluable experience meeting top quality opponents like George Chip, Tom and Mike Gibbons, Al McCoy, Jack Dillon, Battling Levinsky, Mike McTigue and Gunboat Smith.

His big chance came in May 1922, when he was matched with Gene Tunney for the vacant American light-heavyweight title. He inflicted on 'the Fighting Marine' the only defeat of his career. Tunney, later to take the world heavyweight title from Jack Dempsey, suffered an unmerciful beating by Greb over fifteen rounds. His nose was broken and his face bloodied from the early stages. Even the hard-hearted Greb pleaded with the referee to stop it, but Tunney's pride kept him going. In four further meetings between the pair, two of them 'no decision' bouts, Tunney emerged on top.

Greb retained his title in a fifteen-rounder with master boxer Tommy Loughran, before losing it to Tunney on points. 'The Pittsburgh Windmill' stepped down to middleweight to capture the world title from Johnny Wilson in August 1923. After another unsuccessful bid to topple Tunney, Greb defended his world title successfully six times. The most memorable was a savage encounter with another ring great, Mickey Walker, in July 1925. Greb won on points and the fight continued when they met up outside a nightclub later that night.

The effects of his long, gruelling career, especially his worsening eye problems, were clearly telling by February 1926, when he lost his middleweight title. Tiger Flowers, a church deacon from Georgia, took a close decision to become the first black middleweight champion. Greb failed to win his title back six months later when Flowers again outpointed him. He was not to know it then, but that was his last contest.

Despite his poor eyesight, he drove recklessly at high speeds. After the last of many crashes, he was admitted to hospital for an operation on his fractured nose. He suffered a cardiac arrest while under the anaesthetic and died. He was aged thirty-two.

EMILE GRIFFITH

World welterweight champion 1961, 1962-63, 1963-66. World middleweight champion 1966-67, 1967-68.

Born in St Thomas, Virgin Islands, 3 February 1938.

Career: 1958-77.

Total contests: 112. Won: 85 (23 KOs). Lost: 24. Drew: 2. No contest: 1.

Working for a hat-designer is not among the most common of boxers' day-time occupations. So it didn't help Emile Griffith, already taunted by fellow fighters over his suspected homosexuality, that he was employed by one of his managers in a Manhattan millinery business.

His patience finally ran out, however, when Benny 'Kid' Paret made Griffith's alleged sexual preference a big issue before their world welterweight title fight in 1962. The bitter rivals had already met twice, with the score one apiece. In the twelfth round, Griffith trapped him in a corner and unleashed a furious burst of punches. Had he not been held up by the ropes, Paret would have gone down for a count. But he took the pummelling on his feet. The referee,

Ruby Goldstein, jumped in to stop the fight and Paret slumped to his knees, unconscious. He was rushed to hospital and died ten days later.

Unfortunately, this tragic event clouded the career of Griffith. It served to take much of the credit away from a fine professional who took part in twenty-two world title fights and won the world welterweight title three times and the middleweight crown twice.

Emile was nineteen when his family left the Virgin Islands for New York. His millinery shop boss, Howard Albert, noticed his muscular shoulders and tapered waist and encouraged him to take up boxing. He sent him to Gil Clancy, who would later become Emile's co-manager and trainer. Under Clancy's tutelage, he won the New York Golden Gloves and the Inter-City tournament in 1957.

Turning professional at twenty, Griffith won twenty-one of his first twenty-three fights. Among his victims were welterweight contenders Gaspar Ortega, Denny Moyer, Jorge and Florentino Fernandez, Willie Toweel and Luis Rodriguez. Regular television exposure helped build for him a substantial following.

He got his deserved big chance at the Miami Beach Convention Hall on 1 April 1961 – a crack at Paret's world welterweight title. Griffith, slightly behind on points, landed a terrific left hook to score a knockout in the thirteenth round. This was a surprise, as Emile was not noted as a one-punch knockout artist. He lost the title back to Paret on a split decision five months later. Most of those who saw the bout thought Griffith was robbed.

Then came the tragic third meeting, with Griffith champion again, but inconsolable over his rival's death. 'I would have quit,' he said later, 'but I didn't know how to do anything else but fight for a living.' Like heavyweight champion Ezzard Charles when an opponent died, many people felt Griffith never showed the same fiery aggression again. The fight came only a fortnight after featherweight champion Davey Moore was killed in similar circumstances. The double tragedy led to another of the sporadic outcries for boxing to be banned.

Griffith put the sad affair behind him as he went to Austria and won European recognition as world light-middleweight champion by beating Ted Wright. Back home in the States, he engaged in the first of another three-fight series for the welterweight championship, against flashy Cuban Luis Rodriguez. Griffith lost his title in the first meeting in March 1963, regained it three months later, then retained it in June of the following year. All three bouts went to fifteen-round split decisions.

A shock first round knockout by Rubin 'Hurricane' Carter, best known for his long and ultimately successful battle to free himself from jail after being convicted of triple murder, did not discourage Emile from trying his luck in the middleweight division.

On 25 April 1966, the Virgin Islander took a disputed decision over Nigeria's Dick Tiger to become world middleweight champion. He tried to hold onto his welterweight belt as well, but neither the New York Commission or the WBA would allow him to do so. He chose to stay at middleweight. Narrow points decisions were a common feature of Griffith's championship bouts and he twice kept his middleweight belt with desperately tight wins over New York Irishman Joey Archer. In another three-bout series, this time against the Italian Nino Benvenuti, he lost the title, won it back and lost it again. All three fights took place in New York between April 1967 and March 1968. All went to points verdicts.

Though his title-winning days were over, the balding Griffith fought on for another nine years. He failed to regain his old welterweight title when Jose Napoles outscored him. He travelled to Buenos Aires to challenge the great Carlos Monzon for the middleweight crown, but was stopped in fourteen rounds. It was only the second time he had lost inside the distance. He again failed against Monzon, this time in Monte Carlo, but at least had the satisfaction of going the full fifteen rounds.

Griffith lost ten of his last twenty contests, including his final title try, for Eckhard Dagge's WBC junior middleweight title in Berlin. He finally called it quits after being outpointed by Britain's Alan Minter in Monte Carlo in July 1977. He was coming up to his fortieth birthday.

A brutal mugging in 1992, when he stopped off at a Times Square bar and his attacker spotted the $800 he was carrying, almost cost him his life. He spent several months in hospital. On his recovery, he became a freelance boxing trainer. Since he split from his wife and she returned to the Virgin Islands with their daughter, Emile has lived with his mother in a five-bedroom house in Queens, New York. He had bought the property from the biggest purse of his career, the $250,000 he earned from one of his three fights with Nino Benvenuti.

MARVIN HAGLER

World middleweight champion 1980-87.

Born in Newark, New Jersey, USA, 23 May 1952.

Career: 1973-87.

Total contests: 67. Won: 62 (52 KOs). Lost: 3. Drew: 2.

Marvin Hagler thought there was a nice ring to 'Marvelous Marvin'. He insisted on being announced as such. When one American television network refused, he changed his name by deed poll to Marvelous (spelt with one 'l') Marvin Hagler. Never was a fighter so aptly named.

Southpaws are not normally revered, but Hagler is rightly regarded as one of the all-time greatest middleweights. A slick boxer with a sleep-inducing punch in both hands, his shaven head added to his menacing appearance. He reigned supreme as middleweight king for seven years and defended his title twelve times. Only Carlos Monzon, with fourteen defences, bettered that record. A private, moody individual, Hagler put his personality down to his lonely childhood. 'Animals were the only friends I could relate to,' he said. 'Maybe the only friends I really liked. I was always by myself.'

Born in Newark, New Jersey, Hagler moved as a boy with his family to Brockton, Massachusetts. The town had been put on the map by Rocky Marciano, but Marvin's young dreams were to become a baseball player. It was Floyd Patterson's rise to the heavyweight title that turned him on to boxing.

Hagler learned to box at Goody and Pat Petronelli's gym in Brockton and won the national Amateur Athletic Union middleweight championship in 1973. Turning professional that same year, with the Petronelli brothers as his co-managers, he notched up fourteen straight wins before getting his first real test, against former Olympic gold medallist Sugar Ray Seales. He came through with a creditable points win. Though held to a draw in a return with Seales, Hagler remained unbeaten until 1976, when he lost close decisions to two top-ten ranked middleweights, Bobby 'Boogaloo' Watts and Willie 'The Worm' Monroe. He later avenged both defeats in emphatic fashion.

It wasn't until his fiftieth fight that he got his deserved chance at the world middleweight championship. He seemed to have clearly outpointed New York-based Italian Vito Antuofermo in a hard fifteen-rounder in Las Vegas, but the verdict was a draw. When Antuofermo was dethroned by England's Alan Minter, Hagler got first crack at the new champion. He had to travel to London for the fight, at Wembley on 27 September 1980. Had he known what lay ahead, he might have stayed home.

Minter, a southpaw like the American, was prone to cuts and the blood was soon flowing from the attention of Hagler's sharp punches. By the third round, Minter's face was a mess and the referee had no option but to call a halt and lead the dejected Englishman to his corner. What should have been an occasion for rejoicing by the new champion turned into a nightmare. He was subjected to a shower of beer cans and screams of racist abuse from drunken Minter supporters and needed a police escort to reach his dressing room safely. The angry American said later: 'Here I was at the moment of my glory, the things I'd been waiting for all my life, and I was deprived of it by these small people.'

Former British heavyweight hero Henry Cooper summed up the

night of shame: 'I have never experienced anything like it in all my years in boxing. It left me feeling sick to the stomach and fearing for the future of my sport. It made me wonder whether British fair play was a thing of the past.'

Hagler proved a worthy champion. He never ducked a deserving challenger and he put his title on the line in every one of his remaining fights. His first defence was against unbeaten Venezuelan Fulgencio Obelmejias, who took a severe hammering before being stopped in the eighth round. Vito Antuofermo, who had got that lucky draw in their first clash, lasted less than five rounds in the return. Britain's Tony Sibson travelled to Worcester, Massachusetts, and was sent kicking in six. Tough guy Mustafa Hamsho had two goes. He went eleven rounds the first time, then was dispatched in three.

The only man to stay the full course was the legendary Roberto Duran. He gave Hagler all the trouble he could handle over fifteen keenly contested rounds in Las Vegas in November 1983. Marvin finished the fight with his left eye swollen and a cut on his brow. The WBC refused to recognise it as a title bout because they had recently decreed that all championship fights must be over twelve rounds. But Hagler, a close but worthy winner, still earned wide support as world champion.

Few fights in history have ever matched Hagler's war with Thomas 'Hit Man' Hearns in April 1985 for sheer ferocity and excitement. In fact, the first round is regarded as THE most thrilling round ever. Both men came flying out of their corners at the opening bell with a common intention – to get the other guy out of there as quickly as possible. Punches flew hard and fast and most were on target. Anyone else but Marvelous Marvin would have folded under the steam-hammer shots that crashed through his guard. That turned out to be the big difference between them. Hagler could take Hearns' best shots, but 'the Hit Man' didn't have the same cast-iron chin. Though concerned that a badly cut eye could have cost him the fight, Hagler came out best in the fierce second round exchanges and he finished off his lanky opponent with a succession of right hooks in the third.

Hagler didn't fight again for almost a year. He was back at Caesars Palace, Las Vegas, scene of the Hearns thriller, and again engaged in a bitter war of attrition. His challenger, John 'The Beast' Mugabi, took an unbeaten record into the fight and was another big hitter. The Ugandan put up a brave fight, but was knocked out in the eleventh round.

When Sugar Ray Leonard, who had only fought once in five years, announced that he was coming back to challenge Hagler and would do so without a warm-up fight, it looked the height of foolishness on his part. Still, public interest was so keen on the showdown between ring legends that $30 million was spent to put it on. Hagler was guaranteed $19 million and Leonard, a former champion at welterweight and light-middleweight, $11 million for the hugely hyped Las Vegas meeting on 6 April 1987.

At the end of twelve absorbing, sometimes brilliant, rounds the majority decision went to Leonard. Hagler bitterly contested the verdict and never fought again. 'I almost threw a chair at the TV when I watched it afterwards,' he said. 'I know in my heart I won that fight.'

There were occasional reports of a planned comeback, but he resisted the temptation. 'I try to stay out of the gym,' he said in 1997. 'Once you get the smell and start punching the bag, you get tempted to get back in the ring.' He went to live in Italy and went into the movie business, playing action parts. His fans remembered when he shot down guys without a gun!

NASEEM HAMED

Nickname: Prince.

WBO featherweight champion 1995 to present. IBF featherweight champion 1997.

Born in Sheffield, England, 12 February 1974.

Career: 1992–present.

Total contests: 32. Won: 32 (29 KOs).

Love him or loathe him, Naseem Hamed is the face of boxing in the nineties. The loud, arrogant, self-styled Prince, with his outrageous antics and unique fighting style, has, more than any other ringman, transformed the sport into what it truly is today – show business with blood.

From the moment he emerges from his dressing room in a cloud of smoke and flashing laser lights, and his long drawn-out jig to the ring to the accompaniment of loud rap music, Hamed milks the atmosphere for all it's worth. Even when he steps up to the ring, his performance is far from over. He turns to the crowd to acknowledge their applause, then takes his time choosing his spot for a spectacular somersault into the ring. Talk about dramatic entries – Michael Jackson could learn from this guy!

All this over-the-top stuff would be inexcusable if 'Naz' didn't back it up with real fighting talent. This the Sheffield southpaw has in abundance. His combination of speed, defensive skill, strength, punching power, timing and endurance add up to one exceptional ringman. He may even turn out to be the legend he brazenly predicts he will be.

Not surprisingly, boxing's traditionalists recoil in horror at what they see as their beloved sport descending to the odious level of professional wrestling. Former British heavyweight champion Henry Cooper articulated many long-time fans' grievances when he announced he was giving up his job as radio commentator because he was fed up attending shows where the boxers' entries to the ring often took longer than the fight itself. In Our 'Enry's time, a recorded fanfare of trumpets was the only theatrical touch to a Jack Solomons or Harry Levene promotion.

Those who are not enamoured of Hamed's behaviour or ring style live in hope that someone will land a big punch on that ever-inviting chin and send him sprawling on his leopard-skin shorts for the full count. Then, they reason, boxing will be rid of this obnoxious big-mouth once and for all. For the rest, they are happy to sit back and enjoy him while they can.

'I want to be a legend,' boasted Hamed. 'There's nothing too high for me. If there's a challenge, I want to do it. I don't think I can get beat. I've looked at every style, every move, studied it all since I was a kid. I've watched them come and go. The Alis, Robinsons, Haglers and Leonards. All tremendous fighters. But I can be better.'

It was in the early eighties when Brendan Ingle, an Irishman with a deep and abiding passion for boxing, first spotted Naz in action – from the top of a bus. The vehicle was winding its way through the streets of Wincobank, one of the poorer suburbs of Sheffield, where Ingle has a gym. From the top deck, he saw this little youngster fighting off three older kids.

'He was ducking and punching beautifully,' recalled Ingle. 'They couldn't land a shot on him. It struck me, even then, that he had natural movement and a knack of avoiding blows. It should have been no contest, because the other kids were twice his size, but even at that age he showed no fear.'

Ingle wasted no time in tracking down the youngster and inviting him to his gym. The genial Irishman had some unorthodox approaches to training. For instance, he would put a boxer in the ring and not allow him to hit his opponent, but make him concentrate on ducking and diving to avoid getting hit. This suited Hamed perfectly. He would not be forced to abandon his natural style just because the text books taught things differently. As for Ingle, he saw in Naseem someone who could enable him, at last, to laugh at the critics who labelled him an eccentric dreamer.

Hamed, whose parents had immigrated from the Yemen to Britain in the 1950s, won his first national schoolboy title at the age of eleven. Captaining an England youth team against America, he made his way to the ring in a gold dressing-gown, vaulted over the ropes and proceeded to bamboozle his opponent, a junior Olympic champion. The pattern had been well and truly set.

He lost just six times in sixty-seven amateur contests, but spurned a chance of being selected for Britain's Olympic team in 1992 by turning professional in April that year. True to form, his launching on a paid career was no ordinary event. His three-year contract with promoter Barry Hearn was signed in the grand committee room of the House of Commons. And already he had his first sponsor, Joe Bloggs, the clothing manufacturer. Seven years later, he would agree a £7 million deal with Adidas for modelling and promoting their sportswear.

Naz's first professional victim, Ricky Beard, said after being blasted out inside two rounds: 'I'd been fighting for fifteen years and he made me feel junior and inexperienced. I was really surprised how hard his knockout punch was. I reckon it would have put Frank Bruno down.'

That wasn't such an outrageous suggestion. Though he is only five feet, three inches tall, Hamed frequently sparred with bigger men in Ingle's gym and was known to hurt and floor light-heavyweights.

After just three fights, Hamed had already entered *Boxing News'* European ratings at number ten. The 'trade' paper defended him against criticism from the British Boxing Board of Control about his flamboyant style, cartwheel demonstrations and general ring gimmicks. *Boxing News* said he had given the sport a badly needed tonic. Brendan Ingle added his tuppence-worth: 'The modern game, dominated by TV money, demands that something extra.'

By May 1994, Hamed's record stood at eleven fights, eleven wins, ten inside the distance. Not everyone was convinced he was the goods, however. While his amazingly fast reflexes enabled him to make an opponent miss by a twist of the body or a flick of the head, he left himself wide open as he lunged in, often wildly off-target. What would happen when someone eventually did catch him?

European bantamweight champion Vincenzo Belcastro looked as if he might expose the Hamed frailties, if there were any. The Italian was a veteran of over forty fights, including two unsuccessful world title challenges, and he had never been knocked down. That particular record was smashed as Naz dumped him on the floor three times. Belcastro, though he managed to last the twelve rounds, was made to look like a novice by the quicksilver challenger. Two of the judges didn't see Hamed losing a single round, while the other official gave the Italian one round.

Now champion of Europe, Naz looked for new fields to conquer. The WBC international super-bantamweight title, a second-rate prize, was picked up by halting Freddy Cruz in six rounds. Promoter Frank Warren, who had taken over the running of Hamed's affairs from Barry Hearn, managed to lure Welshman Steve Robinson into putting his WBO featherweight belt at stake in September 1995. Naz would have to go to the champion's home town of Cardiff for his big chance, but that didn't worry him in the slightest.

Hamed found a way through the Welshman's tight defence and gradually broke down his brave resistance to finish him off in the eighth round. He again found himself in trouble with the Boxing Board, however, for his goading of Robinson throughout the fight. Lord Brooks of Tremorfa, one of the Board's senior stewards, commented: 'There is universal disquiet among my fellow stewards at some of the antics Hamed got up to with Robinson. I certainly didn't like him waggling his backside or the way he continually verbally taunted Robinson. I found that unacceptable. Hamed has so much talent and ability that there is no need for him to carry on like that.'

The new world champion was unrepentant: 'If that's my style and that's the style to beat an opponent, that's what I have to do. But I never humiliate a fighter. I try to break their concentration by being unorthodox, but that is not humiliating them. Muhammad Ali did it to all his opponents. If you break a fighter's concentration, then you've won.'

Sky TV were delighted at their star fighter's wide appeal with viewers and the Yemen joined Britain in celebrating his championship victory. Hamed, though born in Britain, is proud to be an Arab. 'When I get into the ring, I am fighting for two nations,' he said.

An injury to his right hand caused worries about his future, but he dispelled them in emphatic fashion with a dramatic knockout of Said Lawal with his suspect right hand in thirty-five seconds of his first defence. Next challenger, Daniel Alicea, answered some of the doubts about Naz's ability to take a punch when he momentarily dropped the champion in the first round. Hamed wasn't hurt and made Alicea pay for his impertinence by flattening him in the next round.

A chest infection was blamed for a below-par showing against former IBF featherweight champion Manuel Medina in Dublin, but he managed to floor the game Mexican three times before stopping him in the eleventh round. He was back to his devastating best next time up, dispatching Remigio Molina inside two rounds. More than a few boxing experts thought the brash Sheffielder would get his come-uppance when matched with Tom 'Boom Boom' Johnson, the IBF featherweight champion, in a title unification fight at the London Arena on 8 February 1997. The veteran American, though considered past his peak, was a tough, experienced campaigner who had lost only twice in forty-eight contests and had made eleven defences of the title he had taken from Manuel Medina four years earlier.

Naz came through his acid test with flying colours. He constantly bemused Johnson with his speed and switches of stance. Though he seemed to be playing a dangerous game with his hands held low and his chin stuck in the air, he was only caught once with a really telling blow, a right in the fifth round that made his knees dip and brought gasps of apprehension from the 10,000 crowd. Naz showed his good powers of recovery and it was Johnson who looked most likely to finish on his back. In the eighth round, Hamed staggered the American with a strong right lead and sent him crashing to the canvas with a right uppercut that started inches off the floor. Johnson gamely struggled to his feet, but referee Rudy Battle waved the fight over.

But his first American adventure almost ended in disaster. In a see-saw thriller with Kevin Kelley at Madison Square Garden in December 1997, Naz made several trips to the canvas before he found the power to dispatch the always-dangerous former WBC champion in the fourth round.

An unconvincing points win over durable Irishman, Wayne McCullough, in Atlantic City – Hamed had predicted a third round knockout – was followed by a bitter split with Brendan Ingle. Promoter Frank Warren was also ditched, with members of Naseem's family taking over managerial and other business affairs. Only time would tell if the new Jeam Hamed would succeed or fail.

As for the Prince's outrageous boast that he would win world titles in five weight divisions, who could say for sure what this amazing character could achieve?

One thing was absolutely sure, boxing had never known anyone quite like Naseem Hamed.

LEN HARVEY

British-recognised world light-heavyweight champion 1939-42.

Born in Stoke Climsland, Cornwall, England, 11 July 1907. Died in London, England, 28 November 1976.

Career: 1920-42.

Total contests: 133. Won: 111 (51 KOs). Lost: 13. Drew: 9.

When old-timers talked about the Manly Art of Self-Defence, they had the likes of Len Harvey in mind. A perfect example of the once-revered 'British style' of boxing, the Cornishman relied on masterly skills rather than aggression and a big punch for success. His defence was so difficult to pierce that, after twenty-two years in the ring, his handsome features bore hardly a blemish. He never wore a gumshield and scorned the use of headguards during training, maintaining that they only made boxers careless.

Only twice in 133 fights – historians believe there were many more bouts which went unrecorded – did he fail to last the distance. He was fighting British heavyweight champion Jack Petersen with both eyes damaged when he was forced to retire after twelve rounds. And, in the last bout of his career, he was belted through the ropes by Freddie Mills and failed to get back into the ring to beat the count.

Although he only won recognition in his own country as world champion, Harvey had a remarkable record of picking up domestic titles. He remains the only man ever to have won the British middle, light-heavy and heavyweight championships. And he very nearly made it four. His first try for a British title was at welterweight and he held highly regarded Harry Mason to a draw over twenty rounds.

Len had his first professional fight when he was only twelve years old. Appearing as 'Nipper' Harvey and weighing in at four stone, twelve pounds, he outpointed 'Young' King over six rounds. He earned five shillings, plus a share of the 'nobbins' (coins thrown into the ring by an appreciative audience).

At eighteen, Harvey was already a 'veteran' of sixty-one contests when he drew with Mason in 1926. It took him another twenty-eight outings before he got his second British title chance, at middleweight. He knocked out Scotsman Alex Ireland in the seventh round. Len had three classic encounters with Jack Hood, from Birmingham, in defence of the title. The middle bout of the three was a draw, but Harvey won the others on points over fifteen rounds.

If his fellow Britons appreciated his upright, move and jab style, it didn't exactly go down a treat in America. Judges there were more impressed with the aggressive style of fighting. Harvey was looked upon as a spoiler who didn't give full value for money. He was twice outpointed by Vince Dundee and then by Ben Jeby at Madison Square Garden, New York, in 1931. Both Dundee and Jeby were to win versions of the world middleweight title within the next two years.

Back in Britain, Harvey retained his domestic title against Jack Hood, Jock McAvoy and Len Johnson before getting his first chance at a world title. Frenchman Marcel Thil was recognised by the European-based International Boxing Union as world champion. He put his title at stake at White City, London, on 4 July 1932.

Harvey found himself at an immediate disadvantage when he discovered the referee was a Swiss who did not understand a word of English, but who spoke fluent French. The world champion made it a close quarter fight from the start, burying his bald head on Len's chest and working away to the body. When the referee broke up the frequent bouts of holding, he would wag his finger at the Englishman and speak to him in French. Harvey couldn't understand him, nor could he ask why Thil wasn't being similarly warned.

Frustrated by what he considered unfair treatment, Harvey then picked up a cut eye from the champion's head in the seventh round. He told his cornermen he would quit if things didn't improve, but he stuck it out for the full fifteen rounds. Unable to put his long-range skills into practice for any prolonged period, he was bustled back to the ropes time and again. At the finish, he knew Thil had won and, as the decision was announced, he walked straight across to shake the champion's hand.

After losing his British middleweight title to Jock McAvoy – the only time he was defeated in four meetings with 'the Rochdale Thunderbolt' – Harvey moved up to light-heavyweight and took the vacant British title by outscoring Eddie Phillips in June 1933. He then caused a shock by challenging Welshman Jack Petersen for the British heavyweight championship – and winning it!

The only sour note was that he didn't get paid. His wife, Florence, in a moment of recklessness, had told promoter Jeff Dickson that Len was so keen on challenging Petersen that he would fight him for nothing. Dickson took her at her word and made the match on those terms.

After adding the British Empire heavyweight title to his impressive collection by outpointing Larry Gains, Harvey met Petersen in a rematch. This time he did get paid. But his £5,000 purse hardly compensated for the loss of his championship. Handicapped by a badly swollen left eye from the sixth round, he was unable to keep the eager Welshman at bay. When his right eye also suffered damage, he was practically fighting blind. He retired at the end of the twelfth round. It was the first time in fourteen years of boxing he had failed to last the full course.

Harvey still held his British light-heavyweight title, but he refused to meet his old rival Eddie Phillips when the top bid for the contest only reached £750. The champion told the Boxing Board: 'If you value a British championship at only sixty per cent of £750 (his share), then it isn't worth keeping.' The Board asked him to return his Lonsdale Belt.

After losing to Petersen on points in another bid for the British heavyweight title, Harvey was appointed as matchmaker at Wembley Arena by promoter Arthur Elvin. He promptly showed how good he was at the job by luring world light-heavyweight champion John Henry Lewis to London in November 1936 – with himself as challenger! Though his troublesome right hand 'went' in the third round, Harvey gave the American all the trouble he could handle. There were many who thought Len deserved the decision, but referee Jack Smith, the sole arbiter, had no hesitation in raising Lewis' hand.

Len went back to picking up domestic honours. He regained the British light-heavyweight championship from Jock McAvoy in a 1938 fight that made its mark in history. It was the first contest to be televised, though it only went out on closed circuit. Harvey won the British heavyweight title, which had been vacated by Tommy Farr, by beating Eddie Phillips, who was disqualified for hitting low.

Then, after forcing Larry Gains to retire in thirteen rounds in a bout for the vacant British Empire championship, Harvey signed for a return match with John Henry Lewis for the world light-heavyweight title at White City on 10 July 1939. Lewis, however, was refused permission to fight by the British Boxing Board when he was found to have a serious eye problem, requiring his retirement.

Harvey saw a way over his disappointment. He wrote to the British Board suggesting that the bill should go ahead, with he and Jock McAvoy meeting for the vacant world title. To most people's surprise, the Board concurred. It was evident how much influence Harvey had over boxing in Britain at that time.

With colourful Irishman Jack Doyle meeting Eddie Phillips in a supporting bout, the bill aroused extraordinary interest. All roads to the White City were jammed with traffic by 6 pm. The main event was held up for forty minutes and fans were still streaming into the arena with the fighters already in the ring. The 82,000 attendance created a record for a boxing show in Britain. It still stands.

Like their three previous encounters, it was a closely contested tussle. Harvey, the boxer, and McAvoy, the puncher, each had their periods of ascendancy. The Cornishman weathered a stormy fourteenth round, in which he was almost floored by the always dangerous 'Rochdale Thunderbolt', to earn referee Charlie Thomas' points verdict. Stewards from the British Board presented Harvey with a silver trophy, emblematic of the world championship, even though his status was only recognised in his own country. It meant that Len now held three titles in the light-heavyweight division, plus two at heavyweight.

At thirty-two, Harvey was still fit for several more years of boxing. But in September 1939, as Britain declared war on Nazi Germany, Len packed away his boxing kit to become a sergeant-instructor in the Royal Air Force.

Apart from exhibitions, it was June 1942 before Harvey fought again in the ring. He was paired with twenty-two-year-old Freddie Mills, from Bournemouth, at Tottenham Hotspur's football ground in north London. Harvey's claim to the world title, as well as his British and Empire light-heavyweight championships, were at stake.

Only allowed a week's leave for full training, Harvey knew the odds were against him. Mills was not only twelve years his junior, but he had fought twenty-two times since the outbreak of the war. Len had been idle for almost three years. In the second round, Harvey was dropped flat on his back with a left hook. Up at nine, he was caught by a fierce right uppercut and sent sailing through the ropes and onto the press benches. He was further dazed by hitting his head on the ring apron as he struggled to get back into the ring. By the time he crawled between the ropes, the count of 'ten' had been completed.

It took Harvey a few months to decide his long career was over. After the war, he ran a succession of public houses until he retired from the trade at sixty-five. He died in 1976 from a combination of hardening of the arteries, emphysema and a tired heart.

THOMAS HEARNS

Nickname: the Hit Man.

WBA welterweight champion 1980-81. WBC light-middleweight
champion 1982-86. WBC light-heavyweight champion 1987.
WBC middleweight champion 1987-88. WBO super-middleweight
champion 1988-91. WBA light-heavyweight champion
1991-92.

Born in Memphis,Tennessee, USA, 18 October 1958.

Career: 1977–present.

Total contests: 64. Won: 59 (46 KOs). Lost: 4. Drew: 1.

Nothing is more exciting in boxing than watching someone who hits
with dynamite power, but who is liable to collapse like a pole-axed
steer if the other guy's hit lands first.

It would be unfair to say that Thomas Hearns' chin was made of
delicate porcelain, but even when he was knocking lumps out of an
unfortunate opponent, you never lost the feeling that the whole
course of the fight could change with a desperate punch from the
seemingly doomed man. That's what made Hearns one of the most

exciting fighters of the last two decades. When he fought, anything could happen.

As a single shot knockout artist, no one bettered 'the Hit Man'. The most dramatic evidence of that was his sensational second round knockout of Roberto Duran in 1984. Hard man Duran took a punch as well as anyone, but he was simply destroyed by a powerful right that exploded on his chin and sent him crashing face-first to the canvas. Hearns made the mistake of thinking he could do a similar demolition job on Marvin Hagler a year later. 'Marvelous Marvin' plunged straight into the line of fire and flattened the reckless Hearns in the third round.

At other times, Thomas would seem to be on the brink of defeat, tottering on his spindly legs, only to hit back with devastating punches that would turn the tide in his favour.

Strange as it may seem, Hearns was more of a boxer than a puncher in his amateur days. Born in Memphis, Tennessee, he took up the sport when the family moved to Detroit, Michigan. He won a Golden Gloves title and represented his country before joining Emanuel Steward's Kronk Gym.

The two men were good for each other. Steward discovered that Thomas had a bigger wallop than he had been given credit for. Under Steward's expert coaching, the lanky youngster turned in some exciting performances that really put the Kronk gym on the fistic map. Hearns won his first twenty-six fights, twenty-four by KO, before picking up the first of his record-breaking five world titles. An impressive second round stoppage of Mexican Pipino Cuevas earned him the WBA welterweight belt in August 1980.

A title unification showdown with the brilliant WBC champion Sugar Ray Leonard eleven months later promised to be a classic. It was. Hearns looked set for victory until a desperate Leonard, behind on points and one eye closed, staged a terrific rally in the fourteenth round. He dropped Hearns for a count and forced the referee to call a halt.

It was no disgrace to lose to a modern great like Leonard, and Hearns stepped up to light-middleweight to take Wilfred Benitez's WBC belt on a fifteen-round decision. He defended it four times, including the dramatic knockout of Duran, before increasing weight problems made him move up again.

'The Hit Man' had filled out considerably, but it was still a major surprise when he leap-frogged a couple of divisions to challenge England's Dennis Andries for the WBC light-heavyweight title in March 1987. Hearns halted the strong, but technically limited, Andries in the tenth round, then dropped back to his more natural middleweight.

He made history on 29 October 1987, by winning his fourth world title at a different weight. In a wild punch-up, in which both men were on the floor, Hearns knocked out Argentinian Juan Domingo Roldan in the fourth round to become WBC middleweight champion. The frailties in his fighting make-up were becoming more apparent, however, and he lost his latest title in an upset third-round knockout by Iran Barkley.

Yet another self-elected administrative body, the World Boxing Organisation (WBO) had come into existence, adding to the derisive collective term of 'the alphabet boys'. Hearns won the first contest for the WBO super-middleweight title by outpointing James Kinchen on 4 November 1988. He failed to impress, however, and his multitude of fans called on him to retire gracefully before he suffered another humiliation.

The WBO title having minimal standing in the United States, Hearns decided to take on his old rival Sugar Ray Leonard, who now held the WBC super-middleweight championship. Memories of their great welterweight tussle eight years earlier were rekindled when the two ring legends stepped into the Las Vegas ring on 12 June 1989.

Though both had left their best days behind them, they provided an interesting struggle, with each man taking the upper hand for a spell, losing it and then regaining it. At the end of the twelve rounds, it was declared a draw. Most observers thought Hearns had been hard done by. Leonard acknowledged that he had been somewhat lucky, but later retracted his statement and claimed he had done enough to win. Hearns was more gracious. 'I gave it my best shot,' he said, 'I am not upset about the decision. It was very close.'

Despite concerns about the effects his long, arduous career was having on him, Hearns continued to fight sporadically as he passed his fortieth birthday. Graham Houston wrote in *Boxing Monthly*: 'Hearns still enjoys the game and wants to prove to the critics that he is not a shot fighter. But, more than any of the other ageing ex-greats on the boxing senior circuit, Hearns seems most to resemble a man wandering through the empty rooms of a house where once he had happiness, searching for something that is no longer there.'

His many British fans, sadly, had to wait until Hearns was in the twilight of his career before seeing him in action as a professional (he had beaten George Gilbody as an amateur at Wembley in 1976). Though he charmed everyone with his dignified manner on his trip to Manchester in April 1999, it was an old, tired shadow of the once-feared 'Hit Man' who outscored fellow-American Natz Miller in a twelve-round bore.

'Boxing is my life', said the man who owns a ten-acre mansion in Michigan and a $9 million home in Las Vegas.

LARRY HOLMES

Nicknames: Black Cloud, the Easton Assassin.

WBC heavyweight champion 1978-83. IBF heavyweight champion 1983-85.

Born in Cuthbert, Georgia, USA, 3 November 1949.

Career: 1973-present.

Total contests: 72. Won: 66 (42 KOs). Lost: 6.

It looks great on his record – the only man to beat Muhammad Ali inside the distance. But Larry Holmes was not the first fighter to discover that there is little kudos available for demolishing an icon.

All anyone could think of was how sad it was that 'the Greatest' had stayed on too long in the game and why everyone connected with the affair should be ashamed for letting an obviously unwell man in against an undefeated world heavyweight champion. Holmes admitted he got little joy out of beating the man he idolised and for whom he had once served as a sparring partner. Explaining why he had held back when he had Ali at his mercy, he said: 'I love that man and didn't want to see him getting hurt.'

Only in retrospect has Holmes earned the recognition he deserves as one of the outstanding heavyweight champions. In his prime, he looked well-nigh unbeatable. In fact, he came within one fight of equalling Rocky Marciano's record of forty-nine straight wins, only to drop a disputed decision to Michael Spinks. A clever boxer with one of the best left jabs of all the heavyweight champions, Larry made the most of his eighty-one-inch reach. He was not a great knockout artist, but the cumulative effect of his punches enabled him to equal Tommy Burns' record of eight successful stoppages in title defences. Standing six feet, four inches tall and strongly built, he proved his big heart by climbing off the canvas to win against Earnie Shavers and Renaldo Snipes.

To go with his snappy left jab, Holmes had a sharp tongue. It got him into trouble on occasions, most infamously when he spat out that Rocky Marciano 'wasn't fit to carry my jockstrap'. The gibe was to haunt Holmes for the rest of his career and denied him a place in the hearts of many fight fans. Marciano was a much revered titleholder and Larry's slur, though he later tried to play it down as an off-the-cuff remark, was seen as an uncalled-for lack of respect towards a great champion.

One of a family of nine brothers and three sisters, Holmes moved with his family from Cuthbert, Georgia, to Easton, Pennsylvania, when he was a boy. When his father walked out, leaving mother Flossie to look after her large brood, the family was thrown into a financial crisis.

Larry took on spare-time work as a shoeshine boy to earn cash, then quit school to take jobs sweeping floors in a foundry, and working in a car wash, a wool mill and a steel factory. An admitted hell raiser, he became the father of two girls by the time he was nineteen and continued to support his daughters after the affair ended. To boost his income, he sat in on all-night card games and developed into a master poker player.

Despite all this activity, Larry somehow found time to get involved in amateur boxing. He progressed to the finals of the United States Olympic trials in 1972, but lost on a disqualification for holding against Duane Bobick. Holmes made his professional debut the following year, earning $63 for outpointing Rodell Dupree over four rounds. Over the next twenty-five years, he was to bring his career takings to over $30 million.

A broken hand interrupted his career for eight months in 1976, but he leaped into the limelight with a convincing points win over powerful puncher Earnie Shavers in March 1978. That earned him a shot at Ken Norton for the WBC heavyweight title three months later. In a superb fifteen-rounder, with both men receiving prolonged applause for their efforts, Holmes took a hotly disputed points decision. He later revealed that he had been handicapped by a torn muscle in his left arm, his most effective weapon.

Despite living in the shadow of Ali throughout most of his championship reign, Holmes earned grudging admiration from many fans as a fine champion. His best performance in twenty-one championship title contests was his dismissal of 'white hope' Gerry Cooney in thirteen rounds at Las Vegas in June 1982. The fight attracted huge interest, much of it due, unfortunately, to the racial aspect. Neither fighter, to his credit, played up the colour difference. They pocketed a neat $20 million between them.

A dispute with the WBC and promoter Don King, who had a major influence on that organisation, led to Holmes handing back the championship belt and accepting recognition as champion by the newly-fledged International Boxing Federation (IBF). He became self-managed and part-promoter of his fights. 'Now that I'm with the IBF I don't have to give money to Don King or anybody else,' he declared. 'Every dime I have is mine. You hear a lot of talk coming from the young guys who want my title, but while they're yapping away I'm up here on the top of the mountain with the money I've got in the bank earning me $400,000 in interest. These guys don't get that to fight. I'm a businessman first and a boxer second.'

A good businessman, too, he proved to be. In Easton, where he lived in a mansion with his wife, Diane, and a growing family, he owned a fleet of limousines, a hotel, a parking lot, a restaurant, a garage and a gymnasium. He owned so much of the town that there was talk of changing its name to Holmesville.

All set to equal Marciano's record for a heavyweight champion of forty-nine straight wins, Holmes saw that dream dashed when Michael Spinks took his IBF title on a highly controversial decision on 21 September 1985. Larry bitterly disputed the verdict and got a return match with Spinks seven months later. Once again, Spinks was declared the winner on a debatable points decision.

Disgusted at what he considered a double robbery, Holmes hung up his gloves after the second Spinks bout. His financial status seemingly assured, Larry saw little reason to fight. Then the recession hit. A lot of his vast fortune was eaten away. There was only one way he could make good his losses – a return to the ring for a crack at the fearsome Mike Tyson for the undisputed world heavyweight championship at Atlantic City on 22 January 1988.

His $5 million purse was scant consolation for the humiliation and pain he suffered at the hands of the all-conquering Tyson, who flattened him with a vicious left hook in the fourth round. Ferdie Pacheco, the well-known TV commentator, described Holmes' defeat as 'the kind of beating that makes guys walk funny when they're fifty'.

Larry took no notice of such dire warnings. Three years after the Tyson beating, now forty-two years old and sporting a sizeable paunch, he launched another comeback. Though lacking the speed and power of his younger days, he had enough ring savvy to outscore dangerous Ray Mercer and earn a chance with Evander Holyfield for the WBA and IBF championship belts. Holmes surprised everyone by going the distance with a champion thirteen years younger than himself and by taking Holyfield's best punches without noticeable effect. He even managed to wobble Holyfield twice in the last couple of rounds, but the judges' scores were unanimous in the champion's favour.

That still wasn't the end of Holmes' title chase. On 8 April 1995, at Caesars Palace in Las Vegas, the forty-five-year-old grandfather took WBC champion Oliver McCall all the way in a fine effort. Indeed, for the first eight rounds, he looked capable of registering a sensational upset over the man who had pulverised Lennox Lewis inside two rounds to win the title.

Larry's left jab was a constant problem for the champion and he brought roars from the crowd as he fired right-handers that might not have always landed, but served to discourage McCall from getting too ambitious for a knockout. But the old gladiator, who had won the title at the same venue seventeen years earlier, tired over the last third of the fight. The verdict for McCall was unanimous, but it was close. One judge had them only one point apart at the finish.

'Don't feel sorry for me, I gave it my all,' said Holmes afterwards. 'I fell short in my goal of victory and now I feel it is probably time to give it up. Boxing owes me nothing – I owe everything to boxing.'

Yet, in January 1997, Holmes, at forty-seven, was still good enough to travel to Denmark and only lose by a split decision to unbeaten Brian Nielsen. The twelve-rounder for the so-called International Boxing Organisation (IBO) heavyweight title, which was dismissed elsewhere as a joke, saw the old-timer drilling home an effective left jab and following up with thudding rights. Nielsen, though bleeding from the nose and swollen around the left eye, was the busier over the distance, but he never hurt the American.

Looking back over his life in 1997, Holmes told *Boxing Monthly*: 'There's not much that I would have done differently today. Maybe I'd have made a few more dollars, but I'm fine like I am now. My children are taken care of and my grandchildren. I came from nothing and look at me now.'

Some excitement was stirred when Holmes was matched with George Foreman in January 1999, with *USA Today* calling it 'a pot-bellied fight for the ages'. Larry, at forty-nine, was a year younger than George. But the novelty match fell through. It was probably just as well – it was two decades too late.

EVANDER HOLYFIELD

Nickname: the Real Deal.

WBA and IBF cruiserweight champion 1987-88. World cruiser-weight champion 1988. World heavyweight champion 1990-92. WBA and IBF heavyweight champion 1993-94. WBA heavyweight champion 1996-present. IBF heavyweight champion 1997–present.

Born in Atmore, Alabama, USA, 19 October 1962.

Career: 1984-present.

Total contests: 40. Won: 36 (25 KOs). Lost: 3. Drew: 1.

He was old. He was a 'shot' fighter. There were lingering concerns about a suspected heart defect, even though he had been given the medical all-clear. He was brave, but that could be a handicap rather than a help if he took too much punishment and refused to go down. His handlers and the WBA would face a justifiable outcry if there was a tragic outcome to the fight, as was widely feared.

What happened? Evander Holyfield, the supposed no-hoper, wrote his own chapter in boxing's history book by destroying the 'Baddest Man on the Planet', Mike Tyson, in eleven unforgettable rounds at the MGM-Grand Arena in Las Vegas on 9 November 1996. In the infamous return match, seven months later, Holyfield was again dominating Tyson when Iron Mike vented his frustration by biting the champion on both ears. The amazing assault earned Tyson's disqualification in the third round and won the world's sympathy and admiration for Evander, a decent and true warrior who exposed and chastised the bully.

Holyfield's first win over Tyson made the thirty-four-year-old Holyfield an overnight hero. Though the new WBA heavyweight champion was anxious to give credit to God for his victory, his fitness, strength and marvellous self-belief played a part in allowing him to triumph against all the odds. Above all, he felt no fear for the man who made giants go weak at the knees with nothing more than a menacing stare. 'I'm a Christian,' said Holyfield before the fight. 'I don't have the spirit of fear. I'm a conqueror and such people don't lose from fear. Winners make things happen, while others let things happen. I fear no man and that enables me to fight at my best.'

Holyfield, initially an 18/1 underdog, though the betting was down to 6/1 by fight time, won by beating Tyson at his own game. He refused to be intimidated, came through the rough patches with his will-power undiminished, and frequently beat Iron Mike to the punch. Tyson, floored in the sixth by a sharp left hook, was weary and demoralised, though still on his feet, when referee Mitch Halpern cradled him in his arms in the eleventh round and told him it was all over.

'No matter what I did before,' said the elated new champion, 'you had people saying, "You can't beat Mike Tyson." But they can't say that now. They can't say Mike didn't fight hard or he wasn't in shape. And it's not like I beat him with a lucky punch. People saw what happened. They saw domination.'

Holyfield, whose $200 million-plus career earnings made him one of the richest fighters in history, had first met up with Tyson in 1984, when both were among the favourites to win the National Golden Gloves tournament in Atlanta. Holyfield won the light-heavyweight trophy by halting all his five opponents. But it was Tyson, who stopped four out of five to take the heavyweight prize, who was named the tournament's outstanding boxer.

After winning a bronze medal at the Los Angeles Olympics, Holyfield signed up with the Main Events organisation. He made his professional debut, weighing twelve stone, nine and a half pounds, in November 1984, and scored a unanimous decision over Lionel Byarm. It took him just twenty months to capture his first world championship belt, when, in his twelfth fight, he beat WBA cruiserweight champion Dwight Muhammad Qawi on a split decision over fifteen exciting rounds. It was Holyfield's superior fitness which enabled him to outwork the champion and endure a great last-round rally by Qawi.

The cruiserweight (190 pounds) division had been instituted in 1979 to bridge the gap between light-heavyweight and heavyweight. Holyfield became the first undisputed world champion at the weight by beating IBF titleholder Rickey Parkey in three rounds and Carlos DeLeon, the WBC champion, in eight. Having established his superiority at the weight, he gave up all three belts to aim for heavyweight honours. That was where the big money lay.

He embarked on an elaborate diet and exercise regime to build him up to a magnificently proportioned fourteen stone, six pounds for his heavyweight debut in July 1988. His extra strength and punching power took him to a one-sided win over experienced James Tillis in five rounds. Impressive inside-the-distance victories over former heavyweight titleholders Pinklon Thomas and Michael Dokes, as well as leading contenders Adilson Rodrigues and Alex Stewart, put him in line for a crack at Mike Tyson's undisputed world heavyweight title.

James 'Buster' Douglas upset the agenda by sensationally knocking out Tyson. So it was Douglas whom Holyfield challenged in Las Vegas on 25 October 1990. There were many doubters who felt that Evander was just a blown-up cruiserweight who wouldn't stand up to the bludgeoning punches of Douglas. It turned out to be one of the easiest fights of Holyfield's career. Douglas, weighing fifteen pounds more than he had against Tyson, was plainly in no condition or proper frame of mind to combat a hungry Holyfield. 'Buster' was taking a systematic hiding when a classic right-hand counter from the challenger took him out of his misery in the third round.

It looked like an untaxing first defence for Holyfield against George Foreman, but the forty-two-year-old former champion stayed with him for the full twelve rounds. Although the decision for Evander was unanimous and Foreman was reeling desperately at times, the old guy got most of the credit for his brave resistance. Late substitute Bert Cooper made Holyfield look vulnerable when he staggered the champion with a terrific right in the third round. Evander, out on his feet, somehow survived the crisis and his great fighting heart enabled him to wear down Cooper for a seventh round stoppage. A hard-earned points win over another ancient warrior, Larry Holmes, did nothing to enhance Holyfield's reputation, however.

Holyfield's world came crashing down in November 1992. Riddick Bowe, bigger, younger and unbeaten in thirty-one fights, took the title on a unanimous decision. Only the champion's tremendous courage enabled him to come through a severe battering in the tenth round. Holyfield said after his first defeat in twenty-nine contests: 'I gave my best, but it wasn't good enough. I think I'll finish now.'

But the big-spirited battler had more to offer. Seven days short of a year since his loss to Bowe, he regained the WBA and IBF belts with a magnificent majority points win in a rematch with 'Big Daddy'. The astonishing arrival of a para-glider, who descended into the ring during the seventh round, causing a twenty-two-minute delay, didn't disrupt Holyfield's concentration or rhythm as he went on to outbox and outpunch Bowe.

An upset loss of his titles to Michael Moorer in April 1994 seemed to spell the end of Holyfield's career. 'I gave it all I had. I'm tired and I'm sore,' he said after dropping a majority verdict to the southpaw challenger. Three days later, he officially announced his retirement, after complaining of chest pains. He was diagnosed as having a 'loose heart ventricle'. But the finding proved to be erroneous. After exhaustive medical tests, the Nevada State Commission branded him the 'healthiest fighter in the world'.

Back in action thirteen months after the Moorer defeat, Holyfield became the first man to floor former Olympic gold medallist Ray Mercer in a hard ten-rounder. But there were alarming signs of his physical deterioration in a non-title fight with Riddick Bowe. In the third meeting of the great heavyweight rivals, Evander looked washed-up. But he produced a terrific left hook in the sixth round which sent 'Big Daddy' crashing on his back. Bowe climbed to his feet, but looked all-out. Holyfield, however, didn't have the energy to finish the job. He fell apart after shipping a big right to the jaw in the eighth and the referee called a halt after he had been down twice.

When he struggled to overwhelm much smaller Bobby Czyz before forcing his opponent's retirement after five rounds, there seemed no logical reason why he should have a ghost of a chance against Mike Tyson. But this wasn't Frank Bruno or Bruce Seldon, who had been scared to death in Tyson's last two fights. This was Evander 'Real Deal' Holyfield, the guy with the biggest heart in the business. The 'experts' suffered for a long time from chronic indigestion due to the amount of words they had to swallow that night.

A revenge victory over Michael Moorer in eight rounds added the IBF belt to the WBA trophy he had won by beating Tyson. The stage was now set for the showdown the world wanted to see, a title unification bout against Lennox Lewis, the WBC champion.

The fight, at Madison Square Garden on 13 March 1999 was a huge disappointment and the result of a draw led to accusations of, at least, incompetence by two of the judges and, at worst, a conspiracy to rob Lewis of a deserved win. South African judge Stanley Christoudoulou made Lewis the winner by 116 points to 113, which was about right. England's Larry O'Connell had them all-square at 115-115, but the biggest outcry was over American woman judge Eugenia Williams' 115-113 score in favour of Holyfield.

It wasn't the worst decision in history, as some claimed, but most people were certain justice had not been done. Holyfield and Lewis would have to do it all again.

JULIAN JACKSON

Nickname: The Hawk.

WBA light-middleweight champion 1987-90. WBC middleweight champion 1990-93, 1995.

Born in St. Thomas, Virgin Islands, 12 September 1960.

Career: 1981–present.

Total contests: 61. Won: 55 (49 KOs). Lost: 6.

When a fighter packs the kind of dynamite power in his fists that Julian Jackson did, it makes up for most other deficiencies.

The image many television viewers retain of Jackson is the way he snatched victory from the jaws of defeat against Herol Graham with a magnificent right to the jaw that stretched the Britisher out cold. Describing the punch that brought the Virgin Islander the vacant WBC middleweight title in November 1990, *Boxing Monthly* recorded: 'It was enough to flatten six middleweights, let alone one.'

Graham had been cruising to success, his smooth southpaw skills leaving the crude Jackson floundering as he neatly sidestepped Julian's attacks. Jackson's left eye was so badly swollen that the ringside doctor had a serious look at it after the third round before allowing the fight to continue. But in the fourth round Graham, backing Jackson into a corner, zigged when he should have zagged and took the pay-off wallop flush on the chin. It was one of the most dramatic one-punch knockouts in history.

The Ring ranked Jackson fifth best junior middleweight in history, commenting in its May 1994 issue: 'Power alone catapults him toward the top of the division's ratings. He went on to win the WBC middleweight title, carrying his tremendous punch with him.' Broad-shouldered and long-armed, with the smooth muscles of a natural puncher, Jackson scored an impressive number of wins by clean knockouts. Yet, strangely enough, his first professional fight, in 1981, went the distance. He won his first twenty-nine contests, all but two by the short route. Sixteen of his victims were laid out cold as the referee counted them out.

The capture of the Continental Americas light-middleweight title in 1984 wasn't of much value, except that it brought him attention as a big hitter worth watching. He got his first world title chance in August 1986 and had WBA champion Mike McCallum on the verge of a knockout in the opening round. But McCallum hit back strongly and won in the second round. As has been shown so many times throughout boxing history, a solid hitter doesn't always have a chin to match.

Jackson excused his setback on the excesses of his lifestyle away from boxing. 'I was headed in the wrong direction,' he said. 'I had a girl here, a girl there. I was hanging around with the wrong people. I was living in the fast lane. I was getting involved in sinful things. God spoke to me and I listened. I am now a born-again Christian.'

When McCallum moved up to middleweight, Jackson took the vacant WBA title with a third round stoppage of Korean In-Chul Baek at Las Vegas on 21 November 1987. He defended it three times, scoring short route victories over Buster Drayton, Francisco DeJesus and Terry Norris. The second round dispatch of Norris was especially impressive as the talented Texan went on to win the WBC title three times. Jackson floored Norris with a short, sharp right and though Norris got to his feet, the referee saw how shaky he was and called a halt.

Out of action for surgery on a detached retina in late 1989, Jackson returned for the stunning knockout of Herol Graham to become WBC middleweight champion. The title had been stripped from Roberto Duran for failing to give a written undertaking to defend it. Jackson's first two defences lasted less than a round apiece, Americans Dennis Milton and Ismael Negron both stretched out for the count. He halted Ron Collins in five, but was then taken the distance for the first time in more than ten years by Thomas Tate. Jackson scored a knockdown in the fourth round, but he was shaken several times as the challenger fought back strongly. Nevertheless, the decision for Jackson was unanimous.

In an eagerly awaited battle of the big punchers, Jackson lost his WBC belt to Gerald McClellan in Las Vegas on 8 May 1993. Jackson, in trouble in the opening round and badly cut over the left eye in the third following a clash of heads, was still going strong up to the fifth. Then McClellan, though hurt himself by the champion's hard blows, attacked furiously to drop Jackson twice. The referee, seeing Julian was unable to defend himself, stopped the fight. A rematch the following year proved disastrous for the thirty-three-year-old 'Hawk', who was shot down in one minute, twenty-three seconds of the opening round. Jackson was floored, then subjected to a fierce barrage, culminating in a vicious left hook to the liver. As he stumbled forwards, referee Joe Cortez waved it off.

Serious disquiet was expressed when Jackson was matched with Italy's Agostino Cardmone for the WBC middleweight title, vacated by McClellan on moving up a weight, at Worcester, Massachusetts, in March 1995. Apart from his two poundings by McClellan, he had undergone operations on both eyes for detached retinas, which would have ended his career in other jurisdictions.

The unbeaten Italian southpaw outboxed the slower Jackson in the opening round, then staggered him with a one-two to the head. Jackson was also cut under the left eye. Cardmone's early success proved his undoing. Ignoring the age-old truism that the last thing a fighter loses is his punch, the Italian stood in front of Jackson instead of hitting and moving. Almost inevitably, a Jackson right caught him flush on the chin. Cardmone went down on his back.

Although he got up at 'eight' his legs wouldn't function and the referee signalled the finish.

Jackson's latest title reign lasted just over five months. On the Las Vegas undercard to Mike Tyson's return to action against Peter McNeeley after a four-year absence, the Virgin Islander was dethroned by Quincy Taylor, a clever southpaw from Dallas, Texas. Taylor slipped the champion's big bombs and popped away effectively with his accurate right jab. In the fourth round a left-hander dropped Jackson face-first. He got to his feet by eight and the bell prevented a follow-up by the challenger. When Taylor poured on the punishment in the following round, referee Jay Nady called a halt.

Jackson laid off for a year, returning in September 1996 to win a unanimous decision over Mexican heavyweight champion Leonardo Aguilar, who had slimmed from a roly-poly fifteen stone, two pounds to eleven stone, three pounds for the bout. Jackson looked in fine condition at eleven stone, two pounds, but despite wobbling his opponent several times, he was unable to find the big punch to put him away.

In May 1998, Jackson, washed-up at thirty-seven, was given a bad beating by Anthony Jones. *Boxing News* reported: 'Jackson used to knock out whoever he hit, but just seconds into the first round he seemed creaky and gun-shy, his once-cracking left hook almost always wide and slow.' Floored and badly hurt in the seventh round, he was belatedly saved by the referee from further punishment in the next. Sadly, there was no word of his wish to call it a day.

Boxing Monthly's American editor, Graham Houston, said of Jackson: 'He won't be remembered as a particularly skilled champion, but when the ring's best one-punch hitters are discussed, his name, one feels, will be right up there.'

JAMES J. JEFFRIES

Nicknames: the Fighting Boilermaker, and the Californian Grizzly Bear.

World heavyweight champion 1899-1905.

Born in Carroll, Ohio, USA, 15 April 1875. Died in Burbank, California, USA, 3 March 1953.

Career: 1896-1910.

Total contests: 21. Won: 18 (15 KOs). Lost: 1. Drew: 2.

James Jackson Jeffries made just one major mistake in his fighting career. He allowed himself to be lured into making a comeback in 1910 in a frantic bid by the white establishment to remove the hated Jack Johnson from the world heavyweight championship throne. 'Big Jeff', who had been living the easy life of a retired gent for six years, was no match for the brilliant black champion and took a systematic hiding before being counted out in the fifteenth round. Had he turned a deaf ear to the demands for him to come back, he would have gone down as the first heavyweight king to retire unbeaten.

Photographs of Jeffries give the impression of a huge man. In fact, although six feet, two and a half inches, and weighing around 220 pounds, he would be dwarfed by many of today's behemoths. He negated his height advantage, however, by fighting out of a crouch. Tutored by the great Tommy Ryan, a former world welterweight and middleweight champion, he kept his left arm extended and used his right forearm to protect his face. His best punch was a powerful left hook. A hard left jab thrown from his crouching position would soften up his opponents for the bigger punches that followed.

Born in Carroll, Ohio, the son of a Methodist preacher, Jim was seven when the family moved to a farm in the Los Angeles area of California. The sturdy youngster excelled at sports, especially boxing, wrestling and track events. Jeffries left school at sixteen to work in a boiler-making factory and picked up the nickname 'the Fighting Boilermaker' when he started professional boxing. After winning his first five fights by knockouts, he held two prominent heavyweights, Joe Choynski and Gus Ruhlin, to draws in twenty-round duels during 1897.

Spotted by Harry Corbett, brother of the then world heavyweight champion, James J. Corbett, Jeffries was invited to join the Corbett training camp at Carson City, Nevada. Because of his bulk and ability to absorb hard blows, he was the ideal sparring partner for the champion to practise his nifty footwork and punching repertoire. Corbett didn't spare the raw recruit in their brisk workouts, but later claims that Jeffries vowed to avenge the punishment he took are unfounded. In fact, he was extremely grateful for the lessons he learned. They stood him in good stead when he met his mentor in the ring some years later.

A third round knockout over a fading Peter Jackson, the great black Australian who had once held Corbett to an epic sixty-one rounds draw, was followed by a hard-earned twenty-round decision over Tom Sharkey. Though he outweighed Sharkey, an Irish-born seaman, by thirty-five pounds and was six inches taller, he found 'Sailor Tom' impossible to put away. Now managed by William A. Brady, who had been Corbett's mentor, Jeffries got his big chance at Coney Island, New York, on 9 June 1899, against Bob Fitzsimmons for the heavyweight championship of the world. In only his thirteenth fight, he took the title on an eleventh round knockout.

Jeffries fulfilled a promise to his old rival Tom Sharkey that he would get first crack at the title. Once again, the rugged Irishman took Jim all the way. For twenty-five rounds, they battered each other relentlessly without either conceding an inch. Jeffries bled from the mouth and ear, while the challenger's left ear swelled up so much that Jeffries likened it to hitting a big wet sponge. The champion finished the stronger and had his hand raised by referee George Siler, though many observers felt Sharkey should have got the verdict. It was the first time a world heavyweight title fight was decided by decision. As well as the punishment meted out to each other, Jeffries and Sharkey had to endure the fierce heat generated by 400-watt arc lamps situated over the ring for the filming of the indoor fight. Within days, the hair of both boxers began to fall out.

In the shortest world heavyweight title fight in history, Jeffries knocked out Jack Finnegan in fifty-five seconds in Detroit, Michigan, on 6 April 1900. While some historians maintain this was merely an exhibition bout, Barry J. Hugman, in his *British Boxing Board of Control Yearbook 1997*, said his research showed it was a genuine contest.

The jig-time win hardly served as a warm-up for Big Jeff's title defence against his former boss, James J. Corbett.

For twenty rounds of the fight, at Coney Island on 11 May 1900, Jeffries was still no better than a sparring partner for the old master. Corbett, now thirty-four, dazzled the leaden-footed champion with his speed and snappy punching. But the long distance, and the persistence of Jeffries' attacks, finally wore down the former champion's resistance. In the twenty-third round, Corbett was caught by a straight left, followed by a swinging left to the jaw, which put him down for the full count.

Jeffries gave Bob Fitzsimmons, from whom he had taken the championship, a chance to regain it in July 1902. It almost proved a foolish gamble. The veteran Englishman was all out to make the most of his opportunity. He outmanoeuvred and battered the champion for five rounds, bringing blood from Jeffries' nose, mouth and a cut under his right eye. Only Jeffries' great fighting heart kept him going as he stepped up his attacks. A mighty right that landed over the challenger's heart in the sixth round turned the course of the battle. Fitz was distressed, but he fought back gallantly in a bid to stave off the now encouraged titleholder. Jeffries, disregarding the blood which streamed from his face wounds, ploughed into his tormentor and finished him off in the eighth round with a thumping left hook to the stomach followed by a great clout to the chin.

James J. Corbett was next up for a second chance. Aged thirty-eight and three years out of the ring, 'Gentleman Jim' again gave Jeffries a boxing lesson for nine rounds, but, in the last fight of his career, he was unable to keep the dogged champion at bay. Two of Corbett's ribs were broken from Jeffries' relentless body punches and he went down for the count in the tenth round.

During a nationwide tour, Jeffries was briefly knocked off his feet by Jack Munroe in an exhibition bout. The incident was blown out of all proportion and the granting to Munroe of a world title match in August 1904 was totally unjustified. Munroe, a Canadian miner and former footballer, was no match for a fired-up Jeffries and was sent kicking inside two rounds.

With his unbeaten record intact, Jeffries announced his retirement from the ring. He followed his heavyweight champion predecessors John L. Sullivan, Corbett and Fitzsimmons onto the stage and proved a popular leading man in *Davy Crockett*. A record purse of $101,000, with sixty per cent for the winner and forty per cent for the loser, offered by promoter Tex Rickard, finally convinced Jeffries to come back and face Jack Johnson. The fight was set for Independence Day 1910, at Reno, Nevada.

Rumours that the bout was fixed for Jeffries to win were found to be nonsense as soon as the first bell rang. Johnson was completely on top, his speed and ripping punches proving too much for the old, slow ex-champ. In the fifteenth round, after Jeffries had been floored three times, his seconds jumped into the ring to prevent his total humiliation by being counted out. In a terrible sequel to the fight, whites went on the rampage in the Deep South after hearing the result and nine blacks died in bloody riots. The film of the bout caused further disturbances when it was shown and it was banned in Britain for fear of similar violent outbreaks.

Jeffries returned to his small farm in Burbank, California, and bred prize cattle. He settled for what looked like a comfortable retirement. He had cash in the bank, an interest in a saloon and more than $300,000 invested in stocks and shares. But he lost nearly everything in the Wall Street Crash of 1929 and was forced to declare bankruptcy. As a means of regaining solvency, he turned a barn on his farm into a gymnasium and promoted amateur tournaments there. He also toured in a vaudeville act with his old ring rival Tom Sharkey and acted in movies.

Jim was badly shaken when his beloved wife of thirty-seven years, Frieda, was killed in a road accident in 1941. Friends said he was never the same after the tragedy. Five years later he suffered a stroke that left him paralysed down one side. But he still loved talking about boxing and told one interviewer that he had only one regret: 'I should never have let myself be talked into coming back against Johnson. Too much rust had collected since my retirement. Nobody will know the pressure I was under in that fight. I felt as if every white American was on my back. I would like to have met Johnson at my peak. I'm not saying I would have beaten him, but you would have seen a completely different fight.'

Jeffries was seventy-seven when he died from a heart attack at his Burbank home in 1953.

EDER JOFRE

NBA bantamweight champion 1960-62. World bantamweight champion 1961-65. WBC featherweight champion 1973-74.

Born in São Paulo, Brazil, 26 March 1936.

Career: 1957-76.

Total contests: 78. Won: 72 (50 KOs). Lost: 2. Drew: 4.

The first Brazilian to win a world championship, Eder Jofre had another unusual claim to special attention. He was one of the few vegetarians to reach the boxing peak. In the ring, however, he was a man-eater.

Jofre was a superb all-rounder. He used his long arms to outbox opponents, then struck with lightning speed and dynamite power. His world championship reigns spanned fourteen years and he only lost twice, both times to the same man, Japan's Fighting Harada. When he made a comeback three years after losing for the second time to Harada, few gave the thirty-three-year-old Brazilian much of a chance of success. But he won all of his further twenty-five bouts, including the capture of the WBC featherweight title from Jose Legra, before hanging up his gloves for good at the age of forty.

Eder's Argentinian-born father had been a useful lightweight, boxing as 'Kid' Jofre. After he moved to Brazil and married an Italian, he gave boxing lessons to Eder from the age of five. The youngster progressed to the Brazilian amateur title and represented his country in the 1956 Olympics in Melbourne, Australia. He reached the quarter-finals before being eliminated.

Turning professional on his twenty-first birthday, Jofre put together an impressive unbeaten run, including the capture of the South American bantamweight title from world-rated Ernesto Miranda. On his first trip to the United States, he knocked out Mexico's Jose Medel in ten rounds in Los Angeles to earn the right to meet Eloy Sanchez, another Mexican, for the vacant National Boxing Association title in November 1960. Jofre landed a great one-two to the jaw to win on a sixth round knockout. He further strengthened his claim to be the world's top bantamweight by forcing Italian Piero Rollo to retire in nine rounds.

In the meantime, Irishman John Caldwell had earned recognition in Europe as world champion by outpointing Italy's Alphonse Halimi in London. A decider for the undisputed title was arranged, with Jofre gaining home advantage. Caldwell, winner of all his twenty-five contests to date, was given a hostile reception by the 20,000 crowd at the Ibirapuera Stadium in São Paulo on 18 January 1962. The Irishman put up a brave performance, but he was taking a bad hiding when referee Willie Pep, the former featherweight champion, threw his arms around him and led him to his corner in the tenth round.

Jofre defended his world title five times, winning them all by the short route, before he travelled to Japan in May 1965 to meet the former flyweight champion, Fighting Harada, in Nagoya. Struggling to make the weight, the Brazilian was two pounds over the limit at the weigh-in. He had to go for an hour's run to lose the necessary pounds. The weakened champion had difficulty keeping the aggressive Harada at bay and lost on a split decision.

Jofre didn't take his first defeat well. He complained that the referee, ring legend Barney Ross, lost control of the fight and allowed Harada to use his head and hold throughout the bout. In a return match the following year, in Tokyo, Harada again won on a fifteen round decision.

Jofre announced his retirement, but caused a surprise three years later by donning the gloves again as a featherweight. He looked as good as ever as he notched up fifteen straight wins, culminating in a majority points win over Cuban Jose Legra to capture the WBC championship belt in May 1973.

After scoring a meritorious fourth round knockout over another veteran, Mexico's Vicente Saldivar, Jofre was stripped of his title by the WBC for failing to defend it against mandatory challenger Alfredo Marcano, of Venezuela. He had seven more fights over the next two years, winning them all, before retiring for good in October 1976. Always a hugely popular figure in Brazil, he entered politics and also became a successful businessman.

Rating him second best bantamweight in history, next to Carlos Zarate, *The Ring* summarised Jofre's career: 'Went unbeaten in his first fifty bouts, and in early '60s was considered by many experts to be best fighter in game...Reputation suffered, however, because only two of thirteen world title fights took place in USA...Retired after twice losing to Fighting Harada, then cemented reputation as all-time great by coming back and winning world feather title at thirty-seven...Flawless fighter; boxed beautifully and carried kayo power in both fists...Won last twenty-five bouts of career...Among most under-rated fighters in history.'

JACK JOHNSON

Nicknames: the Galveston Giant, Li'l Arthur.

World heavyweight champion 1908-15.

Born in Galveston, Texas, USA, 31 March 1878. Died in Raleigh, North Carolina, USA, 10 June 1946.

Career: 1897-1928.

Total contests: 105. Won: 68 (40 KOs). Lost: 10. Drew: 10. No decision: 16. No contest: 1.

Rated by many old-timers as the greatest heavyweight of all time, Jack Johnson has rightly dropped a few notches in more recent appraisals of the game's big men.

Watching Johnson on film, one wonders what all the fuss was about. Certainly, he was a master defensive boxer, and he did severe damage with his vicious short hooks and uppercuts from close-in. But modern fans would have dozed off long before he belatedly decided to turn up the heat and go for a decisive win. He could punch, certainly, but he usually waited till his opponent was exhausted or had virtually given up in frustration before going for the kill.

Nat Fleischer saw every world heavyweight champion from James J. Jeffries to Joe Frazier. Right up to his death in 1972, he insisted that Johnson was the pick of the bunch. In his book *The Heavyweight Championship*, published in 1949, Fleischer wrote: 'After years devoted to the study of heavyweight fighters, I have no hesitation in naming Jack Johnson as the greatest of them all. He possessed every asset. He was big and strong and endowed with perfect co-ordination. He was a fine boxer, a good hitter and a powerful counter-puncher. He could block admirably and was a master in the art of feinting. In all-round ability, he was tops.'

Nine years later, Fleischer wrote in *Fifty Years at the Ringside* that only James J. Corbett and Gene Tunney matched Johnson for cleverness and speed. Of course, Cassius Clay was still two years off winning the Olympic gold medal at that time. Fleischer did concede that his hero was not as powerful a hitter as Jeffries, Bob Fitzsimmons, Tom Sharkey, Jack Dempsey, Joe Louis or Rocky Marciano. Whatever Fleischer's high status as a reporter and ring historian, he showed a definite bias towards the fighters of his starry-eyed youth. Who, in all honesty, could rate Marciano behind Sam Langford and Max Schmeling among the all-time best heavy-weights, as did *The Ring* editor? Or place Sugar Ray Robinson no higher than fifth among the middleweights, or Henry Armstrong number eight in the welterweights, or Willie Pep a mere seventh in the featherweight list?

In assessing Johnson's true standing among the greats, it must be conceded that he did not get his chance at the world title until he was thirty, when he was already probably just past his peak. This was due to the blatant 'colour bar' of the period. Johnson had to chase titleholder Tommy Burns half-way around the world before cornering him in Sydney, Australia, in 1908 and finally gaining justice.

Once he was champion, Jack took delight in rubbing the noses of white society into the dirt. In the ring, he taunted and insulted his inferior white opponents while punishing them unmercifully with deadly combinations. Often holding them up so he could administer further humiliation, he would look over their shoulders and flash his golden-toothed smile at the agitated ringsiders.

In his not-so-private life, the Texan courted and discarded a string of white women. He was arrested and charged with abduction under the Mann Act, the name given to the White Slave Traffic Act. Found guilty by an all-male, all-white jury of transporting an admitted prostitute across state borders for immoral purposes, he was fined $1,000 and sentenced to a year and a day in prison. According to Johnson in an interview years later, he bribed border guards to look the other way while he skipped into Canada. His exile, extended to Europe, lasted two years.

The seeds of Johnson's resentment at the lowly place of blacks in a white man's world were sown early. The son of a former slave, he grew up in poverty in Galveston, Texas, where blacks were forbidden to walk on the same footpaths as whites. At twelve, he ran away from home and got a job in Boston exercising racehorses. He broke his leg when thrown from a horse and was sent back to Galveston, where he went to work on the docks. There he learned to fight in 'battle royals'.

Jack, known as 'L'il Arthur' because he was christened John Arthur Johnson, had his first professional contest in 1897. Four years later he was stopped in three rounds by the vastly more experienced Californian Joe Choynski. Both men were arrested for taking part in an illegal prize-fight and Choynski spent his time in jail teaching the younger man the tricks of the trade.

Like the rest of the black heavyweights shunned by whites, Johnson's early bouts were mainly against fellow blacks. He beat talented fighters like Sam Langford, Sam McVey, Joe Jeannette and was proclaimed 'black heavyweight champion' after beating Denver Ed Martin on a twenty-round decision in 1903.

Johnson's talents could not go unrecognised for ever and he defeated leading white heavyweights Jack Munroe, Bill Lang, Fireman Jim Flynn and forty-four-year-old Bob Fitzsimmons, though he dropped a controversial twenty-round decision to Marvin Hart.

The world heavyweight championship was in the hands of Canadian Tommy Burns, who went on a world tour in a bid to escape growing demands for him to face his legitimate challenger, Johnson. The Texan took off in hot pursuit and finally got to grips with Burns in Australia. It took $30,000, an enormous sum for the time, to entice Burns into the ring at Rushcutter's Bay in Sydney on Boxing Day 1908.

Johnson made the titleholder pay for the years of discrimination and humiliation. Burns, at five feet, seven inches, the shortest world heavyweight champion in history, was outclassed by the highly skilled challenger, who outweighed him by twenty-four pounds. Jack teased and tormented the champion as he ripped in punches. In the fourteenth round, the police insisted on the slaughter being called off.

A massive hunt for a 'white hope' to knock the arrogant Johnson off his throne looked as if it might be successful when Stanley Ketchell, the world middleweight champion, dropped him with a swinging right in the twelfth round. Johnson exacted swift revenge. His first punch on rising, a right uppercut, sent Ketchell crashing for the full count. The blow was so severe that it knocked out several of the challenger's teeth. Johnson claimed his opponent had cheated on a prior arrangement that the fight should go the distance for the benefit of the movie camera.

After James J. Jeffries had been shamefully brought out of retirement in a vain attempt to dislodge him, Johnson beat Fireman Jim Flynn on a ninth round disqualification, then jumped bail when given two weeks to appeal against his jail sentence for abduction. He spent three years in exile in Europe and had three fights in Paris before World War One broke out. Fearing he would be called up by the French Army, he accepted an offer from American promoter Jack Curley to defend his title against giant cowboy Jess Willard. The fight was held in Havana, Cuba, on 5 April 1915 and ended in controversy.

Johnson, aged thirty-seven, softened by years of easy living and exhausted by the boiling sun, sank to the floor in the twenty-sixth round. One of boxing's most famous photographs shows Jack allegedly shading his eyes from the sun with his arms as he is counted out. Years later, Nat Fleischer bought a signed 'confession' from Johnson that he threw the fight in return for an extra $50,000 and a promise that the American authorities would allow him home without having to serve his prison sentence. But *The Ring* editor refused to publish the letter. He said he knew its contents were untrue and that Johnson only made the 'admission' because he was hard up for money. Fleischer said he paid up rather than let it go to some less scrupulous publisher.

Had Johnson agreed to take a dive, he would hardly have gone twenty-six rounds in such uncomfortable conditions before doing so. Besides, the film evidence is that his superior boxing against the clumsy, six feet, seven inches challenger had him ahead after twenty rounds. Only his rapidly growing exhaustion caused his downfall. The punch that finished him off was a solid overarm right.

If the promoter did vow to get Johnson off his prison rap, as claimed, he reneged. It was not until 1920 that Johnson returned to the United States, and he was made to serve his full sentence. When he left Leavenworth jail, he had just five dollars to his name. But the strict regimen had kept him in fit condition and he resumed boxing, mainly exhibitions, but occasional fights.

At forty-two, he boldly challenged the current world champion, Jack Dempsey, but in vain. He carried on boxing until he was past fifty and was still appearing in exhibition matches when in his sixties. Many people who watched him drumming a rhythm on a punchball in New York's Herbert Museum, where he was second attraction to a flea circus, had little concept of the great social and sporting impact made by the now elderly black man with the gold-toothed smile.

Johnson always had a passion for fast cars. It was said he had enough speeding tickets to wallpaper a gymnasium and he miraculously escaped three crashes in which his cars were a write-off. On 10 June 1946, while returning home from a speaking engagement, he lost control of his vehicle coming off a bend at Raleigh, North Carolina, and crashed into a telegraph pole. He died the following day, at the age of sixty-eight.

ROY JONES JUNIOR

IBF middleweight champion 1993-94. IBF super-middleweight champion 1994-97. WBC light-heavyweight champion 1997–present. WBA light-heavyweight champion 1998–present.

Born in Pensacola, Florida, USA, 16 January 1969.

Career: 1989–present.

Total contests: 40. Won: 39 (33 KOs). Lost: 1.

You go for speed and you sacrifice power. But not if you're Roy Jones Junior. The multi-gifted American, gently breezing along one minute, whips up into a whirlwind the next. The punches fly in a blinding flurry – and they hurt. Few opponents have weathered the storm.

Just how great Jones, a superstar of the 'nineties, might become is very difficult to gauge. While he has picked up world championship belts at middleweight, super-middleweight and light-heavyweight, his critics point out that he has not really been tested. There just isn't anyone good enough to bring out his full potential. It's not his fault that he came along fifteen years after Sugar Ray Leonard, Roberto Duran, Wilfred Benitez and Thomas Hearns were at their peaks. A match with any of this illustrious quartet would have been one to savour.

'Critics of Jones point to a certain unorthodoxy,' wrote *Boxing Monthly*'s American editor Graham Houston, 'a tendency to lean back from punches or to lunge in with the left hook...But his speed and reflexes let him get away with such breaches of ring convention. In this respect he can, perhaps, be compared with the young Muhammad Ali, who did things "wrong" but made them turn out right.'

Complacency could be the current superstar's downfall. His arrogance in playing a game of basketball on the afternoon of his fight with Eric Lucas, and his taking part in a question-and-answer session with media and fans an hour before he stepped into the ring to dispatch Bryant Brannon in two rounds, showed a contempt for opponents that could prove fatal on another occasion. This is the game of mighty upsets, remember!

In March 1997, he showed an amazing lack of control by hitting Montell Griffin on the ground. The action cost him his WBC light-heavyweight title and his unbeaten record, even if a disqualification is not regarded as a genuine defeat. Jones, who speaks even faster than he hits, admitted he was trying to win at all costs. 'I ain't got time to stop,' he said. 'I gotta do what I gotta do.'

It was the first time he had been declared the loser since a scandalous decision was given against him in the 1988 Olympics light-middleweight final. Jones, who had beaten Britain's Richie Woodall in an earlier round, looked a convincing points winner over Korea's Park Si-Hun. The Games were held in Seoul and it was alleged that judges had been paid to vote for Korean fighters. Nine years after the 3/2 decision against Jones, the International Olympic Committee agreed to an investigation, but said it could find no evidence to support the bribery claims.

Just like the old show business question, 'Who was Sammy Davis Senior?', boxing fans sometimes wonder about the father of Roy Jones Junior. Well, Roy Senior was a useful professional middleweight who fought Marvin Hagler in 1977. Jones the elder actually managed his son for the first three years of his professional career. He adopted such a cautious approach that Roy Junior, tired of fighting low-grade opposition for poor rewards, decided to go his own way.

Jones had built his record to twenty-one straight wins – only Jorge Castro had taken him the distance – when he got his first big chance against Bernard Hopkins for the IBF middleweight title in May 1993. Roy won a comfortable points decision. He defended the championship just once, blasting out Thomas Tate with a single left hook after thirty seconds of the second round. Sugar Ray Leonard drew laughter at the post-fight conference when he said: 'I want to challenge Roy Jones – to eighteen holes of golf.'

A diligent trainer, Jones found it difficult to keep his impressively muscled body down to the middleweight limit, so he decided to move up a division. The IBF super-middleweight champion, James Toney, was regarded by many experts as the best fighter in the world at the time. He was unbeaten in forty-two fights and his hard punching had won him the nickname 'Lights Out'. Jones won as he pleased, totally bewildering the champion with his speed and skill, to earn a unanimous decision. The judges' scorecards read 119-108, 118-109 and 117-110.

First challenger, Antoine Byrd, was brushed aside in the opening round. Vinny Pazienza lasted into the sixth, while Tony Thornton was put away in three. After halting Eric Lucas in eleven rounds and Bryant Brannon in two, Jones, a rich man, could have retired to a comfortable lifestyle on his huge farm just outside his home town of Pensacola, Florida. He could devote more time to his hobbies of collecting vintage cars and breeding fighting cocks. Instead, he decided to move onwards – and upwards.

There was a bizarre background to Jones' meeting with veteran Mike McCallum in Tampa, Florida, on 22 November 1996. The WBC wanted to call it for the vacant light-heavyweight title. Only trouble with that was Frenchman Fabrice Tiozzo was still champion. He wasn't going to abdicate just to suit the whim of the organisation, which would earn a $100,000 sanctioning fee. So the fight went ahead as an 'interim' WBC title bout.

To compound matters, the Florida Commission decreed that it, not the WBC, would appoint the ring officials. The WBC, refusing to back down, parked its three judges in the first row of the Press section. The Florida officials occupied the normal places just outside the ring. As it happened, Jones won by such an overwhelming points margin that there could be no argument. Had it been close, and the two sets of judges had differed in their choice of winner, it would have made an interesting case for the courts. It was generally felt that Jones didn't go for a knockout, out of respect for the forty-year-old McCallum. Several times, he had the former three-weight champion in trouble and he made McCallum touch down with a flashing right in the tenth round, but eased off. When the WBC later stripped Fabrice Tiozzo of the title for failing to defend it in time, Jones was officially declared WBC champion.

Rated by most experts as the best pound-for-pound fighter in the world, Jones was so short of worthwhile opposition that he contemplated trying his luck among the heavyweights – for just once. His preference would be matches with Michael Moorer or Evander Holyfield, but he didn't rule out Mike Tyson. Asked if he had the ability to hurt Tyson, he said: 'I'd have to wear him down first, then I could probably hurt him. But if he was smart, he'd hit me in the arms so I wouldn't be able to use them for a while.'

Angry that the one blot on his record was the disqualification against Montell Griffin, Jones regained the WBC title in August 1997 by blasting out Griffin in the first round. Griffin, offering no excuses for his first defeat in twenty-eight fights, said: 'I don't have nothing bad to say about the man. He's a great fighter. One day I'll sit down with my kids and tell them I fought the man.'

Boxing's superman proved to be mortal after all in July 1998, when Jones was floored for the first time as an amateur or professional. Southpaw Lou Del Valle surprised him with a left to the jaw to cause the knockdown, which Jones later dismissed as 'just a flash thing'. Up quickly, Roy was never really bothered after that and won a unanimous decision, with all three judges giving it to him by wide margins. The win gave Jones the WBA title to add to his WBC prize.

PETER KANE

Real name: Peter Cain.

World flyweight champion 1938-43.

Born in Heywood, Lancashire, England, 28 February 1918. Died in Leigh, Lancashire, 23 July 1991.

Career: 1934-48.

Total contests: 102. Won: 92 (56 KOs). Lost: 7. Drew: 2. No contest: 1.

Likened to the American singer-comedian Eddie Cantor because of his large, bulging eyes, Peter Kane attracted lots of attention for another reason. He could hit – and how!

It is doubtful if there was a harder punching flyweight in ring history. More than half his opponents failed to make it to the final bell.

Only nineteen when he was pitted against the great Benny Lynch for the world flyweight championship in 1937, Kane lost in the thirteenth round after putting up a terrific battle. He held Lynch to a draw in a return, with no title at stake, then went on to capture world honours when Lynch was forced to relinquish his claim.

Kane was born in Heywood, between Rochdale and Bury, but the family moved to nearby Golborne while he was still a baby. He learned the basics of boxing from his dad, but never had an amateur fight. Blackpool manager Jim Turner recalled: 'Peter was punching for pay when he was still wearing a school cap and short trousers. I saw him box Andy Lowe in Len Johnson's boxing booth, when a thousand fans tried to get into the booth which normally held only 300.'

After leaving school, Kane went to work as a blacksmith's striker. Though he weighed less than eight stone, he developed strong muscles from swinging the smithy's hammer. His proper name was Cain, but he was billed for his first professional contest as Peter Kane and that was how it was spelled throughout his fourteen-year career.

Aged just sixteen on his debut, Kane won his first forty-one fights, thirty-three inside the distance. Among those he dispatched early were respected flyweights like Jim Mararg, Phil Milligan and Irishman Jimmy Warnock, who twice upset Benny Lynch in non-title contests. Peter scored points wins over Tiny Bostock, Joe Curran, Ernest Weuss and Frenchman Valentin Angelmann, who was recognised in Europe as world flyweight champion. The International Boxing Union, forerunner of the European Boxing Union, no longer acknowledged Angelmann's title claim after he lost to Kane. Nor did they support the Englishman as his successor.

Kane's impressive fourth round stoppage of Warnock suggested he would not be over-matched against Benny Lynch, the brilliant all-rounder who was now the undisputed world champion. The title fight drew a crowd of 40,000, a new Scottish record, to Shawfield Park, Glasgow, on 13 October 1937.

It looked like it was all over within a minute as Lynch, roared on by his fanatical Scottish supporters, dropped the teenage challenger with a terrific right to the jaw. Kane rose shakily to his feet, and only survived the opening round on instinct. The Lancashire lad shook off the worst effects of his near-disastrous start to match the champion blow for blow in a magnificent contest. But Kane tired as the bout moved into the later stages and he was floored in the twelfth round and twice in the thirteenth before the referee came to his rescue. *Boxing News* reported: 'A big hand must be accorded to Peter. His spirit was unflinching, his courage was amazing.'

There was a return match five months later in Liverpool, but Lynch was no longer able to make the eight-stone flyweight limit. It went on as a non-title affair. The bout went twelve rounds to a draw.

When Lynch weighed in almost seven pounds overweight for a proposed defence against the American Jackie Jurich, the world title was declared vacant. Kane and Jurich were then matched at Anfield football ground, Liverpool, on 22 September 1938 to find a new champion. Kane's relentless pressure was too much for the stylish Californian and he scored half a dozen knockdowns en route to a clear points win over fifteen rounds.

The Lancastrian was champion of the world – but at a huge cost. He so badly damaged the knuckles of his right hand that he had to have his little finger amputated. He had first injured the finger when he took a swing at a punchball in a fairground at Blackpool. Though he was back in ring action four months after his title victory, the handicap meant that Kane never again revealed the great punching power of previous years and relied more on his boxing skills to win. Amazingly for a reigning world champion, Kane fought for, and won, the English Northern Area flyweight title in October 1942 by forcing Paddy Ryan to retire in six rounds.

During World War Two Kane served in the Royal Air Force, while continuing to box. It was June 1943, however, before he made his first defence of the world championship. Since beating Jurich five years earlier, Peter had fought twenty-seven times, winning twenty-five. But he could no longer make the flyweight limit comfortably. It was a weakened champion who stepped into the ring at Hampden Park, Glasgow, to meet his first challenger, the hard-hitting Scottish southpaw Jackie Paterson. Kane went for the kill from the opening bell, but he ran into a neat countering right and follow-up left hook. It was all over in sixty-one seconds, with Peter out for the count.

In a freak accident the following year, Kane was struck in the face with the lapel of a heavy RAF overcoat and was temporarily blinded in one eye. Doctors in the military hospital told him he would never box again, but an operation seemed to cure the problem and he returned to the ring after a three-year absence as a bantamweight. Impressive wins over tough Irishman Bunty Doran, Hawaiian Dado Marino, a future world flyweight champion, and Frenchman Theo Medina led to a return with Medina in Manchester in September 1947, this time with the Frenchman's European bantamweight title at stake. Kane won a fifteen-round decision after a tough, uncompromising battle.

There were signs that the Lancastrian was coming towards the end of his gruelling career when he showed little of his old fire in outpointing his first European challenger, Joe Cornelis, of Belgium. In February 1948, a new European champion was crowned when Italian Guido Ferracin outspeeded and outboxed Kane to take a clear points verdict. A return match five months later resulted in Kane suffering bad cuts in a clash of heads. His vision impaired by the flow of blood, he was floored for a count in the fifth round. Though he made it to his feet, the towel came fluttering in from his corner.

Kane had just one more fight, a final eliminator for the British title against Stan Rowan on 19 November 1948. Rowan won on points over twelve rounds. Satisfied with a career that had shown so much success – though, strangely, he never fought for a British title – Peter went back to work as a blacksmith. Sadly, the accident with the coat had left its legacy and he eventually lost the sight of that eye.

Though he escaped from a car crash with just an ankle injury, his health deteriorated in his later years. He was in and out of Leigh Infirmary in Lancashire for some time before his death in 1991, aged seventy-three.

Oscar winner: enjoying the moment as new WBC light welterweight champion is Oscar de La Hoya after his victory over Julio Cesar Chavez.

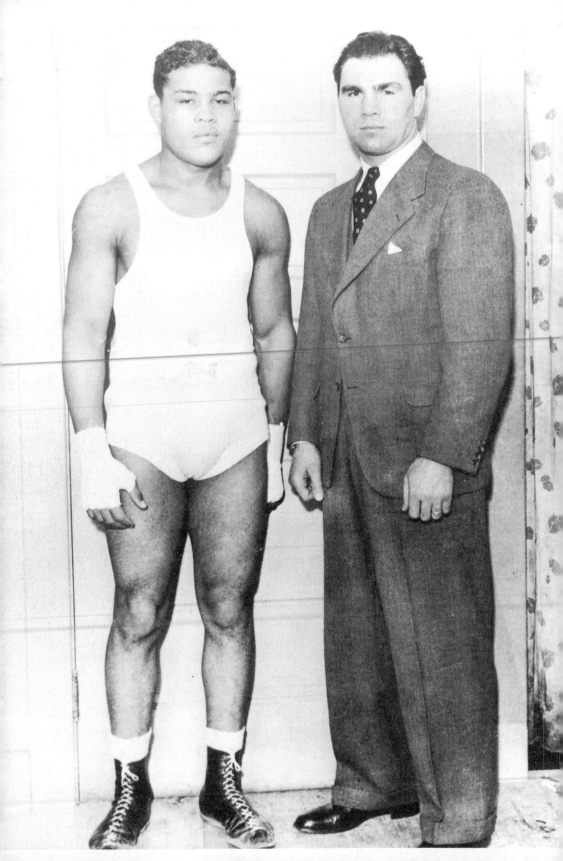

'Brown Bomber' Joe Louis, who made record-breaking defences (*right*) and with Max Schmeling (*left*), before their grudge match in 1938, in which Louis avenged his earlier defeat. (*Below*) Archie Moore let his guard down for this nose-bending right from Yolande Pompey in London, but Moore stopped the Trinidadian in the tenth round to retain his world light-heavyweight title.

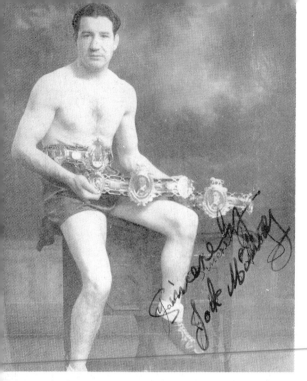

Jock McAvoy *(left)*, fearsome-punching Briton who failed to win a world title and Peter Kane *(right)*, hard-hitting flyweight who stopped more than half his 108 opponents.

Ted 'Kid' Lewis *(below left)*, who fought 282 contests, including a 20-bout series with Jack Britton. Jake LaMotta *(below right)*, one of the toughest middleweights of all, whose life was made into the movie, *Raging Bull*.

Magical match: Irish-born Jimmy McLarnin with his manager, Pop Foster (*right*), who guided him to the world welterweight title, retired him at the top and left him a fortune in his will.

Like this, sonny: Sonny Liston (*below*) takes a break during training for his return match with Muhammad Ali to give some pointers to Richard Hart, aged seven, while former heavyweight kings James J. Braddock and Jersey Joe Walcott look on.

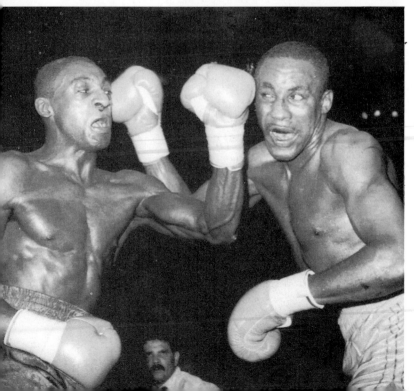

Time to go, Joe: Rocky Marciano (*above*) ducks inside Joe Louis's jab as he pounds his way to an eighth-round knockout in 1951 in Louis's last fight. (*Below*) Mike McCallum (*on the right*) and Britain's Herol 'Bomber' Graham swap blows during their fight for the vacant WBA middleweight title in London.

Busy bee: American Freddie Miller (*right*), who packed 247 contests into his thirteen-year career.

Best Wishes J. Milly

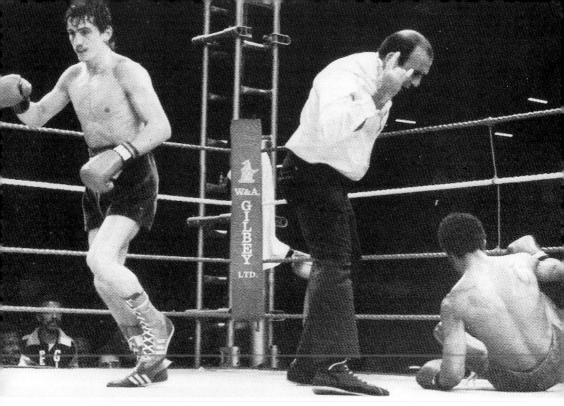

Ireland's Barry McGuigan floors Eusebio Pedroza in the seventh round going on to win a clear decision to become WBA featherweight champion. Returning home, he acknowledges the cheers of the huge crowd that greeted his parade through Dublin on an open-top bus.

STANLEY KETCHELL

Real name: Stanislaus Kiecal.

Nickname: the Michigan Assassin.

World middleweight champion 1906-08, 1908-09.

Born in Grand Rapids, Michigan, USA, 14 September 1886. Died in Conway, Missouri, USA, 15 October 1910.

Career: 1904-10.

Total contests: 64. Won: 52 (49 KOs). Lost: 4. Drew: 4. No decision: 4.

Nat Fleischer, with his customary affection for the fighters of his youth, declared Stanley Ketchell the greatest middleweight of all time. Movies of Ketchell's fights reveal him to have been a wild slugger with a thunderous punch and a great heart, but virtually bereft of technique.

Much of Ketchell's elevated status is due to the fact that he floored world heavyweight champion Jack Johnson, who outweighed him by thirty-five pounds. But, again using the fight film as evidence, Johnson was coasting along in the twelfth round when Ketchell caught him with a surprise right swing. The heavyweight champion sat down briefly, then jumped up to make the smaller man pay for his temerity. A vicious right uppercut left Ketchell spreadeagled on the canvas, out to the world.

Of course, Ketchell never had the benefit of formal training. The son of a Russian immigrant and his Polish wife, Stanley ran away from home in Grand Rapids, Michigan, in his early teens in search of adventure. He reached Chicago, where an ex-boxer named 'Socker' Flanagan gave him a job at his lunch-counter and taught him the rudiments of boxing. His travels took him to the copper mining town of Butte, high in the Montana Rockies. Ketchell became a bouncer at a rowdy dive called the Copper Queen and picked up an extra $20 a week boxing all-comers at a local theatre.

In 1903 he had his first recorded professional contest, flattening Kid Tracy in the first round. One of the scores of legends surrounding Ketchell's life suggests that Tracy had a friend hiding behind a curtain on the stage, waiting for Ketchell to reach the spot where he could knock him senseless with a loaded sock. Unfortunately for Tracy, his pal hit the wrong target.

Ketchell lost only twice in his first forty-six fights, each time to Maurice Thompson, who also held him to a draw. There were four other draws, but the significance of his progress was that not one of his thirty-nine victims lasted the full course. Obviously his mighty punch made up for what he lacked in scientific skill. The middleweight scene was thrown into confusion when world champion Tommy Ryan retired in 1907. While Jack 'Twin' Sullivan earned recognition in some quarters as Ryan's successor, Ketchell's bout with Joe Thomas was billed for the vacant title by California's leading promoter, Jimmy Coffroth.

In an epic battle scheduled for forty-five rounds, Ketchell and Thomas, who had drawn their first meeting two months earlier, each dealt out savage punishment. They took it in turns to hit the canvas and each looked finished on more than one occasion. Finally, in the thirty-second round, Ketchell battered his rival to leave him lying across the bottom rope. As Thomas hung suspended in that position, his seconds threw in the towel.

After just three months' rest, Ketchell and Thomas were at it again. In another bitter war, Stanley had his opponent cut and floored for a count early on, but was dropped himself in the twentieth and final round. Both finished in a state of exhaustion, with Ketchell's arm raised as the winner.

As Jack 'Twin' Sullivan also claimed the middleweight championship, a decider with Ketchell was the obvious way to clear up the mess. Stanley tuned up by dispatching Sullivan's twin brother, Mike, inside a round. Jack did better. He survived until the twentieth round before taking the count. Waiting in the wings for a crack at the now undisputed titleholder was Billy Papke, a tough ex-miner from Spring Valley, Illinois. They were to meet in four gruelling duels that would leave each man with enduring bitter feelings towards the other.

Ketchell got their initial meeting off to a controversial start by hitting Papke with a left hook and flooring him just as the sound of the opening bell faded. Papke later complained that the punch had landed as he went to shake hands. It was customary at that time to touch gloves as the bout commenced, not during the referee's instructions, as is now the case.

Papke, who recovered to lose a ten-round decision, got his revenge when they met again in September 1908. He followed Ketchell into the ring and went straight across to shake his hand. When the bell rang to start the contest, Ketchell held out his glove to repeat the friendly exchange. Papke, remembering what happened in their first encounter, shot a booming right-hander to the champion's head, making him stagger backwards. Papke followed up and battered Ketchell to the canvas three times in the sensational first three minutes. Ketchell never recovered from the initial onslaught and took a savage beating for twelve rounds. Finally Jim Jeffries, who was refereeing the bout, decided he had seen enough and led the bloodied and battered Ketchell to his corner.

The deposed champion took just two months off to lick his wounds before he was back in the ring with Papke again. This time there were no handshakes, before or after the bell. Ketchell, in excellent shape and thirsting for revenge, went after the champion from the start. Papke was in trouble as early as the fourth round. He was floored and saved by the bell in the eighth and was driven backwards in the following round by the ferocity of Ketchell's attacks. A short left hook dropped Papke in the eleventh round. Back on his feet, he took two rights and a hard left to the stomach and sank to the floor again. He just failed to beat the count.

In the fourth match of their series, Ketchell won a disputed twenty-round decision.

Like the others, it was a hard duel, with both men suffering broken hands and absorbing lots of punishment.

Ketchell took off for New York on a publicity stint with his manager, Willus Britt. Decked out in a cowboy outfit by the wily Britt, Stanley took to the Broadway scene with gusto. He was frequently to be seen sipping champagne and smoking a cigar in the company of the regular night-life characters and chorus girls.

Boxing in New York was restricted to no-decision contests in members-only clubs. Ketchell took on the reigning world light-heavyweight champion, Philadelphia Jack O'Brien, at the National. It looked too ambitious an undertaking for the much smaller and lighter man as O'Brien completely outboxed him and had blood streaming from his battered face. In the ninth round, however, Ketchell landed a terrific body blow that sent O'Brien to the floor. He dropped him twice more in the tenth and last session. Then, with just seconds left, a right to the jaw sent O'Brien crashing into his own corner. He lay there unconscious. But, as the count reached 'four', the final bell rang. Ringside newspapermen were divided as to who deserved to win, but all agreed Ketchell would have been the winner on a knockout if he had landed the final blow a few seconds earlier.

In a rematch, Ketchell battered O'Brien to defeat in three rounds. His ability to overcome a much bigger man encouraged 'the Michigan Assassin' to go after the heavyweight crown. Though he had the satisfaction of putting Jack Johnson on the seat of his pants, the big prize eluded him. His failure to whip Johnson sent Ketchell into a depression. He took to smoking opium to add to his considerable list of vices.

At the end of 1909, Ketchell announced he was giving up the middleweight title, as he could no longer make the weight. Then he changed his mind, beating Frank Klaus, Willie Lewis and Jim Smith in bouts billed as championship fights. At the same time, Billy Papke claimed he was the legitimate champion after knocking out Willie Lewis in Paris.

Ketchell longed for another crack at Johnson's heavyweight crown and went to train at a friend's farm in Conway, Missouri, in an effort to increase his weight. While there, he took to poking fun at a temporary ranch-hand named Walter Dipley. Dipley's fury was enhanced when the fighter made a move on his girlfriend, Goldie Smith, who was a housekeeper at the farm.

On 14 October 1910, according to Goldie when she appeared in court later, Ketchell raped her when she resisted his advances. She told Dipley of the incident and, the following morning, as she served breakfast to the champion, Dipley appeared with a .22 Marlin rifle and shot Ketchell in the back. He was rushed to hospital, where he died later that evening. He was twenty-four years old.

Ketchell's body was returned to his birthplace, Grand Rapids, where a Polish military band led the white hearse while young girls scattered flowers along the funeral route. Jewell Bovine, alleged to be the slain fighter's fiancée, was stopped as she made an attempt to kill herself by swallowing carbolic acid.

Dipley and Smith were charged with first-degree murder. They were found guilty and sentenced to life imprisonment. Smith was paroled after twelve years, while Dipley served twenty-four years. On his release, he went to work for a gas company. As part of his rounds, he sometimes called at the farm where he had gunned down Ketchell.

JAKE LAMOTTA

Real name: Giacobe LaMotta.

Nickname: the Bronx Bull.

World middleweight champion 1949-51.

Born in the Bronx, New York, USA, 10 July 1921.

Career: 1941-54.

Total contests: 106. Won: 83 (30 KOs). Lost: 19. Drew: 4.

Jake LaMotta's life story was perfect material for a Hollywood movie. They made it in 1980. Robert de Niro won an Oscar for playing the tough New Yorker in *Raging Bull*.

Like his boyhood pal Rocky Graziano, who also went on to win the world middleweight title, LaMotta was forever in trouble with the law as a youngster and spent some time in reform school. Saved from a life of crime by taking up boxing, he nevertheless got involved with the mobsters who had such a major influence on professional boxing in America in the immediate post-World War Two years.

Many years after his retirement, he told a US Senate antimonopoly sub-committee that the only way he could get a world title fight was to take a dive against Blackjack Billy Fox in 1947. Even then, he had to wait another two years, as well as hand over $20,000 to 'The Mob', to get a crack at Marcel Cerdan's middleweight championship.

Short for a middleweight at five feet, eight inches, LaMotta's bulky body appeared to be hewn out of rock. He was almost impossible to hurt and, after taking a savage beating from Sugar Ray Robinson to lose his world title on a thirteenth round stoppage, his proudest boast was that Robinson couldn't knock him off his feet. Jake's great claim to fame, apart from winning the world crown, was that he was the first man to beat Robinson. He outscored Sugar Ray in a non-title ten-rounder in 1943. It was the only time he emerged victorious in their six matches. After he retired and became a night-club comedian, one of LaMotta's quips was: 'I mixed with Sugar so much I got diabetes.'

LaMotta was not a terrific puncher, as his thirty short-route wins in 106 fights testifies, but his great strength allowed him to swarm all over his opponents and wear them down with non-stop, two-fisted attacks delivered from a crouch. He could be outboxed, but no one beat him for determination and punch resistance.

Jake began boxing in his teens, campaigning as an amateur for two years, then turning professional at the age of eighteen. He stepped between the ropes twenty times in his first year as a pro, winning sixteen, drawing one and losing three. By the following year, 1942, he was already rated sixth among world middleweights by *The Ring*.

That was the year he crossed gloves with Sugar Ray Robinson for the first time. After an exciting ten-rounder at New York's Madison Square Garden, Robinson got the decision. It was the return match, at the Detroit Olympic Arena on 5 February 1943, that gave LaMotta his special landmark in ring history.

Jake, with a fifteen-pound weight advantage, bullied the more stylish Robinson out of his stride and pounded him through the ropes and onto the ring apron in the eighth round. Still, it was close at the end of the ten rounds, but referee Sam Hennessy, the sole arbiter, gave his verdict to LaMotta by five rounds to four, with one even. It was the first time Sugar Ray had lost in forty professional fights. He was to go unbeaten for another ninety-one contests before he lost again.

The third meeting between the pair was another classic, with Robinson boxing and moving while LaMotta tried to catch him with his favourite left hook. He finally succeeded in the seventh round, when Robinson was sent tumbling for a count of 'eight'. Sugar Ray recovered to give the New Yorker a lesson in ringcraft over the last three rounds and wrap up the decision.

LaMotta suffered two more points losses to Robinson in 1945, but while his great rival went on to monopolise the welterweight division for the next four years, Jake cemented his claim to a shot at the middleweight crown with impressive wins over high-ranking men like Bert Lytell, Jose Basora, Tommy Bell, Holman Williams and Tony Janiro. He also won three out of four bouts against former welterweight champion Fritzie Zivic. But 'The Mob', which had such a hold on professional boxing at that time, froze him out of a title shot because he refused to take on their nominee as his manager. In frustration, he faced Blackjack Billy Fox at Madison Square Garden on 14 November 1947, a date that is among the most infamous in ring history.

Fox, managed by underworld figure Frankie 'Blinky' Palermo, was being manoeuvred into a world light-heavyweight title fight with champion Gus Lesnevich. A win over LaMotta, especially if he could be the first man to stop 'the Bronx Bull', would be an impressive step towards that goal. LaMotta seemed to put up little resistance as Fox pounded him to defeat in four rounds, although he was still on his feet when the referee called a halt. There were widespread cries of a 'fix', but it was not until thirteen years later that Jake confirmed to the Senate investigators that he threw the fight.

In an interview with Peter Heller, author of *In This Corner*, LaMotta recalled:

> I purposely lost to Billy Fox because they promised me I would get a shot at the title if I did. Today it's a little different. If a fellow deserves a chance at the title, the people will argue for it,

they will speak up, the newspaper people will speak up. But in my time there were lots of guys that deserved chances to fight for the title. There were a lot of uncrowned champs around at that time that didn't get the shot. And those were the guys I had to fight because nobody else wanted to fight 'em.

LaMotta got his shot at the world title on 16 June 1949, against the pride of France, Marcel Cerdan. His hand was raised as the winner when Cerdan, who had badly injured his left shoulder when thrown to the canvas in the first round, was unable to come out for the tenth round. The scheduled return match never took place. Cerdan died when the plane taking him to the United States crashed in the Azores.

For the devastated French, there was some small crumb of consolation when LaMotta, in his first fight after winning the title, was beaten on points by another Frenchman, Robert Villemain. Unfortunately for them, it was a non-title affair. Jake had taken a hotly disputed decision over Villemain three months before becoming champion. After clearly outpointing Italian Tiberio Mitri in his first title defence, LaMotta took on yet another Frenchman, Laurent Dauthille, in a fight with one of the most dramatic finishes in championship history.

Dauthille, who had beaten LaMotta in a non-title contest a year earlier, was in control for most of the return match and was well ahead on points going into the fifteenth and final round. He then fell for a classic LaMotta con trick. The champion, after pretending to be badly hurt, let loose with a furious barrage of punches. Dauthille was caught completely off guard and collapsed against the ropes to be counted out. There were just thirteen seconds left in the fight.

It was that man again, Sugar Ray Robinson, in the opposite corner when LaMotta put his title at stake for the third time. The sixth and last of their epic series took place at Chicago Stadium on St. Valentine's Day in 1951. The date and venue could not have been more appropriate. Jake took such a savage beating that the headline writers couldn't resist calling it 'Another St. Valentine's Day Massacre'.

Robinson, the reigning world welterweight champion, went into the ring with a remarkable record of just one loss (to LaMotta) in 123 fights. LaMotta had been beaten twelve times in ninety-four bouts. LaMotta, weakened by having to make the middleweight limit, was given a boxing lesson for ten rounds. Robinson then turned up the heat and battered the titleholder to a standstill. In the thirteenth round, LaMotta, leaning against the ropes and unable to raise his hands, but refusing to go down, was rescued, none too soon, by referee Frank Sikora.

Moving up to light-heavyweight, LaMotta seemed to have reached the end of the line when Irish Bob Murphy stopped him in seven rounds. He got revenge over Murphy in a return, but was floored for the first and only time in his career by Danny Nardico, who stopped him in seven rounds. He wisely called it a day after losing on points to Billy Kilgore in April 1954.

Jake owned a night-club in Miami Beach, but he spent time in jail for aiding and abetting prostitution. A painful divorce, a year-long whisky binge and the loss of $300,000 almost did what no ring opponent had managed – put him down and out. He could have been speaking for a thousand rags-to-riches-to-rags fighters down the years when he commented: 'I was unsophisticated about finances. I wasted my money. I went to jail. I lost everything. When they said a fool and his money are soon parted, they were thinking about uneducated street kids with attitudes and wads of cash in their pockets. We think the good times are going to be around forever.'

LaMotta, however, showed the same fighting qualities that won him so many admirers and he pulled himself together. He got some character acting roles in movies and TV programmes and proved such a popular after-dinner speaker that he became a successful stand-up comedian.

It was the huge success of the biographical movie *Raging Bull*, however, that brought Jake LaMotta to the attention of the world at large. The film pulled no punches in its portrayal of the fighter whose life outside the ring was often as violent and brutal as what happened when he was wearing the gloves. Robert de Niro played him as 'a man without any redeeming features at all'. Columnist

Jimmy Cannon called him 'the most detested man of his generation'.

LaMotta was upset at what he saw as a misrepresentation of his life. 'I want people to know I ain't that bad,' he told South African writer Bert Blewett in 1988. 'I'm still trying to get them to do a sequel to put things right.'

SAM LANGFORD

Nickname: the Boston Tar Baby.

World championship contender from lightweight to heavyweight, but never got a title fight. Recognised as 'black heavyweight champion' between 1909 and 1918, but the title had little real significance.

Born in Weymouth, Nova Scotia, Canada, 4 March 1883. (This date is shown in family records, but some historians give the year as 1880.) Died in Cambridge, Massachusetts, USA, 12 January 1956.

Career: 1902-26.

Total contests: 293. Won: 167 (117 KOs). Lost: 38. Drew: 37. No decision: 48. No contest: 3.

How many world championships would Sam Langford have picked up if he was campaigning today? Considering he whipped champions and contenders in every division between lightweight and heavyweight in a magnificent career spanning twenty-four years, the possibilities run into double figures! In the eyes of many boxing historians, Langford was the best fighter who *never* won a world title.

The record books show that Canadian-born Langford did manage to win a couple of minor titles he seemed to have no qualification to fight for. He was Australian heavyweight champion from 1912 to 1913 and, at the tail-end of his career, he held the Mexican heavyweight title for four months in 1923. Neither country had residency requirements for national titles at the time.

Sam was listed as world light-heavyweight champion in 1912 by the European-based International Boxing Union, but no one took the accreditation seriously. He was also recognised as 'black world heavyweight champion' at various periods between 1909 and 1918. This spurious honour was introduced because the notorious 'colour bar' prevented him from getting a genuine title chance. It also meant that he was forced to spend much of his career sharing a ring with fellow blacks. He was involved in an amazing sequence of twenty-two contests with Harry Wills. He also fought Sam McVey fifteen times, Joe Jeannette fourteen times, Jim Barry twelve times and Jeff Clarke eleven times. That was a total of seventy-four fights against just five opponents.

Though he stood only five feet, eight inches and rarely weighed more than the middleweight limit, Langford had a powerfully built upper body and a long reach of seventy-three inches. He was good enough to take Jack Johnson the full fifteen rounds in 1906, when 'the Galveston Giant' was at his peak, but was not yet world champion. Johnson later proved as elusive as any of his white compatriots when it came to giving Sam a title chance.

Langford began his professional career in Boston, Massachusetts, in 1902. According to family records, he was nineteen at the time, although some record books have him as three years older. He made such rapid progress that, within a year of his debut, he beat world light-weight champion Joe Gans on points over fifteen rounds. Unfortunately for Sam, the title was not at stake. He rounded off the year by boxing a draw with Jack Blackburn, another outstanding black fighter, who was to become trainer to Joe Louis. Moving up to welter-weight, Langford fought a fifteen-round draw with Joe Walcott, who had just lost his world title on a disqualification against Dixie Kid.

So much mythology attaches to Langford's life story that it is difficult to know what is true and what is not. Take the fight with Jack Johnson, for instance. Many stories have been written about how Langford floored the future heavyweight king and was unlucky not to get the verdict after fifteen rounds. Investigation does not bear this out. In Randy Roberts' fine biography of Johnson, *Papa Jack: Jack Johnson and the Era of White Hopes*, he described the occasion thus:

> Langford fought Johnson only once. They met in Chelsea, Massachusetts, in late April 1906. Since they were the two great black boxers of the first quarter of the century, and since their only fight against each other was in an out-of-the-way location, myths about the match inevitably arose. Oral tradition – improved on by Langford's manager – holds that it was a close fight and that Langford dropped Johnson for a nine count. But the truth was that Johnson, who outweighed Langford by thirty-five pounds, won rather handily. Several times he knocked down Langford, as well as breaking his nose and cutting his lip. Nat Fleischer's father-in-law, A.D. Phillips, saw the fight and said Johnson was never in trouble. Always upset by the false legends, Johnson himself claimed that he could have knocked out Langford, but the management of the Pythian Rink asked him to prolong the fight. Conscious that good boxing was also good theater, Johnson agreed. The fight ended with Johnson easily winning the fifteen-round decision.

Nat Fleischer, in *Fifty Years at the Ringside*, said that Langford's manager, Joe Woodman, admitted to him that he had made up the story of Langford flooring Johnson as a publicity gimmick and in a bid to goad Johnson into giving Sam a return with the title at stake. Johnson, said Fleischer, would get most upset if anyone mentioned the alleged knockdown or claimed it was a close fight.

If his bid to topple Johnson was a trifle over-ambitious, Langford had little trouble spoiling the title dreams of many of the so-called heavyweight white hopes, such as Sandy Ferguson, Tony Ross and Fireman Jim Flynn. On a trip to London in 1908, he flattened the

British champion, Iron Hague, in four rounds. Two years later Langford fought a tough, six-round 'no decision' bout with Stanley Ketchell, the former world middleweight champion. Sam did most of the early scoring, but Ketchell was on top in the later rounds. The newspapermen favoured Ketchell as the winner, but not by a wide margin. Ketchell had side-tracked Langford when he was champion.

Langford scored an impressive fifth round knockout over former light-heavyweight titleholder Philadelphia Jack O'Brien before taking a trip Down Under. In ten fights in Australia, he lost only once, to Sam McVey. The great black rivals met four more times during that fourteen-month stay. Langford won three of the meetings and drew another. Continuing his globe-trotting, Langford dropped a twenty-round decision to Joe Jeannette in Paris, but proved his true ability to the French when he knocked out Irishman Petty Officer Matt Curran in just seventeen seconds.

Langford, spurned by world champion Jack Johnson, had to make do with the 'black heavyweight title', which he won by outpointing Jeannette in September 1910. The second-rate prize was swapped around by Langford, Sam McVey, Harry Wills, Jeannette and Bill Tate over the next eight years. Langford was forced to relinquish his final claim when he was knocked out in six rounds by Wills. With no hope of a world title chance presenting itself, Langford went on fighting, mainly against his ever-obliging fellow blacks, until he was forty-three. His last recorded fight was a first round stoppage defeat by Brad Simmons at Drumright, Oklahoma, on 2 August 1926.

In the latter part of his career, Sam's eyesight was so bad that he could barely make out the blurred shape of his opponent. Cataracts on both eyes later brought complete blindness. A sad figure as he lapsed into poverty, he was helped by a newspaperman who discovered his plight and wrote an article.

A sportswriters' fund was set up and he lived in relative comfort until his death, at the age of seventy-five, in 1956. Just a few months earlier he had been elected to *The Ring*'s Boxing Hall of Fame, a belated tribute to a great fighter who never got justice.

BENNY LEONARD

Real name: Benjamin Leiner.

Nickname: the Ghetto Wizard.

World lightweight champion 1917-25.

Born in New York City, USA, 7 April 1896. Died in New York City, 18 April 1947.

Career: 1911-32.

Total contests: 212. Won: 85 (69 KOs). Lost: 5. Drew: 1. No decision: 121.

Benny Leonard wore his hair in the popular style of the period, heavily plastered down, parted in the middle and with not a single strand out of place. Old-timers boasted that the New Yorker was so skilful he would finish a fight with his hair as undisturbed as it was at the start.

A rather fanciful yarn, no doubt, but Leonard was undoubtedly a supreme craftsman. In over 200 contests, he only lost inside the distance four times. Three of those were at the outset of his career and the other was in his last fight. A consummate professional who studied himself as closely as he did his opponents, he was a strong puncher as well as a fine technician.

Nat Fleischer rated him second best lightweight of all time, behind Joe Gans. The man who now occupies *The Ring*'s editorial chair, Steve Farhood, also grants Leonard second spot, but behind Roberto Duran. 'For almost fifty years, Leonard was the lightweight all 135-pounders were measured against,' wrote Farhood in 1994. 'He was a brilliant tactician in an era dominated by sluggers Jack Dempsey, Harry Greb and Mickey Walker. He was always a thinking man's fighter, but developed ample power as he progressed. He was a fighter far ahead of his time.'

Leonard is generally accepted as the greatest Jewish boxer of them all. His dazzling footwork, precise timing and hitting strength enabled him to stand out among the many talented lightweights of his era, just as Gans had done a decade earlier and Duran would in the seventies. On the odd occasions when he was caught and hurt, he knew how to bluff his way out of trouble. When he took a hard body blow from title challenger Lew Tendler, he felt his legs give way. He saved himself by talking to Tendler.

Years later, Leonard recalled: 'I'm not sure what I said, but the point was that he thought I was hurt, which I was, and that I wanted to con him, which I did. All I had to do was get his mind off hitting me again, at least for a couple of seconds, or until I could pull myself together – and he fell for it.'

Born in the tough East Side of New York, Benny soon learned how to defend himself in neighbourhood scraps. He made his professional debut at the age of fifteen, but there was little indication of what a glorious career lay ahead when he was stopped in three rounds by Mickey Finnegan. He spent hours in the gym perfecting his moves and punching combinations. The vast majority of his early contests were 'no decision' affairs, but he picked up invaluable experience against respected opponents like Pal Moore, Johnny Dundee, Johnny Kilbane, Rocky Kansas and Freddie Welsh.

Welsh was the reigning world lightweight champion and he thought his title was safe when he agreed to meet Leonard on 28 May 1917 in their third 'no decision' contest. Under the Frawley

Law which regulated boxing in New York City between 1911 and 1920, the only way a champion could lose his title was if he failed to last the distance. He could protect it by stipulating a poundage above the limit for that division. Welsh, from Pontypridd, in Wales, weighed in at a pound and a quarter over the 135 pounds limit. But Leonard, who was two pounds inside the limit, won on a ninth round stoppage and was recognised as the new champion. Welsh, who was floored three times in a decisive defeat, protested at the loss of his championship, but in vain.

Leonard was considered invincible among the lightweights over the next seven years, dismissing challengers Johnny Kilbane, Charlie White, Ritchie Mitchell, Rocky Kansas (twice) Joe Welling and Lew Tendler (twice). He only came unstuck when he tried for Jack Britton's welterweight title. In a curious affair that was never satisfactorily explained, Leonard, ahead on points, dropped Britton in the thirteenth round. He then struck out while the welterweight champion was down, incurring his disqualification.

Well fixed financially, Benny announced his retirement as undefeated lightweight champion in 1925. Four years later, he lost everything in the Wall Street Crash. Though he showed promise as an actor, the money was nothing like what he had earned in the ring.

In 1931, at the age of thirty-five, he pulled on the gloves again. 'I know more about the sock market than the stock market,' he joked.

Enough of the old skills remained for him to go undefeated in nineteen comeback fights, until he met up with hard-hitting Jimmy McLarnin, the future world welterweight champion, in October 1932. The once speedy feet no longer responded to the brain's commands and he was tagged with McLarnin's knockout punch in the sixth round. He never fought again.

Benny continued his association with the sport by becoming a referee. During World War Two he served as a lieutenant in the U.S. Merchant Marine, then resumed his referee duties when hostilities ended. It was while officiating in a bout at St. Nick's Arena in New York City on 18 April 1947 that he collapsed and died from a heart attack.

SUGAR RAY LEONARD

WBC welterweight champion 1979-80, 1980-81. World welterweight champion 1981-82. WBA light-middleweight champion 1981. WBC middleweight champion 1987. WBC super-middleweight champion 1988-90. WBC light-heavyweight champion 1988.

Born in Wilmington, South Carolina, USA, 17 May 1956.

Career: 1977-97.

Total contests: 40. Won: 36 (25 KOs). Lost: 3. Drew: 1.

Perhaps the greatest tribute that can be paid to Sugar Ray Leonard was that he earned the right to be mentioned in the same breath as the original Sugar Ray, one Mr Robinson.

Like Robinson, Leonard was a superb all-rounder. He showed immaculate skill, speed and imagination and finished off opponents with dazzling bursts of combination punching. He had a solid chin and a great fighting heart.

Despite his prodigious talent, he wasn't the most popular ringman in history. His arrogance and his cynical disregard for deserving contenders, preferring 'big name' opponents who would earn him more money, didn't win him any plaudits. He also upset fight fans by ditching his highly respected trainer, Angelo Dundee, on the eve of one of his innumerable comebacks, against Donny Lalonde in 1988. Dundee, feeling slighted when he received a meagre £175,000 from Leonard's $12 million purse for his fight with Marvin Hagler, insisted on a specific percentage for Ray's next fight. He was told his services were no longer required.

Inside the ring, however, Leonard's genius earned ungrudging admiration. Leonard shares with his great rival Thomas Hearns the distinction of winning versions of world championships at five different weights. Outside of this duo, no one has equalled that feat. Throughout a career that spanned twenty years, but was broken by several long periods of retirement, Ray showed a remarkable ability to switch up and down between weight divisions, picking up titles and discarding them as he pleased. His prodigious talent between the ropes was backed by his unquenchable self-confidence. As Harry Mullan put it in his *Ultimate Encyclopaedia of Boxing*: 'His ego matched his genius ... But, then, perhaps without the ego, the genius could never have flourished.'

There were many great performances in Leonard's exciting career, but none topped his astonishing comeback in 1987, after just one fight in five years, to whip the WBC middleweight championship belt from Marvelous Marvin Hagler. The decision was disputed, but it was still one of the greatest upsets in ring history. Sadly, it was Leonard's outsize ego that drove him into making further disastrous comebacks. Like so many of the greats who went before him, he just could not let go of the belief that he could do it again – just one more time. Even Old Father Time's patience runs out eventually.

The natural, instinctive ability was apparent in Leonard from the time he followed one of his six brothers into the sport at the age of fourteen. He lost only five times in 150 amateur bouts and claimed he had achieved all he had set out to do when he returned from Montreal in 1976 with the Olympic Games light-welterweight gold medal. He promptly announced his retirement from boxing – the first of many.

When his parents, who had given him the first names Ray Charles after the blind jazz singer, became seriously ill, young Ray changed his mind about his future. He turned professional fighter to help pay the family bills. Showing considerable business acumen, he engaged a lawyer, Mike Trainer, to handle the business deals, set up a company called Sugar Ray Leonard Inc. to ease his tax burdens, and took on Angelo Dundee, one of boxing's most respected trainers, to hone his natural skills and choose his opponents.

Leonard was determined that he wouldn't be exploited, as so many great fighters of the past had been, and he negotiated lucrative deals with promoters and advertisers, even bringing in his son, Ray Junior, to appear with him in a Seven-Up television commercial. He had, during the Olympics, won his nation's hearts by boxing with his son's photo tucked into his boot. For his professional debut in 1977, Leonard was paid $40,000. That was more than any fighter had ever earned for his first fight. By the time Ray won his first world title, he already had $2 million in the bank.

He was such an outstanding talent and crowd-puller that he need not have taken two years for his first big chance. Ever mindful of his ability to rewrite the boxing history books, he held off until he could become the first non-heavyweight to command a $1 million purse as challenger for a world title.

Winner of all his twenty-four fights to date, Sugar Ray stopped WBC welterweight champion Wilfred Benitez in the fifteenth round at Caesars Palace, Las Vegas, on 30 November 1979. It was a thrilling battle, with Benitez, who earned $1.2 million, fighting back strongly after being floored in the third round and cut on the forehead in a sixth round clash of heads. The Puerto Rican went down for eight in the last round and was out on his feet when the referee, Carlos Padilla, stopped the fight with just six seconds to go.

Leonard easily dismissed overmatched Englishman Dave 'Boy' Green inside four rounds in his first defence, but his next challenger, the rock-hard Panamanian Roberto Duran, was a different proposition altogether. Duran, having beaten off all opposition in a seven-year reign as lightweight champion, had moved up to welterweight.

The two all-time greats provided one of the most thrilling and bitterly fought battles in a division noted for its exciting encounters. Leonard tried to use his better boxing skills to pile up the points, but the swarming, snarling challenger refused to give him any room. Sugar Ray had no option but to engage Duran in the Panamanian's type of fight. Leonard dazzled the 46,317-crowd in Montreal, Canada, in June 1980 with his excellent jabbing and rapid combinations, but Duran kept up the relentless pressure for the full fifteen rounds and was good value for his close, but unanimous, victory.

Five months later, in New Orleans, Leonard regained the title in the infamous 'no mas' encounter with Duran. Ray was slightly ahead on all three judges' cards in a tame match when the Panamanian suddenly quit in the eighth round. Duran later claimed he had a stomach cramp, probably brought on by an eating binge in the hours before the fight, but Leonard commented: 'He must have had heartburn.'

Sugar Ray took a trip up to the light-middleweight division to relieve Ayub Kalule, a stylish Ugandan southpaw based in Denmark, of his WBA championship belt on a ninth round stoppage. He promptly handed it back to concentrate on a welterweight title unification fight with WBA champion Thomas Hearns. The winner would be recognised as undisputed world champion, as the WBC and WBA were the only two organisations in power at the time.

For once, a big fight lived up to all its advance hype. Leonard, on an $8 million guarantee, and Hearns, who earned $5 million, served up an unforgettable battle at Caesars Palace, Las Vegas, on 16 September 1981. The unbeaten Hearns, a skilful boxer with tremendous punching power, used his longer reach to sting Leonard with jabs and sharp hooks. But Leonard wobbled 'the Hit Man' in the sixth round, and forced a standing count as he cut loose in the thirteenth. Coming out for the fourteenth round, Leonard was behind on points, but there was no stopping him now. He punished Hearns without reply until the referee stopped the contest after one minute, forty-five seconds of the round.

Sugar Ray made just one successful defence of his undisputed title, stopping Bruce Finch in three rounds, before he was found to have a detached retina in his left eye. He hung up his gloves in November 1982. Well fixed financially, he enjoyed his more leisurely lifestyle for a while, but got the old bug back when he watched fighters from his ringside commentary seat for Home Box Office TV. Having had corrective surgery on his eye, he announced a comeback early in 1984.

Kevin Howard, a Philadelphia journeyman who had lost two of his last four fights and was unranked by any of the boxing organisations, was the unthreatening choice of opponent for Ray's first fight in over two years. Though he won on a ninth round stoppage, Leonard was floored for a count of three early on. Not even big punchers like Hearns and Duran had managed to knock him off his feet. Now a 'nobody' had done it. He retired again.

He remained inactive for another two years, then startled the boxing world by stating that he was returning for a straight crack at Marvin Hagler's WBC middleweight title, without as much as a warm-up bout. Hagler had been undisputed world champion, but the WBA and IBF stripped him of their titles for fighting Leonard instead of their designated contenders.

The fight, at Las Vegas on 6 April 1987, was over twelve rounds, as stipulated by the WBC. Had it been for one of the other organisations' titles and held over fifteen rounds, Hagler would surely have retained his belt. Leonard edged home on the closest of decisions, but he finished in a state of near exhaustion after an absorbing, often brilliant, encounter. Though the decision was split and bitterly disputed, it was a performance of sheer magnificence by Leonard. He had disproved conventional wisdom that a fighter cannot come back. He had won against all the odds. And, at thirty-one, he had beaten a champion of Hagler's high stature without even a tune-up.

One month later, Leonard announced his fourth official retirement. He was satisfied. He had done what he had set out to do. He had nothing left to prove. Or had he?

Sugar Ray's career was conducted on a stop-go policy. He came back in November 1988, nineteen months after the Hagler triumph, to beat Donny Lalonde for the super-middleweight and WBC light-heavyweight title. He relinquished the light-heavyweight title, but defended the super-middleweight prize against Thomas Hearns, whom he had stopped so dramatically back in 1981. The return bout, in June 1989, was billed as 'The War'. It turned out to be a minor skirmish. Leonard was floored twice and only a big last round, in which he had the 'Hit Man' on the verge of a knockout, got him a draw. Most observers thought Hearns had done enough to win.

Always one to go for the big box office attractions rather than face the logical contenders, Leonard took on Roberto Duran in December 1989. With one win apiece from their previous meetings, and each assured of his place among boxing's all-time greats, the decider was sure to attract huge interest. Ray was guaranteed $13 million, bringing his career gross to over $100 million. Duran's purse was $7.5 million, the biggest of his career.

The fight, at the Mirage hotel and casino in Las Vegas, was a disappointing affair between faded legends. Leonard, the 2/1 favourite, outboxed and outfought a lethargic Duran over twelve rounds, but the pair drew frequent boos for the lack of genuine action. Ray had to go to hospital for sixty stitches in cuts over both eyes and to his lip. Leonard tried to lure Marvin Hagler out of retirement for a return match, but Marvelous Marvin was one of the few fighters who retired and meant it. The same could certainly not be said of Sugar Ray. The old cliche 'He made more comebacks than Frank Sinatra' was never more appropriate than when applied to him.

After a two-year absence, Leonard ducked between the ropes in Madison Square Garden, New York, on 9 February 1991, to challenge Terry Norris for the WBC light-middleweight title. He was unable to match the younger champion's speed and sharper punching. Though he made some impressive short rallies, he was floored twice on the way to a decisive points defeat. Graham Houston, *Boxing Monthly*'s American editor, observed that Leonard 'looked a pathetic, worn-out shell of a once great fighting machine'.

'It took this sort of fight to prove to me that I'm no longer the fighter I was. It just wasn't there,' Sugar Ray told newsmen. They had heard it all before, but this time there seemed to be an air of finality about it. Why then, at the age of forty, with a multi-million dollar fortune tied up in property, commercial ventures and a vast bank account, did Ray feel the need to pull on the gloves again in March 1997?

His excuse for taking on Hector 'Macho' Camacho was that he wanted to give part of his $4 million purse to a foundation he had set up to help underprivileged youngsters. All very noble, no doubt, but the real reason for his umpteenth comeback was that that outsize ego had come bubbling to the surface yet again. He had seen Camacho struggle to outpoint ancient Roberto Duran and was convinced he could beat him. But, since he last fought, he had been divorced, confessed to a struggle with cocaine, and become a grandfather. It was a sad, sad sight as the former superstar was battered into a humiliating fifth round stoppage defeat by a man who, at thirty-four, was no chicken himself.

Boxing News reported: 'Leonard's balance was so atrocious that he looked like a six-round novice. Camacho is hardly a puncher, but this vintage Ray couldn't take any sort of a shot. He was wobbling like a willow in the wind, even from glancing blows . . . With seven fights in the last fifteen years, it was painfully obvious that the once-great fighter should no longer have been in the ring.'

Even more distressing was Leonard's statement a couple of days later that he intended to fight on. 'I can never recapture my prime and go back to the era of 1981,' he said, 'but I can still put on a show. I can't stop because people want me to stop. I need to get out what is still inside me. I can't stop until I get it out.'

Thankfully, no more was heard of his desire to carry on. He seemed to accept, however reluctantly, that even the greats can't go on forever.

TED 'KID' LEWIS

Real name: Gershon Mendeloff.

Nickname: the Crashing, Bashing, Dashing Kid.

World welterweight champion 1915-16, 1917-19.

Born in London, England, 24 October 1894. Died in London, 20 October 1970.

Career: 1909-29.

Total contests: 282. Won: 173 (71 KOs). Lost: 30. Drew: 14. No decision: 65.

Only 'mighty midget' Jimmy Wilde could seriously dispute Ted 'Kid' Lewis' right to be recognised as the greatest fighter ever produced in Britain.

Even the normally sceptical Americans, more used to 'Limeys' who stood bolt upright and poked out less-than-lethal left jabs, took the all-action Londoner to their hearts. No wonder, for almost one hundred of his grand total of 282 fights took place in the United States. That included his remarkable twenty-fight series with New

Yorker Jack Britton. It was calculated that the great rivals spent 222 rounds in the ring together. There was hardly a tactic or a manoeuvre employed by either man that the other hadn't seen before and knew how to counter.

As well as his two tenures as world welterweight champion, Lewis gathered quite a collection of lesser titles. He was British champion at featherweight, welterweight and middleweight, British Empire titleholder at welterweight and middleweight, and European king at featherweight, welterweight and middleweight. He even tried for the world light-heavyweight title, but lost in controversial circumstances to Georges Carpentier on a first-round knockout.

One of eight children born in London's East End to his Russian immigrant parents, Ted was always getting into fights as a youngster, mainly with boys who taunted him over his Jewish background. Never a dedicated scholar, he left school at twelve to take up an apprenticeship in his father's cabinet-making workshop.

Joining the Judean Athletic Club, he had his first professional fight at fourteen on one of the club's promotions. He lost on points over six rounds to Johnny Sharp. For his debut, he earned sixpence and a cup of tea! By the time he won the British featherweight title, three weeks before his nineteenth birthday, he was already a veteran of 115 contests. He added the European championship before heading for Australia, where he took part in five twenty-round contests. America was his next stop.

His first contest in the United States was a ten-round 'no decision' affair with Phil Bloom. Although Lewis was the better man in the judgement of the newspapermen present, he failed to make much of an impression on Bat Masterson, the famed Western marshal, who doubled as a reporter. Masterson wrote: 'Ted Kid Lewis, the much-touted British lightweight, cannot be truthfully called a wonder on this showing. The Englishman was disappointing, but it was his first fight in this country and he might not have been quite himself.'

Good showings in 'no decision' bouts with Young Jack O'Brien, brother of former world light-heavyweight champion Philadelphia Jack O'Brien, and Willie Moore led to his first contest with Jack

Britton, in March 1915. Britton was eight years older than the Englishman and much more experienced. This would be his 150th contest and he had lost just six decisions. A clear majority of ringside reporters made Lewis the winner of a close fight.

By the time they met again, five months later, Britton was world welterweight champion. This time they met in Boston, where the 'no decision' law did not apply, and Britton's title was at stake. Lewis, who had taken to wearing a gumshield to protect his prominent teeth, was astonished when the American refused to fight unless Ted discarded the mouthpiece. Although there was nothing in the rules prohibiting its use, Lewis pulled out the gumshield and threw it at Britton's feet, shouting: 'All right, let the fight start.'

The controversy about Lewis' mouthpiece arose because they were not much used in the States up to then. In fact, the Englishman is credited with being the co-inventor of the device. While sitting in his dentist's chair in London, he had asked the dentist, Jack Marks, if he could design something to protect his teeth. After about eight fittings, a gutta-percha mould was found to suit the purpose. Up to then, boxers had worn orange or lemon peel between their lips and teeth to guard them against mouth injuries.

Lewis was still angry at what he considered Britton's bit of gamesmanship when he emerged for the first round. He carelessly walked into a hard right that put him down momentarily, but he fought back with great spirit and generally had the better of the exciting exchanges. He floored the titleholder for six in the eleventh round and was awarded a unanimous decision after twelve rounds. The new world champion put his precious prize up for grabs just three weeks later. Once again, Britton was the man in the opposite corner. Lewis won more easily than before, flooring the challenger twice and winning another twelve-round decision.

Lewis' American manager, Jimmy Johnston, didn't believe in letting his fighter gather ring rust. He arranged ten contests within a space of fifty-nine days. Modern world champions rarely have that many in three years! Lewis was planning to get married to his English girlfriend and wanted to take a six-week break. Johnston grudgingly conceded, but then telephoned Ted to say he had a fight lined up that couldn't wait. It was a twenty-rounder in defence of his world title against – who else? – Jack Britton.

Troubled by an injury to his right hand that he had picked up several months earlier, Lewis was well beaten on points. His title reign had lasted a few days short of seven months. In two attempts to win the crown back from Britton, he was outpointed over twelve rounds, then held to a draw. There was a series of 'no decision' bouts between the pair before Ted regained the title by winning a twenty-round points decision in Dayton, Ohio, on 25 June 1917.

Lewis did fight some Americans besides Britton. He had the better of top-ranked middleweight Mike Gibbons in a non-title bout and had an intriguing 'no decision' match with world lightweight champion Benny Leonard. Lewis weighed ten stone, while Leonard was five pounds lighter. It was the only time the Englishman had a weight advantage over an opponent in his entire American campaign. It was truly a contest for the connoisseur. Lewis scorned his normal all-out style to match the gifted Leonard in feinting, weaving, ducking and exchanging left jabs. The newspapermen were equally divided on who was the better man after eight rounds.

Disaster struck the Englishman at Canton, Ohio, on 17 March 1919, when he met Jack Britton for the eighteenth time, thirteen of which had been world title fights. Weakened by an anaemic condition, he took a severe hammering and was floored three times before he took the full count in round nine. Bat Masterson, who had been critical of Lewis after his American debut, was full of praise for the Londoner's courage in his title loss. He wrote: 'Ex-champion Ted Kid Lewis will sure go down in boxing history as one of the gamest men to ever scrape his boxing boots in resin. His refusal to admit defeat when a helpless target for Jack Britton's punches stamps him with the guinea gold brand of pluck. Nothing will ever become him better than his behaviour in the hour of defeat.'

Lewis returned to England to win the British, European and British Empire welterweight titles, before heading back to the States for another tilt at Britton. The New Yorker won a fifteen-round points decision to keep his championship.

Back home again, Ted moved up to middleweight and won the

British title by outpointing Jack Bloomfield. He halted Johnny Basham in twelve rounds to add the European championship, then knocked out the British light-heavyweight champion, Boy McCormick, in fourteen rounds at the Royal Albert Hall in London. Lewis could have claimed McCormick's title, but the National Sporting Club, which ruled that all British title fights must be held at its headquarters, would not have recognised it. The NSC was the sport's authority in the United Kingdom until the formation of the British Boxing Board of Control in 1929.

Lewis then made the most audacious challenge of his career, to world light-heavyweight champion Georges Carpentier. The handsome Frenchman was a terrific right hand puncher and had made a habit of demolishing British opponents. He had fought Jack Dempsey for the world heavyweight title a year earlier. The meeting with Lewis, at London's Olympia on 11 May 1922, generated great interest, not least because of the huge weight discrepancy between the two great fighters. The Frenchman tipped the scales at exactly twelve stone, seven pounds, the division limit, while the challenger, fully clothed, weighed in at ten stone, ten pounds.

The fight ended in uproar in less than a round. Lewis, angry at being asked not to hold, turned to the referee, Joe Palmer, to remonstrate. Ignoring the basic boxing rule to defend yourself at all times, he didn't see the right hand that Carpentier smashed into his jaw. Lewis hadn't a hope of beating the count. Some sports writers were suggesting that Lewis was past his best and should retire. But he was still only twenty-nine and he felt there was still good money to be made in the ring. His first two fights of 1923, however, saw him lose his British, European and Empire middleweight titles to Roland Todd, then drop a close decision to Augie Ratner. It seems scarcely credible that Lewis, who had been fighting middleweights and light-heavyweights, could still make the welterweight limit. Yet, in 1924, he successfully defended his British, European and Empire titles at that weight by outscoring Johnny Brown, but lost them to Scot Tommy Milligan in his next fight.

Ted fought on for another five years, but the only championship honour he secured in that period was the light-heavyweight championship of South Africa. He knocked out Alex Storbeck in the first round to take the title. A month later, he drew with Johnny Squires in a fifteen-rounder for the South African heavyweight title.

A farewell trip across the Atlantic didn't win him any kudos. He was disqualified against both Maxie Rosenbloom, a future world light-heavyweight champion, and Canadian Charley Belanger, who outweighed him by thirty-two pounds. Ted made his farewell appearance in London on 13 December 1929. He made a winning exit, knocking out Johnny Basham in the third round.

Lewis had no savings from his long and gruelling career, but he made ends meet for his family by appearing in a revue called *Hello Sweetie* and from refereeing, film work and personal appearances. He was an easy 'touch' for every confidence man he met, however, and he invested money in ventures that hadn't the remotest chance of success. The most extraordinary episode of his colourful life was when he met the British Fascist leader, Sir Oswald Mosley. Lewis, who knew little or nothing about politics and even less about the aims of Fascism, was flattered by Mosley's invitation to become physical training instructor to the 'New Party'.

It was scarcely believable, an East End Jew working for a party which was openly anti-Semitic. In his naïvety, Ted failed to see that he was being used as a publicity stooge to boost the party's image. He even ran for parliament in Stepney and Whitechapel, but got only 154 votes.

Lewis managed fighters, ran a few clubs and got small parts in movies. His craggy features were instantly recognised at London fight nights and, in 1967, the Anglo-American Sporting Club presented him with a silver salver bearing the inscription: 'To the Crashing, Smashing, Dashing Ted Kid Lewis, for winning the welterweight championship of the world. The greatest of them all, for his contribution to boxing.'

Twenty years after Lewis died, aged seventy-six, in 1970, Mike Tyson paid tribute to him as probably the greatest British fighter ever. In an interview with Harry Carpenter for BBC TV, Iron Mike said: 'You rate a fighter by his longevity and for years Ted Kid Lewis beat the greatest American fighters...why, he won the title twice and it's unbelievable, the guys he had to fight! Benny Leonard, Jack Britton, Mike Gibbons, Willie Richie – the *Who's Who* of boxing, the greatest of the great, and yet he still prevailed as number one.'

SONNY LISTON

Nickname: Old Stoneface.

World heavyweight champion 1962-64.

Born in St Francis County, Arkansas, USA, 8 May 1932. Died in Las Vegas, Nevada, USA, 30 December 1970.

Career: 1953-70.

Total contests: 54. Won: 50 (39 KOs). Lost: 4.

If looks can kill, Charles 'Sonny' Liston was the number one expert at intimidating an opponent to defeat. Aptly nicknamed 'Old Stoneface', Liston's menacing appearance was enough to have most of his rivals checking for the exit door before they stepped into the ring to face him. No wonder Jim Wicks, venerable manager of England's Henry Cooper, when asked if his fighter was after a world heavyweight title fight with Liston, replied in the negative: 'If we see Sonny coming along, we'll cross to the other side of the street.'

Writer Budd Schulberg observed in 1964: 'He (Liston) is an inarticulate, primitive, non-card-carrying Muslim, with a fearful suspicion of the white world and a prison-sharp "What's in it for

Sonny?" philosophy...Mrs. Liston and certain small children seem genuinely fond of him, but he is the meanest and most hated man to hold the heavyweight title since Jack Johnson. He is keen-minded, illiterate, and socially scarred. The combination is apt to produce an authority-hating s.o.b. He is the only man I remember meeting who scares you with a look.'

It took a brave, and exceptionally talented, boxer to ultimately demolish the myth of Liston's invincibility. Cassius Clay, as he then was, shocked the world by chastising the bully and taking his championship belt. A bruised and thoroughly demoralised Liston quit in his corner after six rounds, claiming a damaged shoulder. In the return match, Sonny suffered greater humiliation when he was counted out inside a round after taking what looked like a harmless right to the head.

But boxing history judges Liston unfairly. He is remembered mainly for those two disastrous setbacks against Clay, but he was a much better fighter than that indicates. Had Sonny never met 'the Louisville Lip' and had he been judged on his record up to then, he would be hailed as one of the outstanding heavyweights of all time. A powerful hitter with the best left jab since Joe Louis, he had almost effortlessly dispatched the best of the rest on his way to a crack at Floyd Patterson's title in 1962. The awesome knockout of Patterson in the first round, and the repeat performance a year later, stamped him as a destructive force second to none.

The turbulent life of the man who rose from convict to champion ended, almost inevitably, in controversy. He was only thirty-eight when he was found dead in his Las Vegas apartment. Although the cause of death was given as lung congestion and heart failure, traces of heroin were found in his bloodstream. Rumours persist to this day that he either committed suicide or he was murdered by gangster associates.

Life was never easy for Charles Liston. Born one of twenty-five children to an Arkansas cotton farmer who married twice, it was said that he and his brothers were all called Sonny because their father couldn't remember their names. Uneducated, Liston spent his childhood working in the cotton fields. He recalled later: 'My father said if you can go to the dinner table, you can go to the cotton fields to work and help pay for the food going into your belly.'

At thirteen, he ran away from home to St Louis to join his mother, who had separated from his father. There he was constantly in trouble with the police and he was sentenced to five years in jail for armed robbery. It was while he was serving his time that he was directed towards boxing by the prison chaplain. Paroled on the understanding that he took part in the sport, Sonny quickly proved his ability by winning the National Golden Gloves title. He turned professional in 1953, a year after his release from prison.

He won fourteen of his first fifteen fights, his only setback being a points defeat by Marty Marshall, who broke his jaw in the second round. Liston twice beat Marshall and was well on his way into championship contention when he got into a row with a policeman over a parking ticket. The cop finished up in hospital with a broken leg. Sonny finished up back in jail for nine months. If he was building up a following as an exceptional fighter, Liston was not exactly a favourite with the St Louis police. He was stopped and questioned more than a hundred times and was arrested nineteen times on minor charges. Sonny believed he was being victimised and he moved to Philadelphia to start a new life.

He returned to the ring after a twenty-month absence and took his record to thirty-three wins out of thirty-four fights. His chilling punching power saw him dispatch some of the best heavyweights around. Cleveland Williams, one of the hardest hitters of the decade, was twice beaten inside three rounds. Mike De John lasted less than six rounds. Cuba's Nino Valdes went in three. Roy Harris, who had taken world champion Floyd Patterson into the twelfth round and even floored him, was flattened in the first round. Dangerous contenders Zora Folley and Eddie Machen, who had been avoided by Patterson, were eliminated by Liston. Folley was kayoed in three and, while taken the distance by Machen, Liston got the chance to prove he wasn't just a crude slugger by winning on points against a skilful boxer.

Clearly, Liston was in a commanding position for a crack at Patterson's title. But the boxing hierarchy was extremely wary of granting him his deserts. It was felt that as champion, Sonny, with his lingering gangster connections, would show the sport in an unfavourable light. Besides, Cus D'Amato, Patterson's manager, wanted no part of the powerhouse fighter who posed such a major threat to his fighter's continued reign. Patterson, however, was a proud man who was sensitive to the accusations that he was afraid of his number one contender. It was with much reluctance that D'Amato, and the boxing powers-that-be, agreed that the match could be made.

The eagerly awaited clash took place at the Comiskey Park stadium in Chicago on 25 September 1962. After just two minutes, six seconds of the opening round, it was all over. Two solid left hooks and a thunderous right sent Patterson crashing to the canvas to be counted out. President John F. Kennedy and his brother Robert, the Attorney-General who was conducting an all-out war on organised crime in America, might not have liked it, nor would middle-class blacks who feared the ex-jailbird would give their race a bad name, but Sonny Liston was heavyweight champion of the world. When, the following year, Liston repeated his crushing defeat of Patterson, though it took him four seconds longer, he looked booked for a long reign. And it probably would have been so except for the meteoric rise of a good-looking, brash-talking, fast-moving youngster from Louisville, Kentucky, who went by the name of Cassius Clay.

Few took the loudmouth's declarations about what he would do to the man he called 'the big, ugly bear' seriously and Liston was installed as 7/1 favourite when the bout was arranged for Miami Beach on 25 February 1964. Incredibly, Liston was now cast as the good guy who would button 'the Louisville Lip'.

But the thirty-two-year-old champion was made to look a slow, old man as the graceful challenger, ten years his junior, danced out of range of his ponderous punches and ripped in telling counters. At the end of the sixth round, Liston, weary and demoralised and with his right eye badly swollen, quit on his stool. He claimed a shoulder injury, but, while an X-ray did show some damage, it was generally felt that he was too embarrassed to go on.

The humiliation he felt on that occasion was nothing compared to what happened in the return match in Lewiston, Maine, a year later. Liston went down after taking a right cross to the head in the first round. It did not seem a particularly hard punch and many observers missed it altogether. The referee, former heavyweight champion Jersey Joe Walcott, was more confused than anybody as he took up the count.

Clay stood over the fallen challenger, screaming at him, 'Get up, you big ugly bear. We're on television,' and took some time before he retreated to a neutral corner. When Liston regained his feet, Walcott motioned the fighters to continue. Nat Fleischer, *The Ring* editor, yelled that Liston had been down for more than ten seconds and that the fight should be over. As Clay unleashed a flurry of punches on the unsteady Liston, Walcott finally realised his duty and called a halt.

Rumours abounded that the result had been fixed to secure betting coups. Strange as it may seem in retrospect, Liston was favourite to win the rematch. It was also suggested that Liston had been told by gangsters he would be shot if he didn't lie down. Another yarn that hung around was that the Black Muslims, who had Sonny under their influence while he was in jail, wanted Clay (or Muhammad Ali, as he became) to remain as champion to further their cause.

Sonny returned to the ring a year after the Lewiston débâcle and won four fights in Sweden by knockouts. He continued his career in the United States over the next three years, losing only one of his twelve contests. That was a ninth round knockout by Leotis Martin. In June 1970, he stopped Chuck Wepner in ten rounds in Jersey City. That was his last ring appearance.

Seven months later, Liston's wife, Geraldine, who had been one of the few steadying influences in his turbulent life, found him dead in their Las Vegas apartment. She had been away for a week on a family visit. A quarter-ounce of heroin was found in the kitchen, a half-ounce of marijuana in his trousers pocket. Needle marks were noticed on his arm. But those who knew him said he was terrified of needles.

Despite the coroner's verdict that Sonny died from natural causes, sceptics still insist there was something more sinister to it. He could have been bumped off by 'The Mob' because he knew too much, or he was becoming a nuisance. He had become a heavy drinker. When he drank, his tongue got looser. Others were convinced his great heart just gave up trying. Like the mystery that still surrounds his second meeting with Ali, Liston took the secret of his death with him to the grave.

DULIO LOI

World light-welterweight champion 1960-62, 1962-63.

Born in Trieste, Italy, 19 April 1929.

Career: 1948-63.

Total contests: 126. Won: 115 (25 KOs). Lost: 3. Drew: 8.

Dulio Loi wouldn't make it onto everyone's list as one of the outstanding world champions, but the Italian boasted a phenomenally successful record. A solidly built fighter with highly developed skills, he lost only three times in 126 fights and was never stopped. The black mark against him was that he was essentially a home bird. He only ventured outside Italy on rare occasions. In fact, the vast bulk of his ring appearances were in Milan, where he was a huge favourite. He was well paid there, better than he might have been abroad, and this seems to have been the main reason for his reluctance to travel.

Loi, who began professional boxing in 1948, lost only once in his first 110 contests. That was a hotly disputed decision awarded to Denmark's Jorgen Johansen in Copenhagen for the European lightweight title. It was a different story when they met in Milan in

1954. Loi picked up the European title by outpointing Johansen over fifteen rounds. He followed up his success with a trip to Australia, where he won each of his three bouts.

Moving on to America, he outscored world-rated Glen Flanagan at Miami Beach and seemed set to stay on and work his way into a world title shot. Instead, he yielded to a big offer from Milan to face former European featherweight champion Ray Famechon in a non-title match. He beat the wily Frenchman on points and didn't return to the United States for another five years.

Loi only fought once in Britain, when he outpointed Tommy Barnham at London's Empress Hall in 1951, but he notched up victories in Italy over British champions Joe Lucy and Tommy Molloy. One of his rare stoppage wins was over former world lightweight champion Wallace 'Bud' Smith in nine rounds.

Troubled by weight-making, Dulio gave up his European lightweight title on winning the welterweight championship from fellow-Italian Emilio Marconi in 1959. But he wasn't a natural welterweight and it suited him fine when the light-welterweight division was resurrected in America after lying dormant for twelve years. If he was to capture a world championship belt, he knew he would have to journey to the United States. Many observers thought the Italian had done enough to deserve the verdict over titleholder Carlos Ortiz at San Francisco in June 1960, but it went to the Puerto Rican.

Big money was dangled in front of Ortiz to lure him to Milan for the return match three months later. This time it was Loi who emerged as world light-welterweight champion on a fifteen round decision. There would be no more ventures outside Italy.

He retained his title in a third meeting with Ortiz, again on points, but was held to a draw by classy American Eddie Perkins in his second defence. Perkins took the championship belt by outscoring Loi in September 1962, then lost it back to the Italian on points three months later.

Loi, still world champion as well as European welterweight titleholder, caused a major surprise by announcing his retirement from the ring in January 1963. He never made a comeback.

In 1995, *The Ring*'s European correspondent, Brian Doogan, placed Loi second in his rankings of the all-time best Italian fighters. Only Nino Benvenuti beat him to the top spot.

RICARDO LOPEZ

Nickname: Finito (The Finisher).

WBC straw-weight champion 1990–present. WBO straw-weight champion 1997-98. WBA straw-weight champion 1998.

Born in Cuernavaca, Mexico, 25 July 1967.

Career: 1985-present.

Total contests: 48. Won: 47 (34 KOs). Lost: 0. Drew: 1.

A brilliant champion, unquestionably one of the outstanding talents of the nineties, Ricardo Lopez's name means nothing to all but the most dedicated fans. The fact that he's not much bigger than Tom Thumb might be a reason for his failure to be noticed.

As WBC titleholder in the lowest of the seventeen weight divisions, straw-weight, the Mexican master tips the scales at no more than seven stone, seven pounds (105 pounds) for title fights. If he was in the higher sections, he would undoubtedly be in the big money bracket. Because of his low profile and the lack of glamour attached to his weight division, he earns less than woman boxer Christy Martin.

Beautiful to watch, Lopez uses a stiff, accurate jab, good combination punching and can take out an opponent with a single blow. He has a tight defence, and never loses his composure. The only weakness in his fighting make-up is his delicate hands, which have caused several interruptions to his career. At the time of writing, Lopez had never tasted defeat in thirty-seven amateur contests and forty-eight professional outings. Only a technical draw marred an otherwise perfect record.

As a boy, Ricardo's hero was the great Mexican welterweight Jose Napoles. One of his earliest memories is of putting on the gloves with a bigger kid in school and beating him up. He got into so many school fights that he begged his father, Magdaleno, to take him to a gym. In his unstoppable run of amateur successes, he picked up ten titles, including the 1984 Mexican Golden Gloves championship. He turned professional the following year. Twenty-six wins later, he was WBC straw-weight champion after knocking out Japan's Hideyuki Ohashi in five rounds in Tokyo on 25 October 1990.

Naturally, Lopez rates being crowned champion as his career highlight. 'It was a very hard fight,' he recalled, 'and I wasn't the favourite to win. Ohashi was an idol over there. Nobody knew me. I trained hard. At the fight, he was very confident, but I knocked him out with a left hook. That's one of my winning punches. He fell to his knees and couldn't get up.'

Ricardo was in equally devastating form as he knocked out Thailand's future WBC light-flyweight champion, Saman Sorjaturong, in two rounds. Other impressive defences were stoppages of Ala Villamor and Rocky Lin, and a points win over Kermin Guardia. Only four of his first nineteen challengers survived to the final bell.

If Lopez was to win wider recognition for his greatness, as well as earn decent money, he would have to move up in weight. Unfortunately, projected showdowns with light-flyweight title-holders Michael Carbajal and Humberto Gonzalez failed to materialise. Lack of motivation could cause him to walk away from the sport. 'My dream fight would be against my hero, Julio Cesar Chavez,' said Ricardo. 'He's not my weight, but we would make a lot of money together. Then I want to retire with my physical and mental aptitudes well and live in peace.'

Lopez came desperately close to boxing for the first time when he met WBA champion Rosendo Alvarez, of Nicaragua, who was also unbeaten, in a title unification bout in Mexico City on 7 March 1998. A big right sent Lopez onto his back, his legs kicking into the air, in the second round. Up at six, he made an excellent recovery, but it was anybody's fight in the seventh round, when a horrible clash of heads left Lopez with a gaping cut over his right eye and unable to continue. Under WBC rules, the butt being considered accidental, the result was up to how the judges scored it up to the unfortunate finish. One had Lopez ahead, another went for Alvarez, while the third official had them even. So the verdict was a technical draw.

In a re-match eight months later, at the Polo Grounds in New York, Lopez proved himself the king of the little men by outpointing Alvarez, although the decision was split. In an exciting hard-hitting battle, the Mexican suffered cuts over and under both eyes and a bloody nose, but came through for a deserved victory. Though it gave Lopez the WBA belt, he relinquished it shortly afterwards, preferring to remain solely WBC champion.

TOMMY LOUGHRAN

World light-heavyweight champion 1927-29.

Born in Philadelphia, Pennsylvania, USA, 29 November 1902.
Died in Altoona, Pennsylvania, 7 July 1982.

Career: 1919-37.

Total contests: 173. Won: 95 (17 KOs). Lost: 23. Drew: 9. No
decision: 45. No contest: 1.

'How can a fighter who scored 17 kayoes in 173 career bouts be
rated in the top five of any division?' asked *The Ring* in May 1994,
placing Tommy Loughran next to Ezzard Charles, Archie Moore,
Bob Foster and Gene Tunney in its all-time best light-heavyweights.

'A fair question,' the magazine observed, 'but the Philadelphian
belongs, largely because of his considerable skills, but also due to his
record in the talent-laden late '20s ... Often ugly to watch; faced with
an aggressive foe, he'd clinch and remain in a defensive mode from
bell to bell ... Nonetheless, he edges more celebrated champions
Billy Conn and Michael Spinks for fifth spot because of level of
competition.'

Certainly, the Irish-American wasn't scared of pitting his wits against the very best of his era. During his eighteen-year career, he faced fourteen men who held world titles from welterweight to heavyweight. In 1934, he took on world heavyweight champion Primo Carnera, who outweighed him by eighty-six pounds, and lasted the full fifteen rounds.

Loughran, a professional at seventeen, broke his right hand early in his career and learned to rely almost exclusively on his rapier-like left jab. He was undefeated in his first forty-three bouts and picked up invaluable experience in 'no decision' contests with renowned ringmen like Mike McTigue, Harry Greb and Gene Tunney. He suffered his first defeat in a challenge for Greb's American light-heavyweight title. Engaged as a sparring partner by Jack Dempsey as the 'Manassa Mauler' prepared for his first fight with Tunney in 1926, Loughran impressed camp visitors with the way he handled the powerful Dempsey.

Though he notched up victories over Greb, Georges Carpentier, Jimmy Delaney and heavyweight Young Stribling, it wasn't until his 102nd fight that Tommy got a crack at the world light-heavyweight title. At that, it was only the New York version of the championship he won by convincingly outpointing Irishman Mike McTigue. It wasn't until he defeated Jimmy Slattery in December 1927 that he won universal recognition. Loughran added the scalps of Leo Lomski, Pete Latzo, Mickey Walker and James J. Braddock, the future heavyweight king, in title defences before abdicating to compete in the more lucrative heavyweight division.

He thought he might rue his decision when Jack Sharkey, who was to win the heavyweight title three years later, stopped him in the third round. It was one of a series of bouts to determine the successor to Tunney, who had retired undefeated champion. Loughran scored with fast jabs for the first couple of rounds, but he was caught by a hard right and floored in the third. Though he scrambled to his feet, he was in no condition to continue.

Despite the bad setback, Loughran persevered and beat big men like Max Baer, King Levinsky, Paolino Uzcudun, Steve Hamas and Sharkey in a return to earn a chance at Primo Carnera's world heavyweight title at Miami on 1 March 1934. The lumbering Italian, at six feet, six inches, was seven inches taller and eighty-six pounds heavier than the challenger. It remains the greatest weight difference between heavyweight championship contestants.

Tommy later revealed how his manager, Joe Smith, worked out a strategy to prevent the massive Italian's weight from wearing him down in the clinches: 'After we weighed in, he went out and bought a jar of the most sickeningly sweet-smelling hair grease he could get. After we got our instructions in the centre of the ring and went back to the corner, he had this stuff out and he put a big slab of it on the crown of my head. As soon as we'd go into a clinch, I'd put my head right up under Carnera's nose, and I still have pictures of Carnera, in sheer disgust, trying to shove me off.' It wasn't so much the champion's size and strength that bothered Loughran as the number of times the 'Ambling Alp' stepped on his feet, preventing him from using his superior speed. Carnera took the fifteen round points decision.

Loughran never challenged for another title, but fought on for three more years, including a trip to England that resulted in losses to Tommy Farr and Ben Foord and wins over Maurice Strickland and Jack London. His last fight was a points win over Sonny Walker in his home town in January 1937.

He did some refereeing, served in the US Marines during World War Two and died, aged eighty, at a home for former members of the Defence Forces.

JOE LOUIS

Real name: Joseph Louis Barrow.

Nickname: the Brown Bomber.

World heavyweight champion 1937-49.

Born in Lafayette, Alabama, USA, 13 May 1914. Died in Las Vegas, Nevada, USA, 12 April 1981.

Career: 1934-51.

Total contests: 71. Won: 68 (54 KOs). Lost: 3.

Punchers are born, not made. What Joe Louis added to his natural soporific power were fine skills imparted by an old-time fighter, Jack Blackburn, and developed through Joe's willingness to learn and his utter dedication to the job. The sum total was one of the greatest all-rounders in ring history.

Youngsters aspiring to successful fighting careers should study Louis in action. They won't learn to knock a man cold with a single blow, as 'Joltin' Joe' did so often, but they will gain an invaluable lesson in how to open up an opponent's defence and how to deliver a punch to maximum effect. Louis, quite correctly, is ranked high among the hardest hitting heavyweights of all time. But he was a much better boxer than other destructive punchers, such as Jack Dempsey, Rocky Marciano and Mike Tyson. Joe used a stinging left jab to find his range and then opened up with awesome barrages of blows which very few opponents survived. The accuracy of his punches, developed through frequent combat, was phenomenal.

Critics have pointed out that Louis wasn't as good at taking a punch as he was at dishing it out. They explain that he was knocked out by Max Schmeling and Rocky Marciano, and was floored by James J. Braddock, Tony Galento, Buddy Baer and Jersey Joe Walcott. Even light-heavyweight Billy Conn had him badly shaken in their first fight. But only Schmeling and Marciano, in the last fight of Louis' career, were able to stop him in seventy-one fights. He was not badly hurt in any of his other knockdowns.

Louis dominated the sport from the 1930s into the late 1940s. Unlike other great champions who won, lost and regained titles, Joe reigned for an uninterrupted twelve years and made twenty-five successful defences. That remains a record for any weight division.

Born in a ramshackle cabin in a Lexington, Alabama, cotton field, Joseph Louis Barrow was ten when his family moved to Detroit, Michigan. His mother gave him money for violin lessons, but the youngster spent it to work out in a local gym. He won fifty-three of his fifty-six amateur contests, including the 1934 National Golden Gloves light-heavyweight title, then turned professional under John Roxborough, who ran the 'numbers' game in Detroit's black ghetto. Julian Black, a friend and business associate of Roxborough, helped to fund the boxer's training and Jack Blackburn, a former lightweight who had fought Sam Langford, Joe Gans and Harry Greb, was brought on board as trainer.

From the start, the all-black team of mentors drilled into young Joe the message of how to conform to the rules laid down by respectable society. If he wanted to reach the top rung of his profession, he must be everything that the only previous black heavyweight champion, Jack Johnson, was not. He must never gloat after knocking down a white opponent or play around with white women, as Johnson took delight in doing. The easy-going Louis followed the fight instructions to the letter. His unchanged expression when he scored knockout after knockout earned him the tag 'Poker Face'.

The rules concerning his love life, however, were not as easily obeyed. Throughout his life, Joe had an insatiable appetite for women, but somehow his numerous affairs never got into the papers. He even managed to keep secret the fact that, during his climb to the championship, a beautiful high society white woman used to buy him a new limousine every Christmas in return for his occasional company. Among his lovers were singer Lena Horne and movie stars Lana Turner and Sonja Henie. 'I could never resist a pretty girl with a sparkle in her eyes,' he said after his retirement. 'And there were lots of those girls coming on strong, you'd better believe it.'

Louis won his professional debut in 1934 on a first round knockout and continued to demolish all before him when he stepped up in class the following year. Former world heavyweight champions Primo Carnera and Max Baer were chopped down with chilling efficiency.

Another ex-titleholder, Germany's Max Schmeling, was lined up as victim number twenty-eight in the summer of 1936. There was no reason to suspect that Schmeling, now thirty-one and considered to be on the downgrade, would fail to conform to the established pattern of Louis victories. But Max, a keen student of boxing, had discovered a flaw in the American's fighting make-up. Joe dropped his left hand after he jabbed and was thus open to a right-hand counter over the top. It so happened that a right cross was Schmeling's favourite weapon.

Louis, looking sluggish, was floored by a right in the fourth round and took a bad beating before Schmeling knocked him flat on his face for the full count in the twelfth round. Joe sheepishly admitted he had spent more time on the golf course than in the gym and had sneaked away from training camp to be with a girl friend. The bitter lesson was well learned. Louis knew he would have to take this business seriously if he was to fulfil his dreams.

On 22 June 1937, at Chicago's Comiskey Park, 'the Brown Bomber' knocked out James J. Braddock with a crushing right to the jaw in the eighth round to become world heavyweight champion. Braddock only gave him the chance after striking the bargain of a lifetime for himself – a huge guarantee of $300,000, plus a percentage of Joe's earnings for the next ten years.

Louis was given a tough workout in his first defence two months after beating Braddock. Welshman Tommy Farr, though he finished up looking like someone who had been through a threshing-machine, doggedly refused to go down and was still standing at the end of fifteen rounds. Despite claims by some historians that Farr gave him a close fight, the film evidence is that Louis was a clear points winner.

Joe had said he wouldn't consider himself a real champion until he wiped out the one blot on his record, the loss to Schmeling. Before a huge crowd of 75,000 at Yankee Stadium, New York, on 22 June 1938, Louis gave the most ruthlessly efficient performance of his career to pulverise the hapless German inside a round. Upheld as the standard-bearer for all Americans against the representative of Nazi Germany, Louis dropped the challenger three times in the 124 seconds it lasted. The German radio transmission was pulled off the air as Schmeling cried out in pain when a misdirected right caught him in the back and broke two vertebrae.

Despite the bitter propaganda war that had raged around the contest, the fighters bore no lasting ill-will towards each other. Indeed, they became good friends. When Joe hit hard times in his later years and was admitted to hospital for psychiatric treatment, it was Max, then a prosperous businessman in Germany, who helped pay the bills.

Louis proved to be a fighting champion. If someone gave him a decent workout, he could be sure of getting another try. Joe always did better the second time. Inevitably, such an outstanding titleholder ran out of quality challengers. He bowled them over with such effortless regularity that his winning run was tagged the 'Bum of the Month' campaign.

They weren't all bums. Stylish Billy Conn, the world light-heavyweight champion, gave Louis a boxing lesson and was ahead on points after twelve rounds. He got too cocky, however, and tried for a knockout. He finished up flat out after a blistering barrage in the thirteenth round.

Joe served in the US Army during World War Two and donated the entire purses of two of his title defences to the Navy and Army Relief Funds. Against his wife Marva's wishes, Louis continued his boxing career after the war. An extravagant lifestyle, several bad business ventures, a gambling habit and a costly divorce settlement with Marva left him with no option but to carry on fighting. To help pay the alimony, Joe named Marva as his manager so that she would get twenty-five per cent of his purses. He still had John Roxborough as a manager on his payroll and he had signed with yet another manager, Marshall Miles. With the IRS hounding him for unpaid back taxes, he was weighed down with percentage takers.

His first post-war fight was against his old rival Billy Conn in New York on 19 June 1946. Now thirty-two and ring-rusty after his four-year absence, Louis was still too good for Conn, who seemed to have deteriorated even further since their epic encounter five years before. Joe scored a knockout in the eighth round. He remarried Marva, who gave him a second child, and he showed his old dynamic power in knocking out Tami Mauriello in the first round, though the tough New Yorker had sent him stumbling against the ropes with a wild right-hander in the opening minute.

Unsung veteran Jersey Joe Walcott, who was actually four months older than the champion, came desperately close to ending Louis' great reign in December 1947. A crafty, hard-hitting challenger, he constantly confused the slow-moving titleholder by turning on his heel and walking away. Walcott floored Louis in the first and fourth rounds and appeared to have done enough to take the title after fifteen dull rounds. Louis was convinced he had lost and left the ring before the decision was announced. But he remained champion on a split decision. For the first time in his proud championship years, he got more jeers than cheers. Proving he always performed better when he met a man a second time, Louis knocked out Walcott in the eleventh round in June 1948. In March of the following year, he announced his retirement. Everyone hoped he meant it.

But the old money troubles hadn't gone away and now Marva had divorced him for the second time. He was back in the ring in September 1950 to face Ezzard Charles, who had taken the NBA version of the world title by outpointing Walcott. Aged thirty-six and looking bloated at 218 pounds, Louis could not cope with the skilful Charles, who won twelve of the fifteen rounds. It was the only time Louis lost in twenty-seven title fights. In his twenty-five successful defences, only Tommy Farr, Arturo Godoy and Walcott had taken him the distance. Joe won another eight contests after losing to Charles, but the only time he showed a glimpse of his old power was in knocking out Lee Savold, who had been recognised in Britain as world heavyweight champion after stopping Bruce Woodcock.

Unwisely, Louis took on young prospect Rocky Marciano, who had won all his thirty-seven fights, all but five by the short route, on 26 October 1951. For five rounds, the old-timer's still elegant jab kept him in the fight, but he was gradually ground down by the relentless Marciano. It was one of the saddest sights in boxing history as Louis lay sprawled on the ring apron in the eighth round. Referee Ruby Goldstein later explained: 'I couldn't bring myself to count him out, so I stopped the fight.'

It was the end of Joe's glorious boxing career, but he stepped back into the ring in demeaning wrestling matches. That avenue of badly needed resources was cut off when a broken rib pierced his heart muscles. Although his tax bills were finally written off in a belated gesture from the country he had served so well, Louis never got on top of his financial problems. Things got worse when he got into drugs and began to suffer from delusions that Mafia 'hit men' were out to get him. He was admitted to a psychiatric hospital for a spell of intensive treatment.

When his health deteriorated further, he was confined to a wheelchair, but continued to be employed as a 'greeter' at Las Vegas hotels and casinos. Some blamed boxing for the mental infirmity that afflicted him in his later years, but the illness was more likely hereditary. His father, who had never boxed, had been confined to a mental institution in Alabama.

Joe was a month short of his sixty-seventh birthday when he died in Las Vegas in 1981.

BENNY LYNCH

NBA (America) and IBU (Europe) recognised world flyweight champion 1935-37. World flyweight champion 1937-38.

Born in Clydesdale, Scotland, 12 April 1913. Died in Glasgow, Scotland, 6 August 1946.

Career: 1931-38.

Total contests: 122. Won: 90 (34 KOs). Lost: 15. Drew: 17.

The greatest boxer ever produced by Scotland, Benny Lynch was a world champion at twenty-two and a has-been and hopeless alcoholic three years later. By the age of thirty-three he was dead. 'As a fighter he had no weaknesses,' said British historian Ron Olver. 'In his prime he was perfect.'

Lynch beat the best of his era. The one opponent he could never conquer was the bottle. He even tried shutting himself away from temptation in an Irish monastery, but he soon fell off the wagon on returning to Scotland, where he was idolised for his ring exploits. It made sad newspaper reading in 1946 when it was reported that he had been found lying in a Glasgow gutter. His death, on 6 August that year, was due to malnutrition.

Lynch's natural fistic talents were discovered early. He won his first honours as an eight-year-old schoolboy weighing just four stone. He won thirty-seven senior amateur bouts and lost only two. A spell with a touring travelling booth was followed by his turning professional just after his eighteenth birthday.

Tall for a flyweight at five feet, five inches, Benny was the complete fighter, combining ring artistry with stunning power. He won the Scottish title by outpointing Jim Campbell in 1934, then fought a twelve-round draw with Jackie Brown, the world, European and British titleholder, in a non-title fight. His good showing earned him a return with Brown in September 1935, this time with the Englishman's titles at stake. Lynch was in devastating form, flooring Brown eleven times before the referee stopped the slaughter in the second round.

Already, Lynch's careless lifestyle was causing concern to those closest to him. He made a trip to Northern Ireland and lost a decision to Belfast favourite Jimmy Warnock. Luckily for the Scot, his titles were not on the line. But he knuckled down to serious training for a championship defence against Pat Palmer and won in eight rounds. He boxed brilliantly to outscore Small Montana, from the Philippines, in London on 19 January 1937 to earn universal recognition as world flyweight champion. Even with hometown advantage, however, Lynch was unable to avenge his earlier defeat by Jimmy Warnock. Once again, the Scot was lucky it was a non-title affair.

Lynch fought probably the greatest fight of his career in Glasgow in October 1937, when he battered Peter Kane to defeat in thirteen rounds. Kane, unbeaten in forty-one contests, had earned the crack at Lynch's titles by stopping Warnock in four rounds. It was the Scot's last moment of glory. His lack of total fitness was evident when he was held to a draw by Kane in a return and his preference for the bar rather than the gym meant he was fighting a losing battle with the scales.

Scheduled to defend his world title against the American Jackie Jurich at Paisley, Scotland, in June 1938, Lynch caused gasps of astonishment as he weighed in six and a half pounds over the flyweight limit. He was stripped of his championship, but went ahead with the fight and knocked out Jurich in the twelfth round.

Unable to cope with the loss of his world title, Lynch went into rapid decline. He had only two more fights, losing on points to an average American, Kayo Morgan, then being counted out for the only time in his career against Aurel Toma, from Romania. He scaled nine stone, twelve pounds for that pathetic farewell appearance and failed to land a single significant blow in the two and a half rounds it lasted. His licence revoked by the British Boxing Board of Control, Benny really hit the skids. He pawned his trophies to feed his whisky addiction and went back to fighting in the booths, taking on all-comers for the paltry few shillings it brought him.

Divorced from his long-suffering wife, he became homeless when his mother died and he drifted to a slum lodging house in the Gorbals district of Glasgow. After his tragic early death, boxing experts speculated on who was the greatest British flyweight of all time – Lynch or Jimmy Wilde. It's still debated today.

ROCKY MARCIANO

Real name: Rocco Marchegiano.

Nickname: the Brockton Blockbuster.

World heavyweight champion 1952-55.

Born in Brockton, Massachusetts, USA, 1 September 1923. Died in Des Moines, Iowa, USA, 31 August 1969.

Career: 1947-55.

Total contests: 49. Won: 49 (43 KOs).

Forty-nine fights. Forty-nine wins. Rocky Marciano's place in history as the only world champion with a perfect record remains unchallenged.

But his unique achievement doesn't automatically entitle Marciano to be acclaimed as the greatest fighter of all time. He was lucky that most of his well-known victims, such as Joe Louis, Jersey Joe Walcott, Ezzard Charles and Archie Moore, were fading veterans when they faced him. And had Muhammad Ali come along just a few years earlier, few experts would have given the short-armed

Marciano a chance of catching the fastest moving heavyweight who ever lived. Nevertheless, Rocky deserves his place among the outstanding heavyweights on tremendous punch power, heart and resistance to blows. He could be floored, he could be badly cut, but the guy doggedly refused to be beaten.

Anyone who watched one of the roughest fighters of them all in action found it hard to reconcile him with the gentle, easy-going character he was when the gloves were off. He was in the ring to do a job and he did it whichever way he could. If that meant hitting with his elbows, butting, punching low, or after the bell had rung to end a round, then so be it. When 'the Twentieth Century Caveman' said that he didn't foul intentionally, most people took him at his word.

Marciano's initial ambition was to become a baseball star. Incredibly, he was rejected because he didn't have enough strength in his right-arm throw! Legend has it that he discovered his knockout power while serving with the US Army. Stationed in Wales during 1943, he got into a row with a big Australian in a pub and settled the dispute with a mighty right-hander. He represented his army base in competitions and entered the Golden Gloves tournament, where he lost a controversial decision to Coley Wallace, who later played Joe Louis in a movie based on the life of the 'Brown Bomber'. Marciano entered for the 1948 Olympic trials, but had to withdraw with an injured thumb.

Encouraged by his boyhood pal Allie Colombo, Rocky turned professional and signed up with well-known New York manager Al Weill. Veteran trainer Charlie Goldman was brought in as trainer. He threw the clumsy youngster in with a couple of sparring partners and was anything but impressed. 'If you done anything right, I didn't see it,' he concluded.

Goldman saw that Marciano was too short and too light. He had a reach of just sixty-eight inches, the shortest of any heavyweight champion in history. Muhammad Ali, by comparison, had a reach of eighty-two inches. There was no point in teaching him to stand up straight and jab, decided Goldman. But there was one thing that stood out about the eager youngster – he could hit.

With infinite patience, Goldman taught Rocky better balance, how to fight from a crouch and how to dip and punch on the way up. Marciano, a diligent trainer through his career, absorbed the lessons well. He also practised punching under water to develop his strength and spent hours throwing a football left-handed, so that he could hit as strongly with his left as his right.

Through careful match-making, Marciano ran up twenty-four straight wins, twenty-two by the short route, before facing a tough Italian-American, Carmine Vingo, in December 1949. The two slugged it out from the opening bell, rocking each other with big punches, but it was Vingo who crumbled to the canvas to be counted out in the sixth round. The unfortunate victim was admitted to hospital and lay in a coma for a week. He recovered, but never fought again.

Marciano faced his first big test against Roland La Starza, a handsome New Yorker who was unbeaten, like himself. Rocky scored a knockdown in the fourth round, but had a round deducted later for hitting low. After an entertaining contest, it was almost impossible to separate them. But the verdict went to Marciano by the narrowest of margins. On rounds completed, one judge voted for Rocky, another for La Starza and the referee had them even. That would have meant a draw, but, on a recently introduced supplemental points system, to be used in such an instance, the referee awarded nine points to Marciano and six to his opponent.

Though now ranked fifth in the NBA's list of contenders for Ezzard Charles' title, Marciano was an 8/5 underdog when he faced the legendary Joe Louis at Madison Square Garden, New York, on 26 October 1951. Youth and raw strength could not be denied, however, and Marciano sent the once-great Louis tumbling through the ropes in the eighth round as referee Ruby Goldstein stopped the contest. Rocky didn't look too impressive as he laboured to beat another veteran, Lee Savold, who succumbed in the sixth round, but he had little trouble finding a way through crafty Harry Matthews' guard and scoring a second-round knockout.

The way was now clear for Marciano to challenge veteran Jersey Joe Walcott for the world heavyweight title. They met at the Municipal Stadium in Philadelphia on 23 September 1952. Rocky won on a knockout in the thirteenth round, but only after being floored in the first round and cut on the scalp – he was way behind on points after twelve rounds. Walcott, who had won the title at the fifth attempt after losing twice to Joe Louis and twice to Ezzard Charles, looked certain to stay champion until he was caught by a pulverising right to the jaw. Writer A.J. Liebling described Walcott's collapse perfectly: 'He flowed down like flour out of a chute.'

The return match in Chicago eight months later was a huge anti-climax after their magnificent first battle. It was all over in 125 seconds as Walcott crumbled from a left hook followed by a right uppercut. The challenger, coming up to forty, might have risen before the referee reached ten, but he clearly didn't relish another lengthy war with the irrepressible Marciano.

Marciano next took on Roland La Starza, who had given him such a close call before he became champion. For six rounds, the champion was outsmarted by the fast-moving La Starza, but he poured on the punishment to such an extent from then on that referee Ruby Goldstein was forced to call a halt in the eleventh round. Even when he missed the target he caused damage. La Starza was found to have burst blood vessels in his arms from blocking Rocky's blows.

The Rock's two fights with Ezzard Charles in 1954 were classics. In the first, Marciano was taken the full fifteen rounds for the first and only time in his career. Though he won on a unanimous decision, he was given a tremendous fight by the clever, gutsy ex-champion. In the re-match, Marciano overcame a horribly gashed nose to score an eighth round knockout.

Britain's overweight, but game, Don Cockell was next for the Marciano special brand of punishment. The Londoner was battered to defeat in nine rounds, but the manner of his defeat outraged the British. BBC radio commentator Eamonn Andrews observed: 'Marciano is one of the toughest champions who ever rubbed a foot in resin, but he has never read the rule books. He played a different sport from the one Cockell was taught. He butted unmercifully, he hit with the elbows, he hit low. A British referee would have sent him to his corner after three rounds.'

There was only one more ring appearance for Marciano after that. World light-heavyweight champion Archie Moore had been campaigning for years for a crack at the heavyweight prize, but in vain. He even went to the trouble of having posters printed showing himself as a gun-toting sheriff and a photo of Marciano with a 'wanted' sign underneath. He finally snared Rocky in September 1955.

More than 61,000 fans paid nearly $1 million into New York's Yankee Stadium for the eagerly awaited showdown. Though Moore was at least thirty-eight (his mother insisted he was forty-one), he was a ring marvel and was given a great chance of upsetting the unbeaten heavyweight champion. A master craftsman with a knockout punch in both hands, he had won his last twenty-one fights and had stopped a total of 120 of his 190 opponents.

It looked as if Archie was about to fulfil his boast that he could whip Marciano when, in the second round, he floored the champion with a perfectly timed right. But Rocky was up at two and was given the benefit of a standing count of eight, even though there was no mandatory count in the rules for the fight. Moore's great chance was gone. Floored in the sixth and eighth rounds, he was finally knocked out in the ninth.

On 26 April 1956, Marciano announced his retirement. A devoted family man, he felt he had sacrificed enough time away from his loved ones in the long, punishing hours of training. He enjoyed his retirement, travelling a lot, playing golf and setting up deals. A notorious skinflint, he stashed money away in all sorts of odd places – even in biscuit tins – and would frequently invite people to dinner and leave them to pay the bill.

Big offers arrived for him to come back and fight his successor, Floyd Patterson, and later he was invited to take on Ingemar Johansson and Sonny Liston. But he remained adamant that he would stay retired. Apart from a troublesome back injury, he was sickened at how his manager, Al Weill, had creamed off some of the profits from his last two fights without sharing the extra money with him. He swore he would never fight for Weill again.

He did have one more fight – of sorts. He and Muhammad Ali

faked their way through a computerised contest in 1969 in which they simulated seven different finishes for the cameras. The paunchy, balding ex-champion several times held up filming as he adjusted his hairpiece, which had been dislodged by Ali's snappy jabs. He couldn't make up his mind if Muhammad was doing it on purpose or his aim was off.

Two weeks before the film was released – with Marciano 'winning' on a thirteenth round knockout – Rocky took off in a private plane from Chicago on 31 August 1969. He was bound for a personal appearance in Des Moines, Iowa. The Cessna light aircraft crashed, killing all three on board. Marciano was due to celebrate his forty-sixth birthday the next day.

After the boxing world mourned the loss of a great champion, a frantic search began for Rocky's hidden fortune. He died without leaving a will and his family had no way of discovering where he had left much of his money. Ever mindful of his poor upbringing, he had guarded, hidden and invested his treasure as carefully as a squirrel hoarding acorns.

'Rocky must have had from a million and a half to two million dollars stashed away when he died,' said a close friend of the ex-champion. 'The Rock was earning about $1,500 a week for personal appearances for fourteen years after he retired, not to mention all the side deals he had going, and the cash he had stashed away during his boxing career. He made all this money and he never spent a dime, because all the expenses, the phones, the transportation, the hotels, the meals were always taken care of by somebody else.'

JOCK McAVOY

Real name: Joseph Bamford.

Nickname: the Rochdale Thunderbolt.

Leading contender for world middleweight and light-heavyweight championships during the 1930s.

Born in Burnley, Lancashire, England, 20 November 1908. Died in Rochdale, Lancashire, 20 November 1971.

Career: 1927-46.

Total contests: 147. Won: 132 (91 KOs). Lost: 14. Drew: 1.

Though he never won a world title, Jock McAvoy was one of the most outstanding ringmen ever produced by Britain. A terrific puncher, he stopped ninety-one of his 147 opponents and was only on the losing end fourteen times in a career that spanned almost twenty years. Like so many big hitters, he suffered from hand injuries throughout his career. Had he always been able to punch with full power, who knows what his final knockout tally might have reached.

During a trip to America in 1935, he destroyed Eddie 'Babe' Risko, the reigning world middleweight champion, as recognised by the NBA and the New York Commission, inside a round. Unfortunately for McAvoy, the New Yorker's title was not at stake. Risko refused to give him a rematch for the championship. McAvoy did earn a crack at the world light-heavyweight title, but was outpointed by John Henry Lewis, and he had the temerity to challenge Jack Petersen for the British heavyweight championship. Several inches shorter and outweighed by over a stone, he lost on points over fifteen rounds.

Born Joseph Bamford in Burnley, Lancashire, he grew up in nearby Rochdale. He was working as a labourer at the Corporation tramways depot when he got into a row with his strongly built foreman. After knocking the foreman cold with a right-hander, he realised he had natural punching power. Within a year, he was earning one pound for his professional debut, a second round knockout of Billy Longworth.

He bought a 'how to box' book by his idol, Jack Dempsey, and followed every instruction. He knew his mother would be angry if she knew he was boxing, so for his second fight he asked to be introduced as Jack McCoy. The announcer misread the promoter's handwriting and it came out as Jock McAvoy. That was the name that stuck.

His heavy hitting made him a big attraction and by 1932, five years after his debut, he was ready for his first chance at the British middleweight title. He was sent crashing out of the ring in the fifth round by the champion, Len Harvey, but he made up most of his points deficit by the end of the twelfth round. He was badly hurt in the thirteenth and under pressure to the end of the fifteen rounds. Harvey was a deserving points winner.

The great rivals met again a year later. This time McAvoy forced the action throughout and, concentrating mainly on the body, was good value for his points win. It was the only time he beat Harvey in their four meetings. Jock retained his title by knocking out Londoner Archie Sexton in the tenth round, then made a daring bid for Marcel Thil's European light-heavyweight championship in Paris. The

Frenchman, recognised by the European-based IBU as world middleweight champion, proved an awkward target with his peculiar crouching style. McAvoy, who hurt his right hand early on, was floored twice in the latter rounds and lost on points.

Later in 1935, McAvoy decided to try his luck in America and caused a sensation with a dramatic first round knockout of Eddie 'Babe' Risko. When he was unable to secure a title shot at Risko, the British champion gambled on conceding height and weight to world light-heavyweight champion John Henry Lewis. The championship match at Madison Square Garden, New York, went the full fifteen rounds, with the American just in front at the finish. McAvoy, who had to have pain-killing injections in his hands for his third fight in three weeks, tried to work his way in close, but the wily champion was more successful in keeping the exchanges at long range.

Back home, McAvoy faced insurmountable odds when he challenged Jack Petersen for the British and British Empire heavyweight titles at the Empress Hall, London. Once again, he found his lack of height and reach too much of a disadvantage. He was floored for a long count in the last round, but survived to lose on points. Still British champion at middleweight, 'the Rochdale Thunderbolt' knocked out Eddie Phillips in the fourteenth round to add the British light-heavyweight title. Along came his old rival Len Harvey in April 1938 to relieve him of the light-heavyweight prize, but the points verdict was disputed.

McAvoy made his last defence of his British middleweight title, a points win over Arthur 'Ginger' Sadd, before tackling Len Harvey for the fourth time, at White City, London, on 10 July 1939. As well as being for the British and British Empire light-heavyweight titles, the bout was recognised by the British Boxing Board of Control as a world championship contest. As in their previous fights, McAvoy made the running, while Harvey evaded trouble by keeping at a distance. The last two rounds went to 'the Rochdale Thunderbolt' on sheer aggression, but he couldn't quite make up the leeway and Harvey got the decision.

Jock, now nearing the end of his career, had two war-time contests with Freddie Mills, but lost both to the future world light-heavyweight champion. The first fight went the full ten rounds, but McAvoy was forced to retire in the first round of the return with a damaged back muscle. It was the first time he had lost inside the distance since Billy Chew stopped him in the sixth round of his third contest. He was out of the ring for three years, but returned in 1945 to win three fights before hanging up his gloves for good.

A moody, often bad-tempered man, McAvoy was plunged into despair when he was struck by polio two years after his retirement. He spent the last twenty-four years of his life in a wheelchair or walking with the aid of crutches, his legs encased in steel callipers. He set up a stall on Blackpool promenade, where he sold autographed photographs of himself to admirers. Despite his physical handicap, McAvoy, who had given his three wives a hard time because of his womanising, still enjoyed relationships with women. His temper often got him into fights and he even clobbered the inoffensive editor of *Boxing News*, Gilbert Odd, over something he had written about him.

On 20 November 1971, McAvoy's sixty-fourth birthday, he was found lying semi-conscious on the floor of his bedroom by his son-in-law. By the time an ambulance arrived, Jock was dead. The inquest returned a verdict of suicide from barbiturate poisoning.

MIKE McCALLUM

Nickname: the Body Snatcher.

WBA light-middleweight champion 1984-87. WBA middleweight champion 1989-91. WBC light-heavyweight champion 1994-95.

Born in Kingston, Jamaica, 7 December 1956.

Career: 1981–1997.

Total contests: 55.Won: 49 (36 KOs). Lost: 5. Drew: 1.

Mike McCallum was a contemporary of the so-called 'Fantastic Four' – Sugar Ray Leonard, Marvin Hagler, Thomas Hearns and Roberto Duran – but he was denied a place on their 1980s money-go-round. Despite his undeniable talent, he was too low profile, it was said. His biggest purse – $750,000 – didn't come until he was nearly forty and in his seventeenth world title fight. That was his 1996 clash with Roy Jones Junior for the vacant WBC light-heavyweight title, won by Jones on points.

After the fight, Jones expressed his admiration for McCallum and compared him to the big names of his prime: 'Sugar Ray Leonard had a lot of glamour, but he didn't have the skills of Mike

McCallum. Thomas Hearns had a mean right hand, but he didn't have the skills of Mike McCallum. Marvin Hagler was very consistent, but he didn't have the skills of Mike McCallum.'

Mike always had the skills, but it was also his punching power, particularly the body bombardments, which earned him the tag 'the Body Snatcher', his ability to take a solid hit and his longevity that were the ingredients that made him into one of the modern greats. He holds the record for the most punches landed in a single round, as recorded by computer. Ninety-three of his blows (or seventy-three per cent) connected with the target in the fifth round of his bout with Nicky Walker in 1991.

Born in Jamaica, McCallum took up boxing against his parents' wishes. He had an outstanding amateur career, losing only ten out of 250 contests, and reached the quarter-finals of the Olympic Games in 1976. He won a Commonwealth Games gold medal in Edmonton, Canada, two years later.

Turning professional in 1981, Mike, by now based in Tampa, Florida, won twenty-one in a row, nineteen inside the distance, to earn a match with the durable, but limited, Irishman Sean Mannion for the vacant WBA light-middleweight title in New York on 19 October 1984. McCallum won easily on points. He made six successful defences of the championship, including a second-round demolition of dangerous Julian Jackson, a stoppage of Milton McCrory in ten, and a magnificent one-punch knockout of Don Curry in five.

Unbeaten as a light-middleweight, McCallum relinquished the title to try for the WBA middleweight title in March 1988. He was surprisingly outpointed by Zaire's Sumbu Kalambay in Pesaro, Italy. When Kalambay was forced to give up his belt for refusing to meet England's Herol Graham, McCallum was matched with Graham for the vacant championship in London on 10 May 1989. He jabbed his way to a split decision victory over the crafty Sheffield southpaw.

McCallum had to pull out all the stops to outpoint rugged Irishman Steve Collins in his first defence. He scored a brutal eleventh round knockout over England's Michael Watson in London, avenged his only defeat by outpointing Sumbu Kalambay in Monte Carlo, but was then stripped of his title for failing to sign for a return bout with Collins. Mike was already scheduled to meet James Toney, the IBF champion, in a unification contest. The WBA's decision was announced just before that bout was due to take place. *Boxing News* editor Harry Mullan commented: 'There has never been a starker illustration of the way the game is being wrecked by maladministration.' McCallum built up a good lead over Toney, but a strong finish by the IBF champion got him a controversial draw.

It was time to move up again and McCallum took the WBC light-heavyweight title with a points decision over Australian Jeff Harding in July 1994. He only made one successful defence, against little-known American Carl Jones in London, before dropping the championship to Fabrice Tiozzo in Lyon, France, in June 1995.

Though approaching forty and a shadow of the attacking force he was a decade earlier, McCallum was good enough in November 1996 to last the full twelve rounds with the newest superstar, Roy Jones Junior, who had blasted out twenty-eight of his thirty-two victims inside the distance. Mike was subjected to a flash knockdown in the tenth round, only the second time he had ever been floored. Jones might have stopped him, but he seemed to ease up on the man who was his friend. Three months later, McCallum, looking his age and weighing a pound under thirteen stone, the heaviest of his career, challenged for the spurious WBU cruiserweight belt. Though bleeding from a cut over his right eye and also from the mouth, he was even with James Toney after eight rounds. But a strong finish by Toney earned him a convincing points win.

The Ring, rating McCallum second only to Thomas Hearns among the all-time best light-middleweights, concluded: 'A marvellous fighter, but remains low profile to this day ... Biggest problem was he never secured opportunity to face better-known champions Hearns, Duran, Sugar Ray Leonard and Hagler ... Highly skilled, featuring solid tools, strong defense, an exceptional body attack, and one of the best chins of his era.'

TERRY McGOVERN

Nickname: Terrible Terry.

World bantamweight champion 1899. World featherweight champion 1900-01.

Born in Johnstown, Pennsylvania, USA, 9 March 1880. Died in Brooklyn, New York, USA, 26 February 1918.

Career: 1897-1908.

Total contests: 78. Won: 60 (42 KOs). Lost: 4. Drew: 4. No decision: 10.

One of the hardest hitters in the lower weight divisions, Irish-American Terry McGovern had no time for fancy boxing. He just wanted to get in there and finish off his opponents as quickly as possible. When he challenged Englishman Pedlar Palmer for the world bantamweight title in 1899, the timekeeper accidentally hit the bell shortly after the beginning of the contest. The referee, confused, sent both boxers back to their corners. When he signalled them to resume boxing, Palmer extended his glove for a handshake.

McGovern hit him with a tremendous right and scored a knockout after just seventy-five seconds.

McGovern was only twenty when he defeated Palmer, but he had already been a professional boxer for three years. Having never gone to school, he worked as a newsboy and a variety of other jobs before starting work as a labourer in a lumber yard. There he handled himself well in scraps with other workers and was encouraged by his boss to take up boxing.

By the time he beat Palmer for the bantamweight title, he had lost only once – on a disqualification – in thirty-five fights. He made only one defence, scoring a second round knockout of Harry Forbes, before moving up to challenge George Dixon for the world featherweight championship at the Broadway Athletic Club, New York, on 9 January 1900. 'Terrible Terry' was too young and too strong for the thirty-year-old Dixon and gave him a fierce beating. Tom O'Rourke, the champion's manager, threw in the sponge during the eighth round after his man had been floored six times in the round.

American Eddie Santry was recognised as world champion by the British, so McGovern cleared up the dispute by stopping the rival claimant in five rounds.

He ran into trouble in his next defence, however, when only shameful chicanery enabled him to hold onto his title. As was the custom at the time, McGovern chose a referee who could be relied upon to take his side in all circumstances. Terry was floored by a big right-hander from Oscar Gardner in the second round. The referee took up the count so slowly that twenty seconds had elapsed before the dazed champion got to his feet. He was then allowed to wrap his arms around Gardner's waist for the remainder of the round. Fully recovered by the next round, McGovern battered the challenger to the canvas to be counted out.

The Brooklynite scored a great third round knockout over the reigning world lightweight champion, Frank Erne, but it was a non-title affair. A second round knockout of another lightweight king, the great Joe Gans, looked an impressive entry on McGovern's record until Gans admitted that he had thrown the fight to allow his manager, Al Hereford, to collect on bets.

McGovern himself was tricked when he defended his title against Young Corbett at Hartford, Connecticut, on 28 November 1901. Corbett, whose real name was William Rothwell, had adopted the ring name in tribute to his idol, James J. Corbett. He recalled how 'Gentleman Jim' had teased John L. Sullivan before their world heavyweight title fight and made Sullivan so angry that he was an easy target for the cool challenger's punches.

Young Corbett adopted the same strategy. He insulted the champion in a restaurant on the afternoon of the fight, humiliating him in front of his friends. On the way towards the ring, he passed McGovern's dressing room and shouted: 'Come on out, you Irish rat, and take the licking of your life.' McGovern, further insulted in the clinches in the opening round, when the challenger made derogatory remarks about his wife and mother, hurled himself into the attack, scorning defence. He was knocked cold in the second round.

Corbett had vacated the featherweight title due to weight difficulties by the time he met McGovern again in 1903. This time 'Terrible Terry' lasted into the eleventh round before being halted.

McGovern fought infrequently over the next five years, but the fire was gone. He was still only twenty-eight when he made his last ring appearance, a 'no decision' match with Spike Robson, in 1908. By then, his behaviour had become erratic and he spent time in various sanatoriums. He collapsed while serving as a referee at an Army camp during World War One and died, aged thirty-eight, shortly afterwards.

Ranked best featherweight of all by *The Ring*'s original editor, Nat Fleischer, McGovern was relegated to runner-up spot (next to Willie Pep) by the magazine's later chief, Steve Farhood. In the May 1994 edition, Farhood wrote: 'Modern day champions like Carlos Zarate, Wilfredo Gomez and Ruben Olivares owe "Terrible Terry" big-time; the destructive Pennsylvanian was the first lighter-weights champion to prove small fighters can punch too.'

BARRY McGUIGAN

Nickname: the Clones Cyclone.

WBA featherweight champion 1985-86.

Born in Clones, County Monaghan, Ireland, 28 February 1961.

Career: 1981-89.

Total contests: 35. Won: 32 (28 KOs). Lost: 3.

If Barry McGuigan had been nominated for president of Ireland during the mid-1980s, he would have scored a landslide victory. No celebrity ever earned the widespread acclaim and affection that the Irish public bestowed on the gifted ringman from the border town of Clones. At one time, it was thought that McGuigan could help bridge the sectarian divide in strife-torn Northern Ireland. A Catholic married to a Protestant, he entered the ring under a flag of peace, and had fans from both sides of the community. Alas, not even a charmer like 'Wee Barry' could perform miracles.

McGuigan's one-year reign as WBA featherweight champion, with just two successful defences, might not suggest an outstanding titleholder. Perhaps he failed to fulfil his complete potential, but his legion of supporters rest contented with what he did achieve. In 1986, after his brilliant win over Eusebio Pedroza to capture the WBA belt, experts favourably compared him to contemporaries Marvin Hagler, Don Curry and his own idol, Roberto Duran.

He seemed to have everything. A dedicated trainer and student of boxing, he packed explosive power in both fists. He was a skilful pressure fighter, specialising in forcing his opponents onto the back foot and slipping their leads before whipping in wicked left hooks to the body and then to the head. A criticism sometimes levelled at him was that he wasn't so impressive when he was forced to retreat, but very few of his rivals had the strength to carry through this strategy. A fight that would have proved how good McGuigan really was, but unfortunately never happened, was against Azumah Nelson, who held the WBC version of the featherweight title at the same time as Barry was WBA champion. It was considered a fifty-fifty match, but boxing politics was mainly to blame for denying fans the showdown they all wanted to see.

An energetic youngster, McGuigan was encouraged to box by his father, Pat, a showband singer who represented Ireland in the Eurovision Song Contest. He was thirteen when he joined the Wattlebridge amateur club, near his home town, and he later switched to the Smithboro club, where trainers Danny McEntee and Frank Mulligan helped develop him into an Irish senior champion in 1978.

Barry struck gold that same year at the Commonwealth Games in Toronto, Canada. His ambition to capture amateur boxing's premier prize, an Olympic Games gold, was thwarted in 1980 when he boxed below his best form in losing to Winfred Kabunda in a third series bout. Belfast manager Barney Eastwood suggested the three-round amateur bouts were too short for McGuigan to show his worth and he signed up the twenty-year-old prospect to a professional contract. It was the start of a successful, and lucrative, partnership that was, sadly, to turn sour when the Irish hero was at his fighting peak.

McGuigan made his professional debut at Dalymount Park, Dublin, in May 1981, stopping journeyman Selvin Bell in the second round. He came unstuck in his third outing, however, when Peter Eubanks beat him by half a point on the referee's scorecard. Barry had relaxed after flooring the Brighton boxer in the second round and paid the price for his lesser workrate. He learned the lesson well and stopped Eubanks in eight rounds four months later.

A tragic event that almost brought his blossoming career to a premature halt occurred in October 1982. He knocked out Nigerian Alimi Mustafa, who boxed as Young Ali, before an exclusive audience at the World Sporting Club in London. Ali lay in a coma for five months before he died. McGuigan was torn between giving up boxing or carrying on at the sport which was his whole life. He put the sad episode behind him and won the vacant British featherweight title by stopping Vernon Penprase in two rounds, then added the European championship by knocking out Italian Valerio Nati in the sixth round. The British Boxing Writers Club voted him 'Young Boxer of 1983' and *Boxing News* named him 'Fighter of the Year'.

A step up in class saw McGuigan outbox, then turn on the heat to stop Jose Caba, of the Dominican Republic, in seven rounds. Caba had gone fifteen rounds with Eusebio Pedroza in a WBA title eliminator. The Americans got their first look at the young Irish sensation when his bout with Paul De Vorce was televised live from the King's Hall, Belfast, across the Atlantic. His fifth round win prompted Mort Sharnik, boxing consultant for the CBS network, to send this message: 'Your boy has everything ... acceleration, intensity, personality and good looks. He's a real good fighter, the best I've seen in Europe for many a day.'

If proof were needed that McGuigan was world-class, it was provided in his Belfast ten-rounder with Juan LaPorte in February 1985. The Puerto Rican had been WBC champion less than a year before and had mixed with the top featherweights of the day. LaPorte had the King's Hall crowd choking on their 'Here we go' chant when he staggered the local idol with three cracking rights in the fifth round. But McGuigan weathered the storm and hit back with such fury that he won six rounds on referee Harry Gibbs' card, with two rounds even.

It cost Barney Eastwood the best part of £1 million to lure WBA champion Eusebio Pedroza to London to defend against McGuigan at Queen's Park Rangers football ground, London, on 8 June 1985. It was money well spent. The 'Clones Cyclone' swept the highly skilled champion out of his stride and, after fifteen enthralling rounds, he was a decisive winner on all three scorecards by 148-138, 149-139 and 147-140. Pedroza, making his twentieth defence of the title, was almost knocked out in the seventh round, when the challenger threw a right over the Panamanian's lowered guard and caught him flush on the chin. A left hook connected as he sagged to the floor. Pedroza scrambled to his feet at 'four' and managed to survive to the bell.

There were ecstatic scenes of welcome for the new champion on his return to Ireland. In Dublin, over 100,000 people lined the main streets and jammed the route of the open-topped bus, from which he waved his championship belt for everyone to see. A huge crowd also cheered him in Belfast, while in Clones, his home town, the entire population turned out to say 'Well done, Barry'.

He repaid the fans for their loyalty by having his first two title defences in Ireland. Unbeaten American Bernard Taylor gave the King's Hall crowd a scare when he outboxed McGuigan for five rounds, until the champion's heavy body digs began to take their toll. Taylor quit in his corner at the end of the eighth round, claiming heat exhaustion and dehydration. Barry was even less impressive against Danilo Cabrera at the Royal Dublin Society's showgrounds in Dublin. He looked sluggish and was badly marked around both eyes after forcing a fourteenth-round stoppage of the brave challenger from the Dominican Republic.

It was disaster all the way once McGuigan signed to defend his title in Las Vegas on 23 June 1986. The original opponent, Fernando Sosa, had to withdraw when he was found to have detached retinas on both eyes. McGuigan was unhappy with having to face a new challenger, Steve Cruz, as his training had been geared towards a fight with Sosa. Reports from McGuigan's camp that he was unhappy, had suffered ankle and ear injuries and squabbled with his manager didn't ease observers' convictions that it was an ill-advised trip.

A big problem for McGuigan was that the fight took place in the searing heat of the Nevada desert, in the middle of summer, and at a time of day when the sun was at its hottest. In the circumstances, it was little short of a miracle that Barry survived fifteen rounds. He had gambled on a quick finish, before the heat slowed him down, but when that didn't work he hadn't the energy to combat the bustling challenger.

As the ordeal dragged into its final stages, television viewers could plainly hear McGuigan pleading to his cornermen: 'Say a prayer for me.' Cut around both eyes, he was floored three times and could barely remain upright through a nightmare last round. The decision for Cruz was unanimous, although two of the judges gave it to him by only a one-point margin. McGuigan spent the night in hospital suffering from the effects of dehydration and having a brain scan, which showed there was no damage.

A bitter split with Eastwood led to a case in the Northern Ireland High Court, but it was settled out of court. Six years later, McGuigan was ordered to pay £450,000 plus substantial costs to his former manager in libel damages arising from allegations made in a video entitled *The Barry McGuigan Story*. McGuigan tried to get his boxing career back on track after parting with Eastwood. He had three wins as a super-featherweight under the guidance of London promoter Frank Warren, but called it quits after being stopped on a cut eye against Jim McDonnell in May 1989.

While nothing could match the thrill of the ring, McGuigan dabbled in a variety of occupations. He showed promise as a racing driver, but he had less success as a singer and a chat show host. An accomplished after dinner speaker, he earns well from personal appearances, as well as from his boxing column in the *Daily Mirror*. He has also found a happy and successful niche as a perceptive TV commentator and fight analyst and was an enthusiastic founder of the Professional Boxers' Association, which campaigned for boxers' rights.

JIMMY McLARNIN

Nickname: the Baby Faced Assassin.

World welterweight champion 1933-34, 1934-35.

Born in Hillsborough, County Down, Northern Ireland, 19 December 1907.

Career: 1923-36.

Total contests: 77. Won: 62 (20 KOs). Lost: 11. Drew: 3. No decision: 1.

If you're looking for your typical hard-luck boxing story, forget about Jimmy McLarnin. The Irishman re-wrote all the hackneyed Hollywood scripts about the young boxer, exploited by an unscrupulous manager, who finishes up with nothing in his pocket and with his brains scrambled. McLarnin, who was twice world welterweight champion during the 1930s, still had his looks – and his money – when he quit while still at the top. He never needed to make a comeback, becoming a successful businessman. And, to complete the true-life fairytale, he was left a fortune in the will of his manager, Pop Foster.

In a remarkable career, McLarnin beat thirteen world champions. The scalps he took were those of Fidel LaBarba, Pancho Villa, Jackie Fields, Bud Taylor, Louis 'Kid' Kaplan, Sammy Mandell, Young Jack Thompson, Al Singer, Benny Leonard, Young Corbett the Third, Barney Ross, Tony Canzoneri and Lou Ambers. If Jimmy's twenty knockouts in seventy-seven fights don't seem to support the contention that he was a terrific hitter, the explanation is that he faced such high-quality opposition. He carried tremendous power, especially in his right hand, as well as being a skilful boxer.

Born at Hillsborough, near Belfast, McLarnin was not yet three years old when his family emigrated to Vancouver, Canada. One of twelve children, he helped pay for the large food bill by selling newspapers on a street corner. He had to battle to defend his pitch and that was how he learned to use his fists.

At a local gym, he had his fateful first meeting with Pop Foster, an English-born veteran of hundreds of booth fights. Foster saw the youngster's potential and spent long hours teaching him the tricks of the trade. By the time he was sixteen, McLarnin had his first professional fight, a four-round points win over George Ainsworth. Within a year, Foster took him to Los Angeles and put him to the test against Fidel LaBarba, who had just turned professional after winning an Olympic Games gold medal. McLarnin fulfilled his tutor's confidence in his ability by winning the decision. He was held to a draw in a return, but again outpointed LaBarba in their third meeting.

It looked as if Foster might be pushing the kid too hard when he lost to rugged Bud Taylor, a future world bantamweight champion, for his first setback in thirty-two outings. He beat Taylor on a disqualification in a rematch, then came out a loser again in their third clash. Undaunted, Foster pitted his protégé against the reigning world flyweight champion, Pancho Villa, in a non-title ten-rounder. McLarnin came through with a convincing points win, but the fight had a tragic aftermath. The Filipino, who fought with badly inflamed gums following the removal of a wisdom tooth, contracted a throat infection and died ten days after the fight.

McLarnin had grown into a lightweight by 1928. He was

promised a crack at world champion Sammy Mandell if he could dispose of the leading contender, Sid Terris. The Irishman sent Terris crashing for the full count in the opening round, but his bid for Mandell's title ended in a points loss. Moving up to welterweight, he suffered the only inside-the-distance defeat of his career when Ray Miller, later a top referee, sliced open his eyebrow and halted him in the eighth round. McLarnin later got his revenge over Miller and wiped out another blot on his record by twice outscoring Sammy Mandell.

A bad beating by Billy Petrolle, when he showed remarkable courage in lasting the distance, was put to the back of his mind as he won two verdicts over the much-feared Petrolle. Impressive knockouts over Ruby Goldstein, who also became a big-time referee, Al Singer and former great Benny Leonard earned McLarnin his big chance on 29 May 1933. He poleaxed Young Corbett the Third (born Ralph Capabianca Giordana in Naples, Italy) in the first round to become welterweight champion of the world.

His reign lasted exactly one day short of a year. Barney Ross, the current world lightweight titleholder, stepped up a division to take McLarnin's belt on a split decision. It was the first of three enthralling encounters between two of the best welterweights in history. There was never much between the great rivals. McLarnin regained the title, again on a split vote, in September 1934. Eight months later, an eager crowd of 26,599 paid $140,480 into the Polo Grounds, New York, to see the pair square off again. Ross, the more stylish boxer, soon had his opponent's left eye swollen with a succession of accurate jabs, but McLarnin split the challenger's nose with a hard left.

As in their previous encounters, each had spells when they assumed the upper hand. McLarnin, cut over the right eye in the eleventh round, rocked Ross in an all-out attack. But the tough New Yorker weathered the storm. As they emerged for the fifteenth round, it was so close that most observers thought whoever put on the best finish would nick the verdict. McLarnin seemed to have taken the last session, but the two judges and referee Jack Dempsey all made Ross the winner.

McLarnin felt he had been robbed and wanted to quit the ring for good. Pop Foster convinced him to stay on for three more good pay-days in non-title bouts. The Irishman dropped a decision to world lightweight champion Tony Canzoneri, then reversed the verdict in a return. He bowed out of boxing the way all champions should – with a win. He outpointed Lou Ambers, who had just taken the lightweight title from Canzoneri.

Still only twenty-nine, Jimmy took his family to live on the Pacific coast. With more than half a million dollars saved from his ring exploits, he opened a machine shop in Los Angeles and built it into a profitable concern. He acted, lectured and played golf in celebrity tournaments with Bing Crosby. When Pop Foster, a life-long bachelor, died at eighty-three, his will was made out to the fighter he loved like a son. Jimmy inherited his old mentor's life savings of a quarter of a million dollars.

For many years McLarnin ran a profitable tool-and-dye business, operated a travel agency in Hollywood and formed McLarnin Sales to represent firms.

The biggest blow was the death of Lillian, his wife for more than fifty years, in 1989. 'I lost my bride,' he said, 'I didn't think I'd outlive her.'

As he approached his ninety-second birthday in 1999, Jimmy spent his days at a retirement home on the Pacific Coast reading the papers and watching sports on TV. On the wall were photos of the former 'Baby-faced Assassin' in the company of Clark Gable, Jean Harbour and Joe Louis, all of them gone now.

Barney Ross, once asked how he thought his old rival would have fared against Sugar Ray Robinson, rated as the best welterweight of them all by most experts, said: 'McLarnin would have knocked him out. Robinson carried his left hand too low. I know he was fast enough to do that and still beat an opponent to the punch, but no fighter who ever lived could do that against McLarnin's right hand.'

FREDDIE MILLER

NBA world featherweight champion 1933-36.

Born in Cincinnati, Ohio, USA, 3 April 1911. Died in Cincinnati, 8 May 1962.

Career: 1927-40.

Total contests: 244. Won: 208 (45 KOs). Lost: 26. Drew: 5. No decision: 4. No contest: 1.

Modern fighters who consider half a dozen fights a busy year would recoil in horror at the schedule of Freddie Miller. The stylish German-American southpaw won the WBA featherweight title in his first fight of 1933. Far from resting on his laurels, he had another eighteen contests before the year was out. He stepped up his activity the next year with twenty-eight fights and, in 1935, crammed in an astonishing thirty-five ring appearances. A light puncher, Miller only halted forty-five of his 244 opponents. He relied on fine skill and nifty footwork to get him through a thirteen-year career with only one stoppage defeat, in his last fight, when Herschel Joiner beat him in four rounds.

Miller failed in his first bid for the world featherweight title in July

1931, when Battling Battalino went to Freddie's home town of Cincinnati, Ohio, and outscored him over fifteen rounds. A rematch the following year, again in Cincinnati, was a controversial affair. Battalino came in three pounds overweight, so it went ahead as a non-title bout. The referee stopped the contest in the third round after the champion went down from an apparently harmless punch. He raised Miller's hand as the winner. Both the NBA and the New York Commission, however, were not convinced the fight was on the level. They ruled it a 'no contest' and declared the world title vacant.

While Kid Chocolate won the New York version of the title, the NBA belt was picked up by Tommy Paul, who signed to defend it against Miller in January 1933. Any taints of scandal left over from the Battalino farce were soon eliminated when Freddie outscored Paul over ten rounds to become champion.

A worthy champion, too, he proved to be. He retained the title eleven times over the next three years and exhibited his skills for appreciative audiences in England, Ireland, Spain, France, Belgium and Cuba.

He twice put his precious championship belt on the line in memorable contests with British champion Nel Tarleton in England. The first fight, at Anfield Football Stadium, Liverpool, on 21 September 1934, saw Miller put the clever local boy under severe pressure throughout the fifteen rounds. He dropped Tarleton in the sixth round and, though the challenger gamely fought back, Miller almost had him out on his feet in the last round. The victory added recognition for the American as world champion by the Europe-based IBU.

The return, at Liverpool Greyhound Track the following June, looked as if it was all over in the opening round when Miller dropped the Englishman with a body punch. Tarleton, however, got up and survived a rough passage over the next five rounds. He then took the middle rounds with some impressive body punching, before the American staged a storming finish to merit the decision.

Miller was finally dethroned in May 1936 by Petey Sarron, whom he had already beaten three times, once in a title defence. They met twice more in Johannesburg, South Africa, in 1937. Miller won a ten-round decision in a non-title bout, but when they met for the sixth time, with the big prize at stake, it was Sarron who emerged the winner after twelve rounds. Freddie had another twenty-two fights, including wins in England over sometime British champions Johnny Cusick, Ronnie James and Johnny King, before calling it a day in 1940.

CARLOS MONZON

World middleweight champion 1970-74. WBA middleweight
champion 1974-77. World middleweight champion 1977.

Born in Santa Fe, Argentina, 7 August 1942. Died in Santa Rosa
de Clachines, Argentina, 8 January 1995.

Career: 1963-77.

Total contests: 101. Won: 89 (61 KOs). Lost: 3. Drew: 8. No
contest: 1.

It was St Valentine's Day 1988. But there were no flowers from
Carlos Monzon for his lover, Alicia Muniz. In fact, the pair had a
blazing row in the apartment they shared in Mar del Plata,
Argentina.

It ended in tragedy, with the couple plunging off the first-floor
balcony together. Alicia died, although the post-mortem suggested
she may have been dead already from strangulation as she fell.
Monzon, who broke two ribs and a hip, was convicted of her murder
and sentenced to eleven years in prison.

After serving five years, Monzon was released on parole. While
driving back to the Las Flores prison, his car overturned. The

former world middleweight champion died instantly, as did his friend Geronimo Motura. In 1996, they unveiled a statue to Monzon. It opened a debate as to whether a nation should honour a murderer.

If Monzon's private life was a mess, his boxing career was close to perfection. He dominated the middleweight scene for seven years in the 1970s and his record for the division of fourteen successful world title defences still stands. He retired as undefeated champion and is many experts' choice as the all-time greatest middleweight next to Sugar Ray Robinson.

Monzon himself had no doubt that he deserved top spot. He said: 'I'm much better than Robinson. I'm told he won the middleweight title five times and I only won it once. But Robinson kept winning the title only because he kept losing it. He kept getting beat. I won the title just once, because I beat the champion and then kept defending the title without ever losing. That's great.' Tall for a middleweight at just under six feet, he jabbed with power and followed up with crunching right-handers. He only lost three times in 101 fights and was never stopped. There were eight draws, but they all occurred before he won the world title.

Even in his youth, Carlos had an aggressive streak. He was jailed for starting a riot at a football match and again for brawling on a bus. The ring was his salvation. After winning seventy-three of his eighty-seven amateur bouts, he turned professional in 1963. His early form was not particularly impressive and his frustration at not getting a world title shot boiled over at a 1967 Christmas party. He assaulted a photographer and damaged his eye. A series of blazing rows with his first wife ended in his being shot twice. There was no crippling injury, but he carried the bullets in his back for the rest of his life.

Monzon finally got his big chance in November 1970, but he had to travel to Italy to challenge Nino Benvenuti for the world middleweight championship. The Argentinian was in control from the outset and finished off the local hero in the twelfth round with a left hook and a straight right. He dismissed Benvenuti in three rounds in a return, then defended his title anywhere he could earn good money. He beat Emile Griffith in Buenos Aires, Denny Moyer in Rome, Jean-Claude Bouttier twice in Paris, Tom Bogs in Copenhagen, Griffith again in Monte Carlo, and Jose Napoles in Paris.

The WBC stripped him of recognition for his failure to meet top contender Rodrigo Valdes, but Monzon went on the road with his WBA belt, turning back the challenges of Tony Mundine in Buenos Aires, Tony Licata in New York, and European champion Gratien Tonna in Paris.

Carlos again unified the world title by beating Valdes on a unanimous decision in June 1976. Ever the nice guy, he said before the fight: 'I'm going to let him last the full fifteen rounds. That way I can watch him bleed slowly.' He repeated his win over the Colombian a year later before announcing his retirement.

For all his expertise in the ring, Monzon's finger was always poised just above the self-destruct button in his private life. He flopped as a businessman, drank heavily and was jailed for a month for possessing a gun. Frequent rows with his mistress, Alicia Muniz, who had borne him a son, were to end tragically on that fateful St Valentine's Day in 1988.

ARCHIE MOORE

Real name: Archibald Lee Wright.

Nicknames: the Old Mongoose, Ancient Archie.

World light-heavyweight champion 1952-62.

Born in Benoit, Mississippi, USA, 13 December 1916 (Moore insists this date is correct, but many historians accept his mother's contention that he was born three years earlier. As they say, she should know). Died in San Diego, California, USA, 9 December 1998.

Career: 1936-63.

Total contests: 229. Won: 194 (141 KOs). Lost: 26. Drew: 8. No contest: 1.

When assessing the extraordinary career of Archie Moore, you eventually run out of superlatives. He broke so many records and achieved so much in a career that spanned three decades that he ranks as one of the game's genuine legends. The only goal that eluded him was the world heavyweight championship. He twice failed to lift sport's premier prize.

Moore scored 141 knockouts, an all-time record. Some records credit him with 145 inside-the-distance triumphs. Despite such impressive statistics, he was anything but an out-and-out slugger. With his curious cross-armed defence and his ability to land punches with pin-point precision, he was one of the game's great craftsmen. That skill enabled him to complete his career relatively unscathed. He put it this way: 'It's not the length of a career that wears a man out. It's the number of punches he takes. I didn't take too many.

Archie's first listed professional fight was in July 1936, but there is evidence that he was getting paid for so-called 'amateur' bouts before this. Though ranked number four middleweight in the world by *The Ring* as early as 1940, he was disgracefully side-tracked for another twelve years until he got his first world title chance, against light-heavyweight Joey Maxim. After beating Maxim, he held onto the championship for ten years and never lost it in the ring. During that period, he frequently shed up to two stone to make the light-heavyweight limit. He claimed he got his 'secret diet' from an Aborigine tribesman while in Australia in 1940.

To obtain his title opportunity against Maxim, Moore had to agree to a mere ten per cent of the gate. While Maxim was guaranteed $100,000, the challenger ended up with $800, just enough to pay his sparring partners. The deal also gave Maxim's manager, wily old Jack 'Doc' Kearns, who had handled Jack Dempsey and Mickey Walker many years before, a share in Moore's future earnings. At least Archie, four days past his thirty-sixth birthday and in his 159th fight, was finally champion of the world.

Kearns forced him to meet Maxim twice more, with the result the same in all their three encounters, a unanimous decision for Moore, He had to come from behind to stop classy Harold Johnson with a blistering barrage in the fourteenth round, then staked his claim to a crack at the heavyweight title by decisioning top contender Nino Valdes. But champion Rocky Marciano didn't want to know. Moore undertook a self-publicity campaign, bombarding the press with 'Wanted' posters in the name of Sheriff Archie Moore for the 'capture and delivery of Rocky Marciano to any ring in the world'.

Eventually, his drive took effect. Marciano agreed to defend his heavyweight title at Yankee Stadium, New York, on 21 September 1955. Moore dropped the champion for two in the second round, but referee Harry Kessler gave Marciano a mandatory eight count, which wasn't in the rules, and allowed him time to recover. Moore finally sank to the canvas to be counted out in the ninth round. Despite an enormous 'peeper' of a left eye, Archie had the energy to go out night-clubbing after the fight. His earnings for the bout were $270,000, so he had made some decent money for the first time after nearly twenty years at the sport.

When Marciano retired, Moore was paired with Floyd Patterson for the vacant world heavyweight title. He found the speed and power of Patterson's punches too much to handle and was knocked out in the fifth round.

Still light-heavyweight champion, Ancient Archie fought the greatest fight of his life against rock-hard challenger Yvon Durelle in December 1958. Floored three times in the first round and almost counted out, Moore staged an astonishing comeback to batter the Canadian to defeat in the eleventh round. It is rated along with Dempsey vs Firpo, Zale vs Graziano and Hagler vs Hearns as being among the most exciting fights in history. In the inevitable return match, Moore won easily in three rounds.

The NBA withdrew recognition of Moore as champion in 1961 for his failure to defend against number one contender Harold Johnson, whom he had already beaten in four of their five meetings. He defended the New York and European versions of the title against Italian Giulio Rinaldi, who had beaten him in a non-title fight. Archie, in his last championship contest, convincingly outpointed Rinaldi over fifteen rounds. When he still refused to meet Johnson, the other bodies joined the NBA in stripping Moore of recognition as champion. However, he showed there was still some life left in the old limbs by knocking out Pete Rademacher, Alejandro Lavaronte and Howard King. He was unlucky to get only a draw against Willie Pastrano, who won the world title from Johnson a year later.

On 15 November 1962 Moore climbed between the ropes for the

217th time. He was now aged between forty-six and forty-nine (his actual birth-date remained unclear). His opponent was the twenty-year-old Olympic gold medallist from Louisville, Kentucky, Cassius Clay.

Archie had been the youngster's trainer for a while, but quit when Clay wouldn't do what he was told. Now Clay, who had won his fifteen fights to date, was boasting he would finish off the old man with his 'pension punch'. Moore retorted that he had just the thing to settle his cocky opponent – a 'lip buttoner'. Moore couldn't cope with Clay's dazzling footwork and ripping punches and was halted in four rounds. He had just one more fight, a third round stoppage of Mike DiBiase in March 1963, before calling it quits on a magnificent career.

In retirement, Archie did some movie acting and worked with youth organisations. He continued to enjoy his music, playing pool and spending time with his family. Though he underwent a triple heart by-pass operation in 1995, 'the Old Mongoose' still helped out with George Foreman's training.

Married to his fourth wife, Joan, for a good many years, Moore lived happily in a red-bricked house in San Diego, California, with a swimming pool shaped like a boxing glove. He was eighty-two (or was it eighty-five?) when he passed away on 9 December 1998.

Archie once remarked that he had been cheated and hoodwinked many times throughout his life, but he always came up smiling. They should print on his tombstone, he quipped, 'Here lies Archie Moore – smiling.'

JOSE NAPOLES

Nickname: Mantequilla (Butter).

World welterweight champion 1969-70, 1971-75.

Born in Oriente, Cuba, 13 April 1940.

Career: 1958-75.

Total contests: 84. Won: 77 (54 KOs). Lost: 7.

A fast, highly skilled tactician with a venomous punch, Jose Napoles was recognised as the best welterweight since Sugar Ray Robinson was at his peak during the 1940s. The Cuban retained his world title thirteen times between 1969 and 1975 and wasn't afraid to travel, putting his precious belt up for grabs in Mexico, America, England, Switzerland and Canada.

Napoles began boxing as a boy, under the tutelage of his three uncles, who organised promotions. As an amateur, he only lost once in 115 bouts. He turned professional in 1958 and won seventeen out of eighteen fights in Cuba before Fidel Castro put a ban on professional boxing. Married with a young son, Jose moved to Mexico to continue his career.

Though world-rated as a light-welterweight by 1962, it wasn't for another seven years that he got a title chance – against welterweight champion Curtis Cokes at Inglewood, California. Napoles was in devastating form. He brought blood flowing from the Texan's nose and mouth and had both his eyes almost swollen shut by the time the referee called a halt in the thirteenth round.

Napoles proved his superiority by stopping Cokes in the tenth round in a return, then saw off the challenges of Emile Griffith and Ernie Lopez, before losing his world title to 9/1 underdog Billy Backus. The fight was stopped in the fourth round because of Napoles' cut eye. Within six months, Napoles was champion again. He halted Backus, a nephew of Carmen Basilio, in the eighth round. British and European champion Ralph Charles gave the Cuban a few problems, until Napoles cut loose with a blinding barrage of punches to put him down for the count in the seventh round in London.

A step up to middleweight to try for Carlos Monzon's world championship proved over-ambitious. The hard-hitting Argentinian was too big and strong for Napoles, who was rescued by the referee in the seventh round in Monte Carlo. Back in his own division, Jose scored stoppage wins over Hedgemon Lewis and Horacio Saldano in defence of his title, but he was close to surrendering his belt to Armando Muniz, a Los Angeles-based Mexican. Napoles was so badly cut over both eyes that the ringside doctor ordered the fight to be stopped at the end of the twelfth round. But the referee said the cuts were caused by butts and awarded the champion a technical decision.

Napoles, nicknamed 'Mantequilla' ('Butter'), meaning he was as smooth as butter, gave Muniz a return match in Mexico City and won on a unanimous verdict. But there were reports that the Cuban had grown too fond of the high life and was not devoting much time to training. These rumours were music to the ears of Londoner John H. Stracey as he prepared to step into the ring with Napoles in December 1975. The fact that he had to go to Mexico City, Napoles' adopted home base, for his big chance didn't put off the courageous, aggressive challenger. He got off the floor in the first round to score one of the finest victories of any British fighter in history. The referee stopped the bout in the seventh round with Napoles helpless on the ropes as Stacey slammed away with both hands.

Napoles, at thirty-five a pale shadow of the great champion he had been, never boxed again.

AZUMAH NELSON

Nickname: the Professor.

WBC featherweight champion 1984-88. WBC super-featherweight champion 1988-94, 1995-97.

Born in Accra, Ghana, 19 July 1958.

Career: 1979-98.

Total contests: 46. Won: 39 (28 KOs). Lost: 5. Drew: 2

An argument could be made for Dick Tiger as the greatest fighter ever to come out of Africa, but most experts bestow that honour on Azumah Nelson. A world champion at two weights, like Tiger, Nelson first ruled the featherweight division in 1984. Thirteen years later he was still king of the super-featherweights.

'Azumah is very much a man of Africa,' said photo-journalist Arlene Schulman, who visited Nelson at his home near Accra for her book *The Prizefighters*. 'He represents Ghana to the outside world. When he wins, the whole country wins. When he loses, the whole country loses. He's so popular, the people practically kiss the ground he walks on. But it hasn't gone to his head, and he leads a relatively low-key existence. He's not ostentatious, never flaunts his wealth, and is willing to share some of it with his people.'

Fight followers outside of Africa were not so aware of Nelson's nice-guy image in his homeland. They didn't like his arrogance or the way he decried worthy opponents. Inside the ring, however, his brilliance was unquestioned. 'Nelson's fighting style is a strange hybrid,' wrote Nigel Collins in *The Ring*. 'He's best described as a cerebral slugger, and it's what goes on inside of his head that is his greatest asset. He's cool, calculating, with just the right touch of fanaticism. And never, even under the most trying circumstances, does he get discouraged. The decision loss to Pernell Whitaker, who was at the peak of his powers when they fought, was a good case in point. Nelson chased the naturally larger man all over the ring; he just never caught him.'

Although born the son of a wealthy merchant, Azumah was determined to make his own way in the world. According to Schulman, he 'sold dresses, sugarcane, bananas – anything that could be placed on a tray and balanced on his head'. He didn't take up boxing until the relatively late age of seventeen. Within three years, he won a gold medal at the Commonwealth Games and, while doing national service in the Ghanaian army, again struck gold in the World Military Games. Beaten only twice in fifty amateur bouts, he turned professional in 1979. He won the Ghanaian featherweight title in his second fight, the African in his sixth and the Commonwealth in his tenth.

Nevertheless, he dived in too deep against the formidable WBC featherweight champion Salvador Sanchez in New York in July 1982. Coming in as a late substitute, Nelson fought bravely until he was stopped in the fifteenth and final round. Two years later Azumah got his second WBC title chance, but had to go into hostile territory to challenge Wilfredo Gomez in San Juan, Puerto Rico. Unfazed, he powered his way to victory in eleven rounds.

Nelson defended the featherweight title six times, including a chilling first round knockout of Britain's Pat Cowdell in Birmingham, before relinquishing the belt to fight for the WBC super-featherweight title in February 1988. In a fine display of all-round skill and punching power, he outpointed Mexican Mario Martinez for the vacant championship, then halted Martinez in the twelfth round in a return.

Nelson's sights were set on a big-money showdown with Barry McGuigan, but Jim McDonnell sent the Irishman into retirement with a stoppage victory in 1989. So McDonnell was rewarded with a crack at the Ghanaian's crown. The Londoner was knocked cold in the twelfth round.

Azumah's ambitious attempt to win a world title in a third weight division ended in failure in May 1990. He fought well, but could not match the speed and slippery skills of southpaw Pernell Whitaker, holder of the WBC and IBF versions of the lightweight championship, and was clearly outpointed.

Nelson defended the super-featherweight title ten times, including a draw with Jeff Fenech and an eighth round stoppage of the favoured Australian in a rematch in Melbourne, before being dethroned by American Jesse James Leija in May 1994. Leija lost it in his first defence to Gabriel Ruelas and there was Nelson, a year after losing his WBC belt, reclaiming it with a sixth round stoppage of Ruelas. It was yet another remarkable chapter in Azumah's great career. He had been eighteen months away from the ring and most observers thought he had hung up his gloves for good.

It was hard to see what drove the Ghanaian on. A wealthy man, he owned several businesses, including a brick-manufacturing company, a restaurant and import-export companies, and he managed a group of comedians. Yet, at thirty-eight, he still worked so hard at the gym that he frequently fell asleep on the floor after training.

He vowed that 1997 would be his last year in the ring. Yet, after losing his WBC title to Genaro Hernandez in his twenty-fourth championship fight, he would only say: 'I'll have to think about what I want to do.' He did call it a day after a heavy points defeat by Leija in their fourth meeting (two wins for Leija, one for Nelson and the other a draw) but no-one could be sure he meant it.

Over and out: Rocky Marciano (*above*) completes his perfect 49–0 record with a ninth-round knockout of Archie Moore. On the button: Barry McGuigan (*below*) lands a pin-point right to the chin of Ken Buchanan during a sparring session.

Eusebio Pedroza (*top left*), who defended his WBA featherweight title 20 times and 'Durable Dane' Battling Nelson (*top right*), one of the toughest of them all. (*Left*) Jose Napoles, nicknamed 'Mantequilla' (Butter).

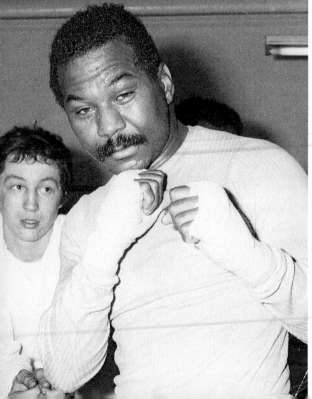

Willie Pep (*right*), perhaps the greatest craftsman the ring has known.

WILLIE Pep, Hartford, Conn.

Winner of

Conn. Flyweight Championship 1938
New England Featherweight Championship - 1942
World's Featherweight Championship . . . 1942
Los Angeles Times, "fighter of Year" . 1944
The Ring, "Fighter of the Year 1945

Mexico's Ruben Olivares (*above*), outstanding bantamweight champion who went on to win two versions of the featherweight crown. Gene Tunney (*opposite, top left*), who won the world heavyweight title from Jack Dempsey, made a fortune and retired a champion. Vicente Saldivar (*opposite, top right*), another brilliant Mexican, who beat Welshman Howard Winstone three times in world featherweight fights. (*Right*) Mike Tyson smashes a right to the jaw of James 'Bonecrusher' Smith during their heavyweight title fight.

Ready when you are: Britain's Randolph Turpin (*above*) looks confident as he shakes hands with Sugar Ray Robinson before their world middleweight title fight in London. Sixty-four days later, Robinson (*below*) regained his lost title after their fight was stopped in the tenth round with eight seconds to go.

Jersey Joe Walcott *(top left)*, world heavyweight champion 1951–52 and Ad Wolgast *(top right)*, world lightweight champion 1910–12. Floyd Patterson *(below left)* was the first boxer to win the world heavyweight championship twice and bantamweight Manuel Ortiz *(below right)* defended world title more than any other champion except Joe Louis.

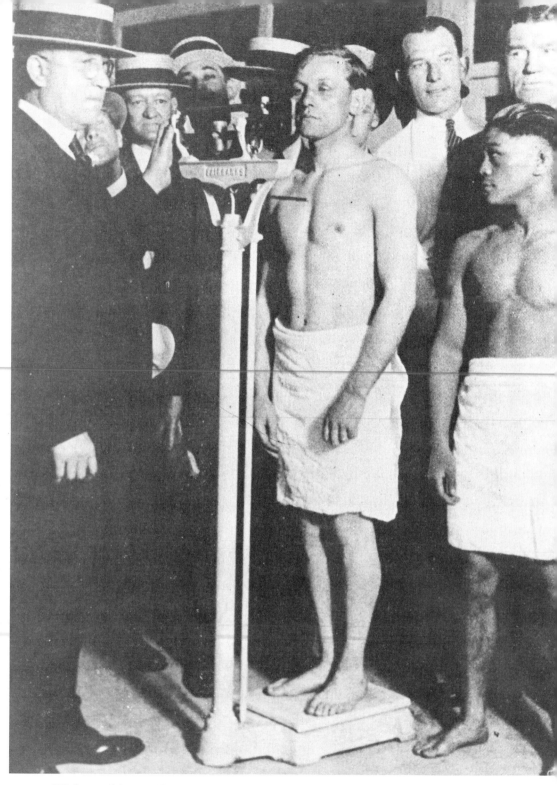

Mighty midgets: Jimmy Wilde steps on the scales for the defence of his world flyweight title against Pancho Villa, of the Philippines. Wilde lost in seven rounds and never fought again.

BATTLING NELSON

Real name: Oscar Matthew Nielson.

Nickname: the Durable Dane.

World lightweight champion 1908-10.

Born in Copenhagen, Denmark, 5 June 1882. Died in Chicago, Illinois, USA, 7 February 1954.

Career: 1896-1917.

Total contests: 131. Won: 59 (38 KOs). Lost: 19. Drew: 19. No decision: 33. No contest: 1.

Truly one of the toughest men to ever lace on a glove, Battling Nelson would use any means, fair or foul, to win a fight. If his orthodox punches failed to do the trick, he would employ his notorious 'scissors hook'. This was a short left hook aimed at the liver, with his thumb and forefinger extended to give a painful pinch. If extra methods were needed, he would gouge his opponent's eyes or knee him in the groin.

Remarkably, 'the Durable Dane' was only disqualified twice.

Either referees were more tolerant then, or they turned a blind eye to Nelson's notorious brand of butchery. Novelist Jack London branded him 'the Abysmal Brute'.

Born in Denmark, Nelson grew up in a suburb of Chicago. He was a professional fighter at fourteen. His ability to absorb pain was made apparent in a fifteen-round contest, during which he broke his arm, but went on to win on points. He gained newspapermen's attention in an extraordinary bout in 1902. Nelson was knocked down seven times, but he floored Christy Williams forty-two times before stopping him in the seventeenth round. In another fight, against Aurelio Herrera, he did an involuntary somersault after being hit on the chin, yet came back to win the decision.

After an impressive eighteenth-round knockout of Jimmy Britt, who claimed the 'white lightweight title' during the reign of the great black fighter, Joe Gans, as legitimate world champion, Nelson challenged Gans in September 1906. Promoter Tex Rickard guaranteed Nelson $23,000, more than twice the champion's purse, to secure the fight for the mining town of Goldfield, Nevada. Nelson, outboxed and growing increasingly frustrated, lashed out with a low blow and was disqualified in the forty-second round.

Nelson waited two years for another crack at Gans' title. This time he bulldozed his way through the champion's stylish defence and knocked him down nine times en route to a seventeenth round win. A third encounter, in 1908, resulted in a knockout win for Nelson in the twenty-first round.

'The Durable Dane' finally met his match in Ad Wolgast, 'the Michigan Wildcat', who was every bit as tough, vicious and unscrupulous as himself. In a bloody, brutal battle to the finish, the Marquis of Queensberry Rules were ignored in an orgy of eye-gouging, rabbit-punching, flying elbows and low blows. During the seventh round, Nelson asked the dumbfounded referee: 'Don't we have any rules at all?'

By the fortieth round, both of Nelson's eyes were closed and he could barely lift his arms. He was sent staggering by two hard rights and the referee, Eddie Smith, called a halt to the slaughter. Nelson, the blood spouting from his mouth as he spoke, protested that he would have finished off Wolgast in the next round if the 'dumb referee' hadn't stopped him.

Nelson never got a chance to regain the title, though he fought on for another seven years. The effects of his long, hard battles were apparent when he was floored five times and knocked out in eleven rounds by Englishman Owen Moran, who was no more than a featherweight. He finally called it quits in 1917 after getting the worst of it in a no-decision bout with Freddie Welsh.

Nelson lost all his hard-earned money and died in poverty, aged seventy-two, in 1954.

RUBEN OLIVARES

World bantamweight champion 1969-70, 1971-72. WBA featherweight champion 1974. WBC featherweight champion 1975.

Born in Mexico City, Mexico, 14 January 1947.

Career: 1965-88.

Total contests: 104. Won: 88 (78 KOs). Lost: 13. Drew: 3.

One of boxing's great one-punch knockout artists, Ruben Olivares halted fifty-six of his first sixty opponents in an unbeaten run. 'When young Mexicans are taught to punch, it is "Rockabye Ruben's" hook that is used as a model of perfection,' declared *The Ring*, rating him third best bantamweight of all time. Olivares didn't need to take up boxing for a living. Son of a successful businessman, he did it because it was something he enjoyed.

An eight-round win over long-time contender Joe Medel earned Olivares a world bantamweight title fight with popular Australian Lionel Rose at the Fabulous Forum in Inglewood, California, in August 1969. He sent the champion crashing for the full count in round five.

British champion Alan Rudkin was brushed aside inside two rounds, and Chucho Castillo outpointed, but Olivares lost his title on a cut eye stoppage in a return with fellow-Mexican Castillo. It was his first defeat. A third meeting with Castillo resulted in Olivares regaining the championship on a unanimous points decision. Ruben made two successful defences before he was upset by another Mexican, Rafael Herrera, who knocked him out in eight rounds.

He returned as a featherweight and took the WBA belt in 1974 with a seventh round stoppage of Japan's Zensuke Utagawa for the vacant title. He lost it in his first defence, however, to the brilliant Alexis Arguello, who scored a knockout in the thirteenth round. Seven months later, Olivares had another world championship belt – the WBC trophy – after disposing of Bobby Chacon in two rounds. Again, his reign was short. David Kotey, from Ghana, outpointed him in a thrilling fifteen-rounder.

Ruben fought for another six years before announcing his retirement. Six of his thirteen defeats occurred during this period. One was a twelfth round stoppage by Eusebio Pedroza for the WBA title. After a five-year layoff, he made two brief comeback attempts, but failed to secure a win.

The Mexican, who liked nothing better than partying with his fans, is remembered as a superb knockout artist and the greatest ever attraction at Inglewood's Fabulous Forum, where he had ten of his thirteen world title fights.

CARLOS ORTIZ

World light-welterweight champion 1959-60. World lightweight champion 1962-65, 1965-68.

Born in Ponce, Puerto Rico, 9 September 1936.

Career: 1955-72.

Total contests: 70. Won: 61 (30 KOs). Lost: 7. Drew: 1. No contest: 1.

Though not the most dedicated fighter, Carlos Ortiz was a fine technician with a strong punch. He resurrected the light-welterweight division in the late 1950s and served two spells as world lightweight champion.

Ortiz left Puerto Rico for New York when he was eight and learned to use his fists in neighbourhood scraps when he was taunted about his ethnic heritage. He joined the Madison Square Boys Club and represented America as an amateur.

Turning professional in 1955, he won his first twenty fights before being outscored by Johnny Busso. He beat Busso in a return and impressed the English with a convincing points win over world-rated Dave Charnley in London. But he was no nearer landing a shot at world lightweight champion Joe Brown, who continued to avoid him.

When an enterprising matchmaker at Madison Square Garden, New York, revived the light-welterweight division in 1959, he paired Ortiz with Kenny Lane, a southpaw from Michigan, for the vacant world title. Carlos, who had been outpointed by Lane a year earlier, became the division's first champion for twelve years when Lane suffered a badly cut eye in the second round, forcing a stoppage.

Ortiz defended the title against Battling Torres and Dulio Loi, but lost it to Loi on a controversial decision in a rematch in Milan. When the Italian won the 'rubber' meeting between the two, Ortiz decided to resume his quest for a crack at Joe Brown's lightweight belt. He finally got his wish on 21 April 1962. Brown, champion for six years, had made eleven successful defences. The seasoned veteran tried to lure Ortiz into slugging it out, but the challenger peppered him with jabs and completely outboxed him in winning fourteen of the fifteen rounds.

Ortiz risked his precious championship belt in Tokyo, Puerto Rico and Manila, against dangerous challengers such as Doug Valliant, Flash Elorde and his old rival Kenny Lane. But a trip to Panama City proved ill-advised. He lost his title on a split decision against smart-moving local Ismael Laguna. Ortiz was able to lure Laguna to Puerto Rico for the rematch and Carlos was in top form, winning a unanimous decision. He made five defences, including two stoppages of former world featherweight champion Sugar Ramos, before being dethroned in an upset by Dominican Republic journeyman Carlos Teo Cruz in Santo Domingo.

Ortiz fought just once in 1969, was inactive the following year, then had one bout in 1971. Down on his luck, he made a big effort in 1972, winning eight fights before Scotland's Ken Buchanan halted him in six rounds in New York. It was the end of the line.

In retirement, Ortiz battled a drinking problem. He invested his money in bad businesses and lost all his ring earnings. He later drove a taxi-cab in New York City. Nowadays he lives in a cozy apartment in the Bronx with his wife, Maria, and enjoys travelling around the world.

MANUEL ORTIZ

World bantamweight champion 1942-47, 1947-50.

Born in Corona, California, USA, 2 July 1916. Died in San Diego, California, 31 May 1970.

Career: 1938-55.

Total contests: 127. Won: 96 (49 KOs). Lost: 28. Drew: 3.

For a notorious playboy whose prime-time fighting years were shortened by his lifestyle, Manuel Ortiz didn't do too badly. Deservedly ranked as one of the finest world bantamweight champions, he was quite tall for his division at five feet, four inches. Yet he preferred to fight inside, where he could score with ripping uppercuts. He reigned for eight years, except for a two-month break when he lost and regained the title against Harold Dade, and made nineteen successful defences.

'Manny was the first man I ever sparred with,' said the great Willie Pep. 'That experience alone should have been enough to make me hang up my gloves right there and then.' Pep outpointed Ortiz in a non-title fight in 1944.

Born in California to Mexican immigrants, Ortiz was nineteen before he took up amateur boxing. He won the California Golden Gloves and a national title before deciding to punch for pay in 1938. There was little indication of future greatness as he lost nine of his first twenty-six fights, but a knockout win over Jackie Jurich earned him a number four flyweight rating by *The Ring*. He was well looked after by his manager, Tommy Farmer, who, as well as coaching and seconding him, cooked his meals and lived with him during training.

A move up in weight paid off, when he outscored world bantamweight champion Lou Salica in August 1942. Though Ortiz was recognised as titleholder by the NBA, the New York Commission insisted that, as the fight had been over twelve rounds instead of the regulatory fifteen, Salica was still champion. Manuel cleared up the dispute the following year by knocking out Salica in eleven rounds. The Californian defended his title twelve times before dropping it to Harold Dade, a 12/1 outsider, in January 1947. Two months later, he was back on the throne, having outpointed Dade over fifteen rounds. That year he also suffered the only knockout defeat of his 127-bout career, at the hands of Manny Ortega, in a non-title fight.

Though an outstanding champion, Ortiz could be an indifferent performer when his title was not at stake. During his reign, he lost nine times in non-title contests. Among those who outscored him was British featherweight champion Ronnie Clayton, in Manchester, although he made amends to his European fans by outpointing Jackie Paterson in Glasgow and Theo Medina in Paris. His most exciting bouts were five wars with his drinking buddy Carlos Chavez. The score was two wins apiece and a draw.

Ortiz's glorious championship term finally came to an end in Johannesburg, South Africa, in May 1950, when home-towner Vic Toweel beat him convincingly on points. Toweel, twelve years the younger man, was having only his fourteenth fight. It was Ortiz's 116th. Manuel won six more fights and lost six before hanging up his gloves for good at the age of forty-two.

Strangely, Ortiz had never attracted much media attention throughout his extraordinary championship reign. This was mainly because he never boxed in New York, where most of the leading

American boxing writers were based. Yet he earned $150,000, a considerable sum for the period.

In retirement, he owned a farm, a ranch and a night-club. When these ventures failed, he worked at a series of odd jobs until his death from a liver ailment in 1970.

FLOYD PATTERSON

World heavyweight champion 1956-59, 1960-62.

Born in Waco, North Carolina, 4 January 1935.

Career: 1952-72.

Total contests: 64. Won: 55 (40 KOs). Lost: 8. Drew: 1.

When Floyd Patterson appeared on Ireland's long-running *Late Late Show* years after his retirement, he was dismayed that the only videotapes available were of his two one-round knockout defeats by Sonny Liston. 'Next time I'll bring my own tapes – of fights that I won,' he quipped to apologetic host Gay Byrne.

It is a sad fact that so many people remember Patterson for the two worst nights of his career. He deserves better. After all, he did become the youngest world heavyweight champion in history when, at twenty-one, he knocked out Archie Moore. (That record was later beaten by Mike Tyson.) And he was the first heavyweight to regain the title.

Patterson was an amazingly fast puncher, with power in both fists. Unfortunately, he wasn't big enough, never weighing more than 200 pounds. And his curious 'peek-a-boo' style, leaping in with rapid, two-fisted bursts, left him open to good counter-punchers. He was knocked down seventeen times in his thirteen title bouts. Henry Cooper, who fought Patterson in a non-title fight in London in 1966, later recalled: 'I went looking for him with my faithful left hook, but he found me instead with a corker of a straight right and it was goodnight nurse. I'd been hit harder in my life but never with quicker punches.'

The third of eleven children, Floyd was only one year old when the family moved from North Carolina to Brooklyn, New York. As he grew up, he was caught up in petty crime and spent two years at a home for emotionally disturbed city delinquents. It was only when he joined the Gramercy Gym, on Manhattan's Lower East Side, that the painfully shy kid found a way of expressing himself – with his fists. The gym's owner, Cus D'Amato, quickly recognised Floyd's talent and gave him the chance he gave to another troubled youngster, Mike Tyson, many years later.

At the age of seventeen, three years after first walking into D'Amato's fight factory, Patterson won the middleweight gold medal at the 1952 Olympic Games in Helsinki, Finland. He turned professional under the close, almost suffocating, control of D'Amato. Carefully matched, he lost only once, a disputed decision to Joey Maxim, in his first thirty-six fights. An excellent points win over Tommy 'Hurricane' Jackson shot him into the number two spot in the heavyweight ratings.

When Rocky Marciano retired as undefeated champion, Patterson was picked to meet 'Ancient' Archie Moore on 30 November 1956 for the vacant crown. At twenty-one years and ten months, Floyd became history's youngest ever heavyweight king by knocking out Moore in the fifth round.

D'Amato, who was waging war with the International Boxing Club, then the monopolistic force in world heavyweight boxing, refused to consider any challenger who had ties with the IBC. The result was that Patterson engaged in a series of defences against unworthy opponents, such as the 1956 Olympic champion Pete Rademacher, who was having his first professional fight. Floyd had to climb off the floor to win on a sixth round knockout. Tommy

Jackson, Roy Harris and Britain's timid Brian London were bowled over before D'Amato imported another apparent pushover in Swedish playboy Ingemar Johansson. But Patterson had no answer to 'Ingo's Bingo', as the European champion's lethal right hand was known. He was knocked down seven times before referee Ruby Goldstein rescued the totally bemused champion in the third round.

A year later, Floyd bounced back to regain the title with a crushing left hook that stretched the Swede on the canvas, his left foot twitching oddly as he was counted out in the fifth round. The pair met for a third time and, in a wildly exciting battle, with both men taking turns to visit the floor, Patterson won on a sixth round knockout. Waiting ominously in the shadows was the legitimate number one contender, Sonny Liston. D'Amato wanted nothing to do with the menacing Liston and it was only when Patterson, tired of being accused of cowardice for refusing to meet Sonny, insisted that the match be made that his mentor relented.

He should have listened to Cus. The champion was bludgeoned to defeat in two minutes, six seconds of the first round in Chicago on 25 September 1962. So ashamed of his performance was Floyd that he sneaked out of the arena by a back door wearing a false beard and glasses so that no one would recognise him.

Ten months later, in Las Vegas, Patterson was given the chance of revenge. He lasted exactly four seconds longer than the first time.

Floyd got another chance at the title in November 1965 against Muhammad Ali, who had dethroned Liston. A convert to Catholicism, Patterson denounced Ali's acceptance of the Muslim religion, which preached racial separatism, and to this day refuses to call him anything else but Cassius Clay. He was further hurt by Ali's gibes that he was 'a frightened rabbit'. Badly handicapped by a back injury, Patterson was cruelly tormented and beaten by Ali before the referee stopped the fight in the twelfth round.

Patterson's final grab for glory, at Jimmy Ellis' WBA heavyweight belt in Sweden in 1968, almost came off. He was considered by most observers to have been robbed of a points victory. Floyd won his next nine fights, then called it quits after losing to Muhammad Ali for the second time. The contest, in New York on 20 September

1972, was for the North American heavyweight title. Patterson suffered a badly cut eye and the fight was stopped in the seventh round.

Having finally outgrown the psychological problems that caused him to be labelled 'Freudian Floyd', he was happily settled into his second marriage and lived on his large estate in upstate New York. He decided to give something back to boxing and served with distinction as New York State Athletic Commissioner. In his sixties, Patterson continued to work out at his own gym and looked fit enough to take on any of the young contenders.

But the boxing world was shocked in 1998 when Patterson was forced to resign from his $76,000-a-year job as Commissioner. Giving testimony in a court case, he was found to be suffering from such severe memory loss that he couldn't recall who he had beaten for the world title, failed to recognise the name of his secretary, and thought that world title fights were still scheduled for fifteen rounds. He even said that he had only just heard about AIDS, even though his brother had died of the disease. Floyd's condition was attributed to his long boxing career.

EUSEBIO PEDROZA

WBA featherweight champion 1978-85.

Born in Panama City, Panama, 2 March 1953.

Career: 1973-92.

Total contests: 49. Won: 42 (25 KOs). Lost: 6. Drew: 1.

Tall for a featherweight at five feet, nine inches, Eusebio Pedroza used exceptional skills and savvy, backed up by hurtful punching power. During a seven-year reign as WBA titleholder, the Panamanian gave true meaning to the term 'world champion'. His twenty defences took him to such far-flung places as Puerto Rico, America, Japan, New Guinea, Korea, Venezuela, Italy, St Vincent and England.

Pedroza began his career as a bantamweight, but he was pitched in too soon with WBA champion Alfonso Zamora in April 1976. In only his sixteenth fight, he was put away in the second round by the big-hitting Mexican. When he was then knocked out in six rounds by Oscar Arnal, it looked as if his career was over almost before it started.

But Pedroza bounced back as a featherweight and stayed

unbeaten throughout his next twenty-six contests. In April 1978, the Spanish holder of the WBA featherweight title, Cecilio Lastra, was lured to Panama City to meet Pedroza. The local boy didn't let down his fans, stopping Lastra in the thirteenth round. Eusebio stopped fading great Ruben Olivares in twelve rounds, but was given two close fifteen-rounders by Rocky Lockridge, a future WBA super-featherweight champion. Boxing master Bernard Taylor gave him an even bigger fright by holding him to a draw. Otherwise, the Panamanian's dominance of his challengers was total.

For all his undoubted talents, Pedroza picked up an unenviable reputation as a dirty fighter. As the Americans put it, he 'parked the rule book at the gate'. In his title defence against Jose Caba, won by Pedroza on points, he was guilty of using his shoulders, elbows, hitting low, kidney punching and pulling Caba's head down onto right-hands. He was also involved in a foul-filled fifteen-rounder with Juan LaPorte.

But the champion behaved impeccably in his twentieth defence, against Irishman Barry McGuigan, in London on 9 June 1985. Though he fought skilfully and bravely, he was unable to subdue the fired-up challenger. Floored and almost stopped in the seventh round, he managed to survive the fifteen rounds, but was well behind on all three judges' scorecards.

At the age of thirty-two, Pedroza announced his retirement. He made a short-lived and unsuccessful comeback as a lightweight in 1992.

WILLIE PEP

Real name: William Guglielmo Papaleo.

Nickname: Will o' the Wisp.

New York-recognised world featherweight champion 1942-46.
World featherweight champion 1946-48, 1949-50.

Born in Middletown, Connecticut, USA, 19 September 1922.

Career: 1940-66.

Total contests: 242. Won: 230 (65 KOs). Lost: 11. Drew: 1.

In 1997, Oscar De La Hoya tried an experiment in his WBC light-welterweight title fight with Miguel Angel Gonzalez. He set out to win the third round without landing a punch. It failed. All three judges gave the round to Gonzalez. Only one man could perform such an outrageous feat. That was Willie Pep, a ringside guest of De La Hoya that night.

Pep, perhaps the greatest craftsman the ring has ever known, bobbed and weaved and danced throughout three minutes of his bout with Jackie Graves in 1946. He didn't land a single blow.

Neither did his opponent. The judges, who had to give the round to someone, decided Pep had shown his mastery and deserved the points.

The aptly named 'Will o' the Wisp' was not a devastating puncher – he only scored sixty-five quick wins in 242 fights – but relied on the skill he polished through regular practice. Modern boxers can never hope to match such ring artistry. They simply don't fight enough to work on what they have learned. No amount of gym work can equal the real thing.

Pep was introduced to boxing when his Sicilian immigrant father took him to watch an earlier featherweight champion from Connecticut, Bat Battalino. Willie won his state's flyweight and bantamweight championships and lost only three of his sixty-five amateur bouts. One of these was a three-round decision defeat by a youngster named Walker Smith, who later took the ring name Sugar Ray Robinson. Turning professional at seventeen, Pep was an incredibly consistent winner. Between his debut in 1940 and his loss to Sandy Saddler eight years later, he fought 137 times. The score was 135 wins, one loss and one draw. Only Sammy Angott, a future world lightweight champion, managed to outpoint him. The drawn bout was with Jimmy McAllister.

He became the youngest featherweight champion in forty years when he outpointed Chalky Wright for the New York version of the title in November 1942. It wasn't for another four years that he won universal recognition by knocking out NBA champion Sal Bartolo in twelve rounds. A plane crash in 1947 which caused him serious injuries seemed to spell the end of Pep's fighting career. But he was back in the ring within five months.

His fabulous run was brought to a shock halt in October 1948 by the lanky, but vicious-punching, Sandy Saddler. The champion was floored three times before being knocked out by a sweeping left hook in the fourth round. Because of Pep's feeble effort, and the fact that lots of money was bet on the challenger just before the fight, the two fighters were summoned to the offices of New York Commissioner Eddie Eagan on the afternoon of their rematch in February 1949. He told them he was holding them both responsible 'for upholding the good name of boxing'.

He needn't have worried. Pep gave the greatest performance of his long career as he dazzled the aggressive Saddler throughout fifteen rounds of scintillating boxing to earn a unanimous decision. He didn't emerge unscathed. In fact, with cuts over both eyes and on both cheeks, it was he who looked like the loser. It was the only time Pep won in four memorable clashes with his great rival.

The third meeting ended with Pep failing to answer the bell for the eighth round, claiming a dislocated shoulder. The final match between the two warriors was a foul-filled affair that Nat Fleischer labelled 'a disgraceful brawl'. The crowd of 13,781 witnessed a wild mêlée complete with heeling, gouging, tripping, butting, pushing, shoving and wrestling. Pep, his face a grotesque mask of cuts and bruises, quit after the ninth round. The recently appointed New York Commissioner, Bob Christenberry, took such a dim view of the affair that he suspended Saddler for thirty days and banned Pep from ever boxing again in New York. The ban was eventually lifted, but reimposed in 1954 after Pep lost in questionable circumstances to Lulu Perez.

Willie should have been a wealthy man, but gambling and business losses, together with alimony payments to three ex-wives, pushed him into continuing his career. He got himself back into championship contention by winning sixty of sixty-four fights after his last defeat by Saddler. He was rewarded with a crack at new world champion Hogan 'Kid' Bassey in September 1958. But the Nigerian's title was not at stake. It didn't matter, as Bassey came from behind to stop Pep in the ninth round.

After losing his next fight, to Sonny Leon, Pep announced his retirement. He made a comeback, however, in 1965 at the age of forty-two. He still had the skill to win nine bouts against moderate opponents, but hung up his gloves for good after being outpointed by Calvin Woodland in March 1966. The man remembered as the consummate boxer took to refereeing, still buzzing around the ring like the old 'Will o' the Wisp'. Among the title fights he worked was the first Johnny Famechon vs Fighting Harada bout, in Sydney, Australia, in 1969. Nineteen years earlier, Pep had outboxed Ray

Famechon, Johnny's uncle, in defence of his title. Willie was also the referee when gallant Irishman Johnny Caldwell lost to Eder Jofre in São Paulo, Brazil, in 1962.

The Ring placed Pep on the top rung of the featherweight ladder. 'Undeniably the greatest defensive fighter of all time,' the magazine declared. 'Simply didn't like to get hit, and used quick, subtle movements to frustrate foes.'

PASCUAL PEREZ

Nickname: El Terrier.

World flyweight champion 1954-60.

Born in Tupungate, Mendoza, Argentina, 4 March 1926. Died in Argentina, 22 January 1977.

Career: 1952-64.

Total contests: 92. Won: 84 (57 KOs). Lost: 7. Drew: 1.

Pascual Perez was a miniature Rocky Marciano. Though he stood only four feet, eleven inches, and weighed around seven stone, eight pounds (106 pounds) the Argentinian packed a sleep-inducing wallop in both hands. He was the first of his countrymen to win a world title and rates as one of the flyweight division's outstanding talents.

Inspired by his idol, Argentine heavyweight Luis Angel Firpo, who knocked Jack Dempsey flying out of the ring, Perez topped a fine amateur career by winning a gold medal at the 1948 Olympic Games in London. In recognition of his achievement, Argentine dictator Juan Perón presented Perez's family with a large house and persuaded Pascual to stay in the amateur ranks upholding his country's honour. Despite Perón's continuing interest, Perez took four years to decide that he would have a better future as a professional fighter than in his job as a janitor in a government office block.

He notched up twenty-three straight wins, twenty-two inside the distance, before taking on world flyweight champion Yoshio Shirai in a non-title fight in Buenos Aires. The result was a draw. That set the stage for a return in Tokyo, in November 1954, with the Japanese holder's belt up for grabs. Perez, seven inches the shorter man, defied the odds by repeatedly getting inside the champion's long arms and hammering away to earn a fifteen-round decision.

Perez knocked out Shirai in five rounds in his first defence, again in Tokyo, and dominated the flyweight division for the next six years. Welshman Dai Dower took a trip to Buenos Aires in 1957 and was sent crashing on his face for the count by a fierce 'one-two' from Perez in the first round. European champion Young Martin, of Spain, was dispatched in three.

Perez finally lost his grip on the title in his tenth defence. Conceding eight inches in height and home ground advantage to Thailand's Pone Kingpetch in Bangkok on 16 April 1960, the Argentinian fought hard but was beaten on a split decision. It was only his second defeat in fifty-six fights. The return match, five months later in Los Angeles, was a bigger disaster for Perez. He failed to mount an effective attack and was stopped in eight rounds. It was the first world flyweight title fight to be held in America in twenty-five years and Perez's only ring appearance in the United States.

Clearly, Pascual's glory days were over. He continued to fight until he was thirty-eight, mainly because his wife, who had been his business manager, divorced him and he was left with little money. He retired after losing four of his last six bouts.

He died, aged fifty, from a liver complaint.

AARON PRYOR

Nickname: the Hawk.

WBA light-welterweight champion 1980-83. IBF light-welterweight champion 1983-85.

Born in Cincinnati, Ohio, USA, 20 October 1955.

Career: 1976-90.

Total contests: 40. Won: 39 (35 KOs). Lost: 1.

One of the most exciting fighters of the late seventies and early eighties, Aaron Pryor looked like a reincarnation of Henry Armstrong for the speed and ferocity of his attacking style. He was unbeaten during an electrifying ten-year spell and would have gone on longer but for a self-destructive lifestyle. When he first retired, he had the perfect record – thirty-six fights, thirty-six wins. He returned to the ring after less than a year, already hooked on drugs, all but blind in one eye and financially broke, to suffer the only defeat of his career. Happily, he later 'found God' and tried to make amends for the wasted years.

One of seven children born into a troubled home, Pryor spent much of his early life on the streets. Boxing brought him a level of stability. He had a brilliant amateur career, winning 204 of 220 contests and two national Golden Gloves titles. He lost out on an Olympic Games place when Howard Davis twice outpointed him. For his professional debut in 1976, Pryor earned $400 for beating Larry Smith. Davis, who won the Olympic gold, got $250,000 for his first fight. Yet it was Pryor, not Davis, who went on to win a world title.

A hard hitter who went after his opponents with reckless abandon, Pryor notched up twenty-two knockouts in his first twenty-four fights. He battered veteran Antonio Cervantes, the greatest fighter ever to come out of Colombia, to a fourth-round knockout and captured the WBA light-welterweight title. An attempt to set up a title unification bout with WBC holder Saoul Mamby was scuppered when Pryor was shot in the forearm during a row with his second wife. Another large scar on his hand is a legacy of a shot fired by Jamaican drug-dealers who held him hostage in Miami.

His eight defences of the WBA title included two classics with Alexis Arguello. The first fight, in November 1982, is remembered as one of the best of the era. Arguello, who had held titles at featherweight, super-featherweight and lightweight, was attempting to become the first fighter to become a champion at four different weights. Pryor set off like a human buzzsaw, throwing a recorded 130 punches in the first round. He survived a terrific right in the second round that 'would have decapitated anyone else', according to Arguello's agent, Bill Miller. Pryor was ahead on two of the judges' cards after thirteen rounds. In the fourteenth, he cut loose with a blistering barrage to force a stoppage. Arguello, on the canvas for four minutes, collapsed again on the way to his dressing room.

After beating Arguello again, on a tenth round knockout, Pryor announced his retirement and handed back the WBA belt. Somehow, it had escaped detection that he had been fighting with a detached retina in his left eye. To add to his drug problems, his marriage was disintegrating and he was in dispute with his manager, Buddy La Rosa.

Within a year he was back in the ring and was awarded the newly formed IBF's light-welterweight title. But the comeback was principally to feed his addiction to crack cocaine. He made two defences of the IBF title, but the news that his mother wanted to commit him to a drugs rehabilitation centre, followed by the revelation of his eye problem, led to the organisation declaring the championship vacant.

In 1986, Pryor finally admitted his addiction, but said he had kicked the habit. He passed a drug test for a fight with a journeyman welterweight, Bobby Joe Young, in Sunrise, Florida. Eight pounds over the light-welterweight limit, Pryor was floored in the first round, staggered twice and knocked out in the seventh. It was the first time he had tasted defeat in thirty-seven fights. He had three more fights against mediocre opponents over the next three years, winning each by a knockout, then hung up his gloves for good. But he should not have been licensed for those final bouts. He had already been declared functionally blind in one eye after surgery.

Finally banned from boxing, Pryor went on what he later called 'the biggest crack binge of my life'. In 1991, he was jailed after pleading guilty to a reduced charge of drug abuse. Drained of all his earnings due to his habit, he lived on the streets, often going without food or sleep for days. He was found, close to death from bleeding ulcers, in a hallway in 1993.

'God saved my life,' he recalled. Having reached rock bottom, the only way was up. He conquered his addiction, became a church deacon in his old home town of Cincinnati, Ohio, and eked out a living as a boxing trainer with the city's Golden Gloves organisation. The millions he earned in purse money now a distant memory, Pryor told *Boxing Monthly*'s Graham Houston in 1997: 'I'm not bitter. When I turned my life over to God it took the bitterness out of me.'

SUGAR RAY ROBINSON

Real name: Walker Smith Junior.

World welterweight champion 1946-51. World middleweight champion 1951, 1951-52, 1955-57, 1957, 1958-60.

Born in Detroit, Michigan, USA, 3 May 1921. Died in Los Angeles, California, USA, 12 April 1989.

Career: 1940-65.

Total contests: 202. Won: 175 (109 KOs). Lost: 19. Drew: 6. No contest: 2.

Some say there's no such thing as the perfect fighter, but Sugar Ray Robinson came as close to it as makes no difference. This was the man who could do it all. Muhammad Ali said: 'He's the only one who was better than me.'

Widely acknowledged as the greatest pound-for-pound ringman in history, Robinson transformed a brutal game into an art form. Perfectly poised, he struck with speed and precision. If skill was required to outscore an awkward opponent, he turned it on in style. If the opening presented itself, he could take a man out with a blistering combination or a single blow. The left hook he exploded on Gene Fullmer's jaw was perhaps the best knockout punch ever delivered.

Defensively, Sugar Ray was masterly. He used the ring well and his ability to pick off opponents' punches would have made Jack Johnson envious. Robinson could be hit and hurt, even floored, but he had great recuperative powers. The only time he failed to last the distance in 202 contests was when he challenged Joey Maxim for the world light-heavyweight title. Even then, it was the effects of the excessive heat and exhaustion that brought about his collapse more than Maxim's punching. Some experts say he was at his best as a welterweight, but his feat of winning the world middleweight title five times was hard to top.

Sadly, the genius in gloves wasn't such a master of managing his private life. Despite a reputation as a hard negotiator who drove promoters mad with his demands, he blew $4 million and was forced to fight into his mid-forties to make ends meet. A fondness for gracious living, together with bad investments, tax problems and alimony payments to his first two wives, combined to keep him in the ring until he was long past his best. He finally quit in 1965 after losing to Joey Archer. He had fought as a professional for twenty-five years. He had lost only nineteen times. Most of his defeats were in his twilight years.

Born Walker Smith Junior, he became Ray Robinson when his amateur trainer, George Gainford, gave him an official card with that name on it. The original holder had retired and Smith didn't have a card allowing him to box. Gainford fished the disused card out of his pocket – and passed off Smith as Ray Robinson.

Gainford managed him throughout his professional career. It was he, too, who came up with 'Sugar Ray'. A reporter who saw the kid in action remarked: 'That's a real sweet fighter you've got there.' Gainford replied: 'Yeah, sweet as sugar.'

Some historians credit Robinson with winning all of his eighty-five amateur contests. Others say he lost a couple, one of them to future welterweight contender Billy Graham. He made his professional debut at Madison Square Garden, New York, in 1940 with a second-round knockout. He made such good progress that within a year he was already ranked top contender for the world welterweight title.

Past and future champions who were brushed aside included Sammy Angott (twice), Marty Servo (twice), Fritzie Zivic (twice), a fading Henry Armstrong and Jake LaMotta. After forty consecutive wins, however, he dropped a decision to LaMotta in a return. It was the only time he lost to LaMotta in six meetings. Successive welterweight champions were in no hurry to accommodate the menacing young contender and it wasn't until 1946, when Marty Servo retired, that Robinson got the chance to contest the vacant title with Tommy Bell. He survived a second round knockdown to win a unanimous decision over fifteen rounds.

His first defence ended in tragedy, when knockout victim Jimmy Doyle died the next day. At the inquest, the coroner asked Robinson if he meant to get Doyle in trouble. 'Mister,' he replied, 'it's my business to get him in trouble.'

After defeating four more challengers, he cast his sights on the world middleweight championship, held by his old rival Jake LaMotta. The sixth and final meeting between them took place in Chicago Stadium on 14 February 1951. LaMotta was butchered in thirteen rounds in another St Valentine's Day Massacre.

The Sugar Ray show was now truly up and running. Ever the flamboyant character, he sailed for Europe with his wife, Edna Mae, a former night-club dancer, along with a 'travelling circus' that included his hairdresser, a trumpeter, a French tutor and a midget who acted as 'court jester'. He also took his open-top flamingo-pink Cadillac, which caused traffic jams wherever he drove, as fans scrambled to get a look at the famous champ.

All of this cost money. To pay for it, the champion took part in non-title fights in Paris, Zurich, Antwerp, Liège, Berlin and Turin. A £30,000 offer from English promoter Jack Solomons persuaded him to risk his title against British champion Randolph Turpin. The Robinson entourage, together with fifty-three suitcases and garish Cadillac, arrived in London to prepare for the fight at Earl's Court on 10 July 1951. A mighty fall was in store for the supposedly unbeatable American.

Turpin, more noted for his punching power, surprised Robinson with his powerful left jab and awkwardly effective boxing style. Sugar Ray, cut over the left eye in a clash of heads in the seventh round, was clearly beaten on points over fifteen rounds. It was only his second defeat in 132 contests.

Robinson blamed his hectic European tour, which included six fights in fifty-two days, on his loss and got himself into excellent shape for the return match, just sixty-four days after the London fight. A crowd of 61,370 packed New York's Polo Grounds, the biggest attendance outside of the heavyweight division. Robinson again had trouble coping with the strong Englishman and there was little between them up to the tenth round, when Sugar Ray again suffered a nasty cut on his left eye. Like a wounded tiger, Robinson pounced on his tormentor and sent him crashing to the canvas with a terrific right. Turpin rose shakily at nine and was backed to the ropes, where he took a pounding until referee Ruby Goldstein intervened. The British camp complained there were only eight seconds left in the round, but most observers believed the referee acted correctly.

Following defences against Carl 'Bobo' Olson and Rocky Graziano, Robinson made a bold bid to lift Joey Maxim's world light-heavyweight title in June 1952. It took place at New York's Yankee Stadium in the middle of a heatwave. It was so hot that the referee, Ruby Goldstein, had to leave the ring after the tenth round and hand over to Ray Miller. Robinson, sixteen pounds lighter than his opponent, came close to the finest victory of his career. He was well ahead on points when, totally exhausted and dehydrated by the 104-degrees heat under the ring arc lights, he couldn't rise from his stool for the fourteenth round. Maxim had endured the conditions better because he was slower and expended less energy. He had also been belting Robinson around the ribs in the later rounds.

Sugar Ray then retired as undefeated middleweight champion, but came back three years later and blasted out Bobo Olson in two rounds to reclaim his championship belt. He caught Olson with the same pay-off left hook five months later, this time in the fourth round. An ex-champion again after being outpointed by Gene

Fullmer, he climbed back on the throne for the third time with that classic knockout of Fullmer, the Mormon from Utah, in May 1957.

But the years were beginning to tell and Sugar Ray, now thirty-six, failed to hang onto his title against the teak-tough welterweight champion Carmen Basilio. The decision in what British writer Peter Wilson called 'an X-certificate fight' was split. It was the same when they met in another fifteen-round war, only this time the verdict was in Robinson's favour. Sugar Ray's cup finally ran dry when he lost his title on a controversial split decision to Paul Pender, and was again outpointed by Pender in a return. He still didn't give up, however, and was unlucky to get only a draw in a challenge for Gene Fullmer's NBA title. His final championship bout, in March 1961, ended in a decisive points defeat by Fullmer.

It was only a shadow of the once great Sugar Ray who lost to Terry Downes and Mick Leahy on a British trip, but he did manage to knock out Johnny Angel for his only success in four appearances in the United Kingdom. London *Evening Standard* writer George Whiting commented: 'I honestly wish Robinson would leave us with our memories of more regal days.'

The man who had fought for huge purses was reduced to swapping punches with journeymen for around $400 a go as he climbed between the ropes in such far-flung places as Jacksonville, Tijuana, Richmond, Norfolk, and Steubenville, Ohio.

At least he got a decent payday – $7,500 – for his farewell appearance, at the Civic Arena, Pittsburgh, on 10 November 1965. His opponent, Joey Archer, was the number one contender for Dick Tiger's world middleweight title and the winner was promised a crack at the champion. Robinson, floored for nine in the fourth round, lasted the full ten rounds, but he was well beaten on points.

That was it. At forty-five, he hung up his gloves for the last time. He acted in several films, ran a popular Harlem night-club and set up the Sugar Ray Robinson Youth Foundation to counter juvenile delinquency. It helped thousands of deprived youngsters.

Stricken by Alzheimer's disease in later years, Robinson was sixty-eight when he died. A tearful Mike Tyson said at his funeral: 'When you think of the name Sugar Ray Robinson, you think of class and style and dignity.' Sugar Ray Leonard, who adopted Robinson's appellation, said: 'Someone once said there was a comparison between Sugar Ray Leonard and Sugar Ray Robinson. Believe me, there was no comparison. Sugar Ray Robinson was the greatest.'

BARNEY ROSS

Real name: Barnet David Rosofsky.

Nickname: the Pride of the Ghetto.

World lightweight champion 1933-35. World junior welterweight champion 1933-35. World welterweight champion 1934, 1935-38.

Born in New York City, New York, USA, 23 December 1909. Died in Chicago, Illinois, USA, 17 January 1967.

Career: 1929-38.

Total contests: 81. Won: 72 (22 KOs). Lost: 4. Drew: 3. No decision: 2.

Only the third fighter in history to win world titles in three weight divisions, Barney Ross is best remembered as an outstanding welterweight champion, even though he only weighed 138 pounds (nine pounds under the limit) in capturing the title. Not a particularly heavy puncher, he relied mainly on sharp attacks, clever counter-punching, a sound defence and one of the best chins in ring history. He was never beaten inside the distance in eighty-one fights.

Ross's first fight started at birth, when doctors feared he would not live because of arthritis and a weakness of the lungs. But he battled through. The family moved from New York to gangster-ridden Chicago during the twenties. His Orthodox Jewish parents wanted him to become a Hebrew teacher and opposed any form of fighting.

Nevertheless, Ross was taught to box by former lightweight contender Packey McFarland at the Catholic Youth Centre and he won the 1929 Inter-City Golden Gloves championship. When his father was shot dead during a hold-up at his grocery store, Barney convinced his mother he could help out by making money in the ring.

His busy style overwhelmed most of his opponents and he compiled a record of forty-five wins, two losses and two draws by the time he challenged Tony Canzoneri at Chicago Stadium in 1933. Canzoneri held both the world lightweight and junior welterweight titles. Both passed to Ross on a ten-round split decision, but the result was hotly disputed. If Ross had hometown advantage on that occasion, he allowed the return match to go ahead on New Yorker Canzoneri's home turf. Once again Ross emerged the winner on a split verdict.

Weight difficulties forced Ross to relinquish the lightweight prize, but he held onto the junior welterweight championship. He defended it nine times before giving it up in December 1935. By then, he was welterweight champion of the world.

His three encounters with Jimmy McLarnin all went the full fifteen rounds – and all were classics. The Irishman had built a reputation of never failing to beat a Jewish fighter. Ross smashed that record by taking the title in May 1934. Though he lost it back to McLarnin four months later, Ross came out on top in the final clash.

Barney thwarted the challenges of Izzy Jannazzo and Ceferino Garcia, who went on to become middleweight champion, but he faced his toughest opponent yet in Henry Armstrong. 'Hammerin' Hank' was moving up from featherweight, bypassing the lightweight division for an audacious attempt to grab the welterweight crown.

Ross could do nothing to fend off Armstrong's relentless attacks and took a sustained hiding. Although the fans were screaming for the referee to stop the massacre, Ross refused to go down. In the last few rounds, Armstrong, full of admiration for his rival's courage, eased up to let him last the distance.

Although he was only twenty-eight, Ross hung up his gloves. He played bit parts in movies and entered the advertising business. He joined the US Marines immediately after the Japanese attack on Pearl Harbor. Declining a desk job, he became a sergeant and was decorated for bravery after being wounded in action at Guadalcanal. Unfortunately, he became addicted to the morphine used to ease the pain from his war injuries. Showing the same fighting qualities he did in the ring, he overcame his drug habit and told all about it in his autobiography, *Monkey on my Back*. It was turned into a movie, with Cameron Mitchell in the starring role.

Ross was finally beaten by cancer. He died following a long illness at the age of fifty-eight.

SANDY SADDLER

Real name: Joseph Saddler.

World featherweight champion 1948-49, 1950-57. World junior lightweight champion 1949-51.

Born in Boston, Massachusetts, USA, 23 June 1926.

Career: 1944-56.

Total contests: 162. Won: 144 (103 KOs). Lost: 16. Drew: 2.

With his skinny legs and long, spidery arms, Sandy Saddler looked anything but the phenomenal puncher he was. But over a hundred knockouts on his record show the devastation he wreaked during the 1940s and '50s.

Abnormally tall for a featherweight at five feet, eight inches, Saddler used his long left jab to soften up opponents before moving in for the kill with rapid clusters of hooks and uppercuts. Unfortunately, he sullied his reputation by unnecessary dirty tactics. Even amateur sparring partners were not spared the notorious Saddler treatment. The last two of his four-fight series with Willie Pep for the world featherweight title were among the roughest brawls in ring history. Saddler finished up with a three-to-one victory score over 'Will o' the Wisp', no mean achievement.

The son of a West Indian immigrant, Joseph Saddler was reared in the tough Harlem district of New York. He got the name 'Sandy' from his manager, Charley Johnston, who, in a bizarre publicity stunt, tried to pass him off as a Scotsman. He dressed the fighter in a kilt and dyed his hair blond. Not many people were fooled.

Saddler had about fifty amateur bouts before turning to the paid ranks at seventeen.

After winning his first fight, he was knocked out in his second outing by Jock Leslie, an experienced bantamweight. It was the only time he lost inside the distance in 162 contests.

An extremely busy fighter, he had forty-six fights in his first two years of activity. Yet he had to wait until his ninety-fourth contest to get a crack at Pep's title in October 1948. He made the most of his opportunity with a sensational fourth round knockout over the 5/2 favourite. Pep regained the championship in the return, which drew 19,097 spectators, a record for the featherweight division, to Madison Square Garden, New York, on 11 February 1949. But in the third and fourth clashes between the arch-rivals, Saddler scored short-route victories.

In the meantime, Sandy had added the world junior lightweight championship to his achievements. He won the title, which had been dormant for sixteen years, by outpointing Cuba's Orlando Zulueta in December 1949. He defended it twice, halting Lauro Salas, a future lightweight champion, and Diego Sosa, but, in 1951, he relinquished his claim to what was then regarded as a second-rate honour.

The featherweight championship was put into cold storage while Saddler served two years in the US Army. He was based mainly in West Germany, keeping in shape by training with the Army boxing division. On his discharge, he took up where he left off. Teddy Davis, who had been regarded as interim champion during Sandy's absence, was unanimously outpointed in a title clarification fight. Flash Elorde's challenge ended on cuts in thirteen rounds. Frenchman Ray Famechon, who had gone fifteen rounds in a title fight with Pep, was cut up and stopped in six rounds by Saddler in a non-title bout.

Saddler was still at his peak as a fighter when, in 1956, he was a passenger in a New York taxi-cab which was involved in a crash. He suffered injuries that threatened his eyesight. It meant his boxing career was over at the age of thirty. He had been a great world champion, but never got paid his true worth. He fought for as little as $100, and his biggest earnings were around $10,000 for each of the Pep fights. 'He was cheated out of a lot of money,' said trainer Ray Arcel. 'He never reaped the rewards.'

In retirement, Saddler worked as athletic director of the National Marine Union, giving boxing and athletic instruction to merchant seamen, until the building was sold. He also trained amateur fighters at Gleason's gym on New York's 30th Street. His life later took a turn for the worse. Estranged from his wife and their two grown children, he lived alone in a dingy apartment, afraid to open the door after being robbed and hit on the head with an iron pipe. Late one night he was found by police wandering through Brooklyn, dazed and confused after muggers had stolen his wallet and spectacles. Ring Eight, an organisation that looks after veteran fighters in New York, arranged for him to live in a nursing home.

When Willie Pep heard about his old rival's situation, he told writer-photographer Arlene Schulman: 'I wish him the very best of luck in the world. Tell him to keep punching. He was a helluva fighter.'

VICENTE SALDIVAR

Real name: Vicente Samuel Saldivar Garcia.

World featherweight champion 1964-67. WBC featherweight champion 1970.

Born in Mexico City, Mexico, 3 May 1943. Died in Mexico City, 18 July 1985.

Career: 1961-73.

Total contests: 41. Won: 38 (27 KOs). Lost: 3.

Though he was only five feet, three inches tall, featherweight Vicente Saldivar had the strength of a welterweight. His awkward southpaw stance and his non-stop aggression, made possible by an abnormally slow heart and pulse rate, proved too much for most of his top quality opponents. He is remembered principally by British fans for his epic three-fight series with Welsh wizard Howard Winstone. Saldivar won each time, but only on desperately close verdicts in the first two encounters. He won the third clash on a twelfth-round stoppage, but he was behind on points at that stage.

One of a family of nine raised in the poorest quarter of Mexico

City, Vicente saw boxing as a way out of the poverty trap, as did so many of his countrymen. He won a Mexican Golden Gloves bantamweight title, then turned professional at seventeen.

The Mexican featherweight title was his after twenty-four fights and he qualified for a crack at Sugar Ramos' world championship in September 1964. He was the underdog against the Mexican-based Cuban, but his non-stop attacking and decisive punching took him to an eleventh-round win.

Saldivar proved to be a fighting champion. In eight defences, his victims included American Raul Rojas, Floyd Robertson of Ghana, and Mitsunori Seki of Japan, all top-rate opponents. He travelled to London for the first of his three duels with Howard Winstone in September 1965. The Welshman, renowned for his stylish boxing and brilliant footwork, surprised everyone by trading with the heavier-punching champion. His strategy worked until the latter stages, when Winstone tired, and the Mexican's constant pressure just had him in front at the final bell.

There had to be a return. It didn't take place for another two years, but Saldivar showed immense self-confidence by agreeing to meet the Welshman at Ninian Park, Cardiff. Just as in the initial clash, Winstone carried the fight to the champion and was ahead on points until he began to run out of energy. The Mexican, fighting with fury to hang onto his title, scored a knockdown in the fourteenth round. He wasn't able to finish it, but he just about deserved the decision after fifteen enthralling rounds.

Winstone had to go to Mexico City for his third attempt to lift the championship belt. Saldivar was kept at bay by effective jabbing for eleven rounds, but his persistent aggression paid off when he floored the British champion for a long count in the twelfth. The Mexican battered Winstone with both hands, causing damage around both eyes, before the towel was thrown in. As often happens with great fighting rivals, Saldivar and Winstone became good friends. The Welshman was a personal guest at Vicente's home during the 1968 Olympics in Mexico City.

Saldivar caused a shock by announcing his retirement from boxing immediately after the third Winstone bout in 1967. He was only twenty-four years old, was still world champion and had only lost once, on a disqualification, in thirty-four contests. Within two years, he had itchy fists and returned to outscore Jose Legra, a former WBC titleholder. Then, in only his second comeback fight, he beat Australian Johnny Famechon on points in a hard fifteen-rounder in Rome to become WBC champion. He surprisingly lost the title in his first defence. Japan's unheralded Kuniaki Shibata outpunched him and badly cut his eye in Tijuana, Mexico. The referee stopped the fight in the thirteenth round to save Saldivar from further punishment.

That was effectively the end of Saldivar's career. He made an ill-advised comeback in 1973 after a two and a half year lay-off, but was knocked out in the fourth round of a WBC title challenge to the brilliant Brazilian Eder Jofre.

Mexico and the boxing world were stunned at the news in 1985 that Saldivar had died from a heart attack at the age of forty-two.

SALVADOR SANCHEZ

WBC featherweight champion 1980-82.

Born in Santiago Tianguistenco, Mexico, 3 February 1958. Died in Queretaro, Mexico, 12 August 1982.

Career: 1975-82.

Total contests: 46. Won: 44 (32 KOs). Lost: 1. Drew: 1.

Much of the $2 million Salvador Sanchez earned in the ring went on the nine cars he owned. His favourite was a red Porsche 928. On 12 August 1982, he was speeding the Porsche along the highway between Queretaro and his training camp at San Jose Iturbide, about 160 miles north of Mexico City. The car ploughed into a heavily loaded pick-up truck. Sanchez was killed outright. He was only twenty-three years of age.

Had he not died so young, the Mexican might well have gone on to be the greatest featherweight in history. He had won the WBC featherweight title from the much-feared Danny 'Little Red' Lopez and defended it nine times against top-grade fighters. Three of his challengers, Juan LaPorte, Wilfredo Gomez and Azumah Nelson, went on to win the title after his death.

In contrast to most Mexican fighters, Sanchez was more of a patient stylist than an out-and-out knockout artist. Although he scored thirty-two short route wins, he relied more on snappy counter-punching, a strong jaw and exceptional stamina. He said: 'The KOs come through undermining my opponents.'

A professional boxer at sixteen, the curly-haired Sanchez won seventeen of his first eighteen fights inside the distance, before being outpointed by Antonio Becerra in a bout for the vacant Mexican bantamweight title. It was the only time he ended up a loser in his seven-year career.

Moving up to featherweight, he put together another impressive winning run to earn a crack at Danny Lopez's WBC title in February 1980. Sanchez handed out a savage beating to 'Little Red' and forced a stoppage in the thirteenth round. England's Pat Cowdell gave Sanchez an unexpectedly tough time in Houston, Texas, fifteen days before Christmas in 1981. The British champion boxed brilliantly, but suffered a badly cut eyebrow in the ninth round, which affected his overall performance. Sanchez scored a knockdown in the fifteenth round and won on a split decision.

Strangely, the Mexican showed no real desire to meet WBA champion Eusebio Pedroza in a title unification fight. It would have been an intriguing match-up between two great featherweights. He considered his WBC belt to be the more significant trophy. Yet, shortly before his death, he talked about stepping up to challenge lightweight titleholder Alexis Arguello.

Sanchez put his title on the line for the ninth time at Madison Square Garden, New York, on 21 July 1982. Ghana's Azumah Nelson had won his thirteen fights to date, but he came in as a late substitute and wasn't experienced enough to take his big chance. The challenger fought his heart out, but was floored and stopped in the fifteenth and last round.

That was Sanchez's last fight. Five months later, while training for a return title defence against Juan LaPorte, he was killed in the head-on crash. Just what the champion was doing driving fast at 3.30 in the morning was open to speculation. He normally went to bed at 9 pm. There were suggestions that he was visiting a woman and was rushing back to his training camp before anyone noticed his absence. This would have been out of character, for he was not known as a womaniser. He left a wife and two sons.

MAX SCHMELING

Nickname: the Black Uhlan.

World heavyweight champion 1930-32.

Born in Brandenburg, Germany, 28 September 1905.

Career: 1924-48.

Total contests: 70. Won: 56 (39 KOs). Lost: 10. Drew: 4.

Happily for Max Schmeling, he is not remembered primarily for the
pair of highly controversial fights against Jack Sharkey in which he
won and lost the world heavyweight title. His greatest claim to fame
was his knockout over an up-and-coming Joe Louis, one of the most
sensational upsets in ring history. On that magnificent performance
alone, the German deserves his place among the greats. Louis, at the
time, was looked upon as unbeatable. He had notched up twenty-
seven straight wins, twenty-three by knockout. The merit of
Schmeling's achievement can be gauged by the fact that the 'Brown
Bomber' campaigned for another fourteen years before suffering his
second loss.

A cool, calculating boxer with a strong chin, Schmeling was like two other Europeans who made an impact on the world scene, Georges Carpentier and Ingemar Johansson, in that he used his left mainly as a measuring tool for his pulverising right hand.

Max was inspired to take up boxing after his father took him to see the film of the Jack Dempsey vs Carpentier fight. Dempsey became his idol. The beetle-browed German even looked like the Manassa Mauler, although he didn't fight with quite the same fury. His professional career began in 1924 as a light-heavyweight. He won the German and European titles, but a shock first-round knockout by Welshman Gypsy Daniels convinced him to move up to heavyweight. After winning the German championship in that division, he embarked on an American trip in pursuit of the world title, which had been vacated by Gene Tunney.

Schmeling found himself in a long queue, but he made rapid progress with five straight wins to earn a match with Jack Sharkey for the crown. More than 80,000 fans crammed into New York's Yankee Stadium for the decider on 12 June 1930. They were none too pleased the way it ended, with the German writhing in agony on the canvas after being struck low in the fourth round. Sharkey was disqualified.

In a 1992 interview for Norman Giller and Neil Duncanson's book *Crown of Thorns*, Schmeling, then eighty-seven, recalled the occasion vividly:

> I was terribly hurt, but also embarrassed. This was not the way I wanted to become champion of the world. In the dressing room after the fight, I announced that I would not accept the title, but the distinguished writer Paul Gallico got hold of me and said that I should not be so foolish. 'You won it within the rules," he said. 'Now you must defend it with pride.' My idol Jack Dempsey, who had become my friend and promoter, also said that I was entitled to keep the championship. So I went home to a hero's welcome in Germany as heavyweight champion of the world. It was a boyhood dream come true.'

Schmeling showed the Americans his true worth when, in his first defence, he landed a perfect short right to send Young Stribling crashing in the fifteenth round. Though the challenger barely made it to his feet at nine, the referee saw he was in no condition to continue and stopped the fight, even though there were only fourteen seconds to go to the end. Stribling was a dangerous challenger with a devastating punch. He compiled a career total of 125 knockouts, a record only bettered by Archie Moore (141).

The powers-that-be pressed the German into a return match with Jack Sharkey at Long Island, New York, in June 1932, exactly two years after winning the title on a foul. This time it was Max's turn to feel hard done by. At the end of fifteen keenly contested rounds, he looked a definite winner. But the split decision went to the American, who had fought with a half-closed eye for most of the fight, whereas Schmeling was unmarked at the finish. The result gave rise to the quote that has become part of ring folklore. Joe Jacobs, Schmeling's American manager, screamed: 'We wuz robbed. We shoulda stood in bed.'

Back at the same venue three months later, Schmeling gave former world welterweight and middleweight champion Mickey Walker such a battering that the crowd cried out for the fight to be stopped. The referee finally agreed in the eighth round. Walker, though he had held Jack Sharkey to a draw the previous year, had no place in the ring with Schmeling, twenty-five pounds heavier and six inches taller. It looked like the end of the big time for the German, however, when he was stopped in ten rounds by future world champion Max Baer, then lost on points to Steve Hamas and was held to a draw by Spain's Paulino Uzcudun. But he made up lost ground by knocking out Hamas in a return and outpointing Uzcudun.

Schmeling found himself embroiled in a political storm after the second Hamas fight, which took place in Berlin in 1935. His Jewish manager, Joe Jacobs, was pictured giving the Nazi salute – but with a cigar stuck between his fingers. Such was the uproar over what was seen as a calculated insult that Schmeling requested, and was granted, a meeting with Adolf Hitler to defend his mentor. The Fuehrer wasn't satisfied with the fighter's explanation that Jacobs had been good for him and that racial or religious prejudices had no part in boxing. When he saw there was no way Max was prepared to dump Jacobs, Hitler stormed out of the room.

Back in America, promoter Mike Jacobs (no relation to Joe Jacobs) was building up his sensational young heavyweight Joe Louis for a world title chance. 'The Brown Bomber' had already accounted for two former world champions, Primo Carnera and Max Baer, and the thirty-one-year-old Schmeling was chosen as just another soft touch. But Max ruined the script with a brilliant power display at Yankee Stadium, New York, on 19 June 1936. He had noticed a flaw in Louis' fighting make-up that others had missed – Joe dropped his left hand after throwing a jab. As a fast, accurate straight right over the top was Schmeling's best punch, he knew he was capable of causing a mighty upset. He took the American's left jabs and countered with a terrific right to the jaw in the fourth round. Louis, floored for the first time in his career, rose at two, but was clearly hurt. Schmeling continued to score with heavy rights until his final blow put Louis down for the full count in round twelve.

The German was shamefully denied a chance to take on world champion James J. Braddock. Instead, Louis got the job and knocked out Braddock. For his fourth defence, he faced Schmeling at the Polo Grounds, New York, in June 1938. A huge propaganda war was built around the contest. Schmeling was portrayed as a symbol of the Nazi ideal of white supremacy, while Louis represented 'the American way'.

Schmeling was unlucky to meet a hyped-up champion at his destructive best. The fight lasted just 124 seconds and Max spent every one of them in agony. Louis threw more than forty punches and not one missed the target. A right that caught him in the back as he tried to use the ropes for support fractured several vertebrae. Schmeling was sent crashing to the canvas three times and referee Arthur Donovan stopped the slaughter just as the towel came fluttering in from the challenger's corner. Schmeling was stretchered out of the ring and spent several months back in Germany recovering from his savage beating. It was nearly a year before he could return to action, scoring a first round knockout over Adolf Heuser to win the European heavyweight title in July 1939.

When World War Two broke out in September of that year, Schmeling was called up as a German Army paratrooper. He was invalided out in 1944 after being injured while making a parachute landing during the Battle of Crete.

After the war, he faced a grim future. The 3,200-acre estate he had accrued from his ring earnings had been wiped out and refereeing boxing matches wasn't enough to make ends meet. By 1947, he realised there was only one way to make real money – by coming back as a fighter. Though he was now forty-two, and had not boxed for eight years, he knocked out Werner Vollmer in seven rounds in Hamburg. Still a big attraction, he fought four more times, winning two and losing two, before hanging up his gloves for good.

With his earnings from his comeback bouts, he bought a property near Hamburg. He became a successful mink farmer and had interests in poultry and fish ponds. Showing more shrewd business acumen, he took over the franchise to bottle and distribute Coca-Cola for West Germany. He became a rich man. Schmeling paid several visits to the United States and quietly helped his old rival Joe Louis get over his financial problems. He even paid the bill for one of Joe's spells in hospital.

Though he lost the love of his life, the former Czech film star Anny Ondra, after fifty-four years of marriage, Max continued to prove a marvellous example of a healthy lifestyle. He never drank alcohol or smoked, although he once owned a tobacco factory. Now in his nineties, the oldest living former world champion still does light workouts every day and pays regular visits to the Coca-Cola plant in Hamburg that he helps to run.

Despite the success of tennis stars Boris Becker and Steffi Graf, Schmeling was voted Germany's outstanding sports personality of the century. 'If I had my life to live over,' he said, 'there is nothing I would change. It has been a wonderful life. Ja, wunderbar.'

MICHAEL SPINKS

WBA light-heavyweight champion 1981-83. World light-heavyweight champion 1983-85. IBF heavyweight champion 1985-87.

Born in St Louis, Missouri, USA, 13 July 1956.

Career: 1977-88.

Total contests: 32. Won: 31 (21 KOs). Lost: 1.

It seems amazing that it was not until 1985, when Michael Spinks beat Larry Holmes, that a world light-heavyweight champion took the giant step up to capture the heavyweight crown. The awkward, but effective, Spinks succeeded where Philadelphia Jack O'Brien, Georges Carpentier, Tommy Loughran, John Henry Lewis, Billy Conn, Joey Maxim, Archie Moore and Bob Foster had all failed. Bob Fitzsimmons did hold light-heavyweight and heavyweight titles, but he took the lower weight honour after he had lost his heavyweight crown.

Spinks also helped create another record. He was one half of the only two brothers to win the heavyweight title. Leon, three years the elder, won and lost the premier prize in two bouts with Muhammad

Ali within seven months in 1978. And Michael only just lost out on equalling Rocky Marciano's unique achievement as the only heavyweight champion to retire with a perfect record. He was foolish enough to step into the ring for his last fight against the all-conquering Mike Tyson, who flattened him inside a round. It was the only defeat of his career. The Spinks brothers did a lot of things together, like picking up gold medals at the 1976 Olympics, but they had quite contrasting personalities. Whereas Leon was never able to cope with wealth and fame, Michael was a much more sober character who enjoyed his spell at the top and was able to retire a rich man.

Michael did not turn professional immediately after striking middleweight gold in Montreal, but took a job in a chemical plant. Flamboyant promoter Butch Lewis, who liked to get attention by wearing a dress-suit and tie without a shirt, convinced him he would be better off using his fighting talents. Spinks made his pro debut in April 1977, knocking out Eddie Benson in the first round.

Just over six feet, two inches tall, Spinks based his style on an authoritative left jab and solid follow-through right. He could annoy spectators with his negative tactics, including 'going walkabout' during contests, but his common-sense philosophy was to hit without getting hit.

After sixteen straight wins, including an impressive fourth round knockout of former champion Marvin Johnson, he was matched with WBA light-heavyweight champion Eddie Mustapha Muhammad, who had taken the title from Johnson. Spinks had trouble coping with the powerful, but ungraceful, Muhammad for the first four rounds. After that he used his superior repertoire of punches to take control. He cut the champion over both eyes and knocked him down in the twelfth round. Three rounds later Spinks was the new titleholder on a unanimous decision.

He defended the WBA version of the title five times, then became undisputed champion by taking a fifteen-round verdict over WBC holder Dwight Muhammad Qawi (formerly Dwight Braxton) in March 1983.

Four successful defences convinced Spinks and manager Lewis

that Michael could rewrite the history books by winning the heavyweight crown. The trouble with past light-heavyweights trying for the top division title had been that they were simply too light. Spinks went on a special weight-building programme, so he put on twenty pounds for his challenge to IBF titleholder Larry Holmes in September 1985.

Holmes, winner of all his forty-eight fights to date, was one step away from going on par with Rocky Marciano's perfect record of forty-nine wins. It was not to be. Spinks won the battle of unbeaten heavyweights on the slimmest of margins after fifteen rounds. He used his wide variety of unorthodox tactics to prevent Holmes from getting his vaunted left jab on target and did most of the scoring from odd angles.

The decision was angrily disputed by Holmes and he demanded a rematch. It took place seven months later and was almost a repeat of the initial encounter. Spinks overcame a poor start to use his skills and score while staying out of trouble. He was caught and hurt by a hard right in the fourteenth round, but came back well in the last round to snatch another controversial verdict.

An easy win over Norway's European champion Steffan Tangstad set Spinks up for a big-money fight with Gerry Cooney in June 1987. But the IBF refused to sanction it as a title fight, insisting Spinks should meet mandatory contender Tony Tucker instead. When he refused, he was stripped of his championship belt. The fight with Cooney went ahead anyway, with Spinks having little trouble in recording a fifth round win.

Exactly a year later, Spinks made the one mistake of his career. He took on the fearsome Mike Tyson, who had unified the heavyweight title for the first time since Michael's brother, Leon, was undisputed champion nine years earlier. Michael froze in front of a rampaging Tyson and he was knocked spark out in just ninety-one seconds. There was no way back after such a crushing defeat. He retired, with $12 million in the bank.

DICK TIGER

Real name: Richard Ihetu.

WBA middleweight champion 1962-63. World middleweight champion 1963, 1965-66. World light-heavyweight champion 1966-68.

Born in Amaigbo, Orlu, Nigeria, 14 August 1929. Died in Aba, Nigeria, 14 December 1971.

Career: 1952-70.

Total contests: 81. Won: 61 (26 KOs). Lost: 17. Drew: 3.

English fight fans who watched Dick Tiger perform in small-hall shows in the late 'fifties never dreamed that the strong, but unexceptional, Nigerian would go on to win world titles in two weight divisions. Painfully homesick, he lost his first four fights in England on points. But there was a hint of better things to come when he forced 5/1 favourite Terry Downes to retire after six brutal rounds. The fight between the two future world champions took place at London's Shoreditch Town Hall in May 1957. Downes earned £125, while Tiger, then working part-time in a paint shop, took home £75.

It was not until Tiger switched his base to America that his real talent began to shine through. Regular fights against top-rate opposition sharpened up his skills and he developed an effective two-fisted attacking style. Dedicated and always in top condition, his five foot, eight inch frame was impressively muscled and he could take a punch.

Tiger, who bore the tribal scars that were a sign of manhood among the Ibo in Nigeria, was attracted to boxing by the success of his country's first world champion, Hogan 'Kid' Bassey. After a brief amateur career, he turned professional at the relatively late age of twenty-three. He lost just once in sixteen contests before sailing to England to further his career. Once he got over his unsettled period, Tiger scored some useful wins and took the British Empire middleweight championship from Pat McAteer on a ninth round knockout. He lost to the classy American Spider Webb, outpointed tough Trinidadian Yolande Pompey, and won and lost in bouts with another top American, Randy Sandy.

Soon after, he moved to the United States. 'America made me a better fighter,' he said. 'There I got good training and sparring, but best of all I could go to many fights. I watched and I learned.' Managed by the influential sportswriter Jersey Jones, Tiger lost a few decisions, but he beat world-rated middleweights Joey Giardello, Gene Armstrong, Holly Mims, Florentino Fernandez and avenged his London loss to Spider Webb with a sixth round knockout.

When he wasn't trying to knock men's heads off in the ring, Tiger was a quiet, gentle person known for his frugal lifestyle. He wore old, patched clothes and lived in a cheap hotel. He sent most of his earnings to his wife, Abigail, a former teacher, and their family in Nigeria.

On 23 October 1962 Tiger finally got his big chance. Facing the rugged WBA middleweight champion Gene Fullmer in San Francisco, he used his effective short-range punches to counteract the wider swings of the American. At the end of fifteen gruelling rounds, Tiger proudly accepted the championship belt. He was held to a draw in a return with Fullmer, then stopped the Utah Mormon in seven rounds to win universal acceptance as world champion.

This was the first major sports event ever staged in Ibadan, Nigeria, and 25,000 spectators saw their hero put on what *Boxing News* described as 'a frightening display of scientific slaughter'.

Tiger lost the title in his third defence to the veteran American Joey Giardello, whom he had beaten and lost to before he became champion. The verdict was disputed, but the Nigerian had to wait two years before Giardello gave him a chance to regain the championship. This time it was Tiger who emerged the winner on points. Six months later, he was an ex-champion again, after being outscored by Emile Griffith. Now thirty-six, Tiger seemed to be close to retirement. Instead, he moved up to light-heavyweight and caused a major upset by toppling Jose Torres off the world championship throne. To prove it was no fluke, he outpointed the Puerto Rican for a second time.

Though he owed his fighting success to America, Tiger never lost touch with his homeland. Much of his earnings were sent back to help finance the cause of his Ibo tribe, who were fighting to gain independence from Nigeria and had set up the new state of Biafra. A bloody civil war had ensued and thousands were massacred on both sides, but the Ibo suffered most. Tiger sent $100,000-worth of food and medicine on the 5,000-mile journey to Aba in a private plane. As the war dragged on, thousands more were threatened with starvation from an economic blockade.

Desperate to help out, Tiger agreed to defend his light-heavyweight title against American Bob Foster in May 1968. Foster, a gangling six feet, three inches, towered over the champion by seven inches, and was nine years younger. He was also a pulverising puncher. In the fourth round, a single left hook knocked out the Nigerian for the only time in his career. Even worse was the news from home that members of his family had been imprisoned and his property, comprising a nine-room house, seven apartment buildings, a ranch and shops, confiscated. Angered at the lack of support from Britain for the Biafran cause, he returned the CBE he had been awarded by the Queen. When the Ibo fight eventually ended in defeat, Tiger said in New York: 'Nothing matters any more.'

He fought four more times after the Foster defeat before retiring at the age of forty-two. He lived in a low-rent room in Brooklyn while working as a guard at the Metropolitan Museum of Art. One day in October 1971 he was stricken with a severe pain in his back. He was diagnosed as suffering from cancer of the liver. With the civil war over, the Nigerian government allowed him home to die. His old rival Gene Fullmer said: 'He was a great competitor and champion and, most important, a gentleman.'

GENE TUNNEY

Real name: James Joseph Tunney.

Nickname: the Fighting Marine.

World heavyweight champion 1926-28.

Born in New York City, New York, USA, 25 May 1897. Died in Greenwich, Connecticut, USA, 7 November 1978.

Career: 1915-28.

Total contests: 83. Won: 61 (45 KOs). Lost: 1. Drew: 1. No decision: 19. No contest: 1.

One of the most under-rated of the world heavyweight kings, Gene Tunney was a highly skilled boxer who planned his success, inside and outside the ring, to perfection. Having twice outsmarted the great Jack Dempsey and made his fortune, he retired as undefeated champion and married a multi-millionairess. He became a highly successful industrialist and had the satisfaction of seeing his son become a US Congressman.

Because of his intellectual pretensions, he wasn't a great favourite with fight fans, who liked their heroes more rough and ready, like Dempsey. Tunney was well-read, liked to quote Shakespeare and was a close friend of writers George Bernard Shaw, Thornton Wilder and Ernest Hemingway. When someone suggested he was becoming a snob, Tunney retorted: 'If being a snob is about trying to improve my mind and to learn anything I can from reading books and meeting writers and artists, then I am happy to own up to being a snob.'

Despite his lofty ideals, he didn't come from a privileged background. His Irish immigrant father worked in New York City as a longshoreman, who struggled to provide for his wife and six children. When Gene was three months old, the family moved to an apartment above a grocery store in Greenwich Village. Born James Joseph, he became Gene because of his baby sister's inability to pronounce 'Jim'. As he grew up in an area well known for its artists, musicians and writers, Tunney determined that, one day, he would be as articulate and literate as these people. He didn't have the benefit of a good education, however. He left school at fifteen for a $5 a week clerical job in a shipping company. Correspondence courses in English and maths helped him progress to costing clerk, a prestigious job with the firm.

Attracted to boxing by a neighbour who fought professionally, Gene saw the sport as a sweet science. He couldn't see the sense of taking punches if he could avoid them, and spent countless hours practising defensive techniques. He also learned how to perfect his left jab and developed a strong, if not devastating, right cross. He began professional boxing at eighteen and was unbeaten in his first twelve contests when America entered the First World War. He joined the Marines and won the US Expeditionary Forces light-heavyweight title in France just after the war ended.

Back in civvies in 1919, Tunney continued to progress and manager Billy Roche got him a bout on the undercard to the Dempsey vs Carpentier heavyweight title fight in 1921. He disposed of Soldier Jones in seven rounds, then joined the 90,000 audience for the first million-dollar contest. He saw enough of Dempsey to think that, one day, he could beat him.

Tunney's first championship contest, against Battling Levinsky for the American light-heavyweight title, broke the attendance record at New York's Madison Square Garden with a crowd of 14,428. He won clearly on points. But he learned a painful lesson in his first defence, when Harry Greb gave him a brutal beating and inflicted on him the only defeat of his entire career. In the opening round, Tunney's nose was broken by a head-butt and he suffered a bad cut over his left eye. Two rounds later his other eye was cut. For fifteen rounds, Greb hit him with every punch in the book – and quite a few that weren't – but he couldn't knock him down or make him quit. Tunney lost so much blood that he collapsed in the dressing room afterwards.

Such a display of courage earned him the admiration of many who had considered him a 'Fancy Dan'. While a lot of fighters might have given up the sport after such a savage mauling, Tunney immediately sought a rematch with his conqueror. He got his revenge in February 1923 in a close fifteen-rounder to regain the American title. When they met for the third time, Tunney won by a wider points margin. Their two subsequent meetings were 'no decision' affairs, with Gene having the edge.

Tunney, who left no stone unturned in his efforts to improve his all-round ability, took advice from two past masters of the art, James J. Corbett and Benny Leonard. When he began having trouble with brittle hands, he chopped trees to strengthen them and to develop his upper body. An excellent win over Frenchman Georges Carpentier in fourteen rounds was followed by an even more impressive knockout of Tommy Gibbons, who had taken Jack Dempsey the full distance in a world heavyweight title fight. It was clear Tunney had strength as well as skill.

Gene's elimination of the other leading contenders led him to Dempsey's door and the championship contest was set for 23 September 1926. A crowd of 120,757 braved the driving rain in Philadelphia to see Tunney lift the title on a unanimous decision after ten rounds, the maximum allowed under Philadelphia law. Tunney stunned the champion with a hard right to the head in the first minute and was the master throughout. Promoter Tex Rickard, a master of ballyhoo, beat the drums for a return match. It took place in Chicago, a year after the first clash, and attracted 104,943 spectators who paid a world record $2,658,000. Tunney, who earned $990,445, asked Rickard to write him a cheque for $1 million and paid the promoter the difference. He had the $1 million cheque framed and hung in his office.

Tunney's skills again carried him to victory, but he came perilously close to losing on a knockout in the famous 'long count' incident in the seventh round. A desperate Dempsey had finally caught the champion against the ropes with a barrage of punches to send him to the canvas. 'The Manassa Mauler' had a habit of standing over fallen opponents, ready to strike them the second they got to their feet. Dave Barry, referee in the Tunney fight, insisted that Dempsey go to a neutral corner before he started counting.

Dempsey eventually obeyed, but precious seconds had been lost. Tunney, in the meantime, regained his senses and took full advantage of the delayed count. Although he was upright by the time Barry reached 'nine', he had actually been on the floor for fourteen seconds. Gene, who had practised running backwards for such an eventuality as this, used his nifty footwork to keep out of harm's way for the rest of the round. He again earned a unanimous decision over ten rounds.

Tunney had just one more fight, an easy eleventh round stoppage of New Zealander Tom Heeney, before making his shock announcement to quit. A few weeks later came the news that he was to marry Polly Lauder, heiress to a $40 million steel fortune.

Just as his fighting career had been, except for the one glitch against Greb, success all the way, his venture into the business world was equally profitable. He became chairman of a large insurance corporation, a director of seventeen other companies, and invested well in property. He had a luxury summer house in Maine, which he often loaned to his friend President John F. Kennedy. Gene was a proud man when one of his four children, John, became a US Congressman for California. But he suffered great heartache in 1970 when his daughter, Joan, was convicted of murdering her husband in England, where they had set up home, and was committed to Broadmoor, the hospital for the criminally insane.

Tunney, who suffered from a bad back problem in his latter years, was eighty-one when he died in 1978. Jack Dempsey, who had become a close friend of his old rival, said: 'We were as inseparable as Siamese twins. As long as Gene was alive, I felt we shared a link with that wonderful period of the past. Now I feel all alone.' Dempsey lived for another five years.

RANDOLPH TURPIN

Nickname: the Leamington Licker.

World middleweight champion 1951.

Born in Leamington Spa, Warwickshire, England, 7 June 1928.
Died in Leamington Spa, 17 May 1966.

Career: 1946-64.

Total contests: 73. Won: 64 (45 KOs). Lost: 8. Drew: 1.

The stark statistic that shows Randolph Turpin was world middleweight champion for only sixty-four days should not detract from his right to be regarded as one of Britain's outstanding ringmen. Had he taken greater control of his private life, he would undoubtedly have enjoyed a longer career at the top. His emphatic win over the fabulous Sugar Ray Robinson to capture the world title in 1951 is probably the finest single performance by a British fighter in history. He rather foolishly gave the American a quick return in New York, when he could have made easy money in less demanding defences. Even so, he was on pretty even terms in the rematch until he succumbed to a blinding barrage from a badly cut Robinson.

Turpin had natural knockout power in both hands. His well-developed upper torso was due to weight-training, at a time when this form of exercise was not considered beneficial to boxers. It was thought it would tend to make them muscle-bound rather than supple. He also developed a peculiarly effective boxing style, operating from a wide-legged stance, pulling back from the waist to avoid punches rather than ducking inside them, and leading off with a left jab that American writer A.J. Liebling described as being 'like a man starting his run for the pole vault'.

Randolph was the youngest of five children born to Lionel Turpin, an immigrant from British Guiana, who was the first black man to live in Leamington, and his white wife, Beatrice. Lionel died when Randy, as he became known, was three, and Beatrice had to scrub floors to bring up her family.

The three boys all boxed. Dick, the eldest, was a clever stylist without his youngest brother's punch. He won the British and British Empire middleweight titles and at one time seemed to be on a direct collision course with Randolph. But they had promised their mother they would never meet in the ring. The middle brother, Jackie, was an extremely busy featherweight, but never fought for a title.

Randolph's talent was soon apparent to Police Inspector John Gibbs when the energetic youngster joined his Leamington Boys' Club. Under Gibbs' valuable care, Turpin's aggressive style took him through a very successful amateur career. He won the British ABA junior and senior welterweight titles in the same year. At seventeen, he was the youngest boxer to win a senior title. He won the middleweight prize the following year and caused a sensation in an international match by knocking out highly regarded American Harold Anspach in ninety seconds. Professional managers were queuing up to sign up the exciting teenager, but he decided to join the man who guided his brother Dick's career, Leamington grocer George Middleton.

Turpin made his professional debut at Harringay Arena, London, in September 1946, on the undercard to British heavyweight champion Bruce Woodcock's knockout of world light-heavyweight champion Gus Lesnevich. *Daily Express* writer Peter Wilson reported that the way Turpin leapt on Gordon Griffiths, 'like a bronze tiger devouring a tethered kid, battering him half-way through the ropes until the referee intervened in the first round, was enough to prove that a new middleweight menace had already arrived'.

Though, at nineteen, he was not eligible to fight for a British title, he outpointed Vince Hawkins, the British champion, in an eight-rounder. But woman troubles, which were to loom large throughout his career, led to his first defeat. Accused in court of striking his pregnant wife, he got off on a dismissal, but his mind wasn't on his contest with Albert Finch, who beat him on points. Increased doubts about his dedication to boxing were expressed when he retired in five rounds against tough Frenchman Jean Stock. By 1949, however, he was back on track with eight wins, only one bout going the distance.

When Dick Turpin lost his British middleweight title to Albert Finch, all eyes turned to Randolph to avenge his brother's defeat, as well as his own loss to Finch, and win the title back for the family. Within five rounds, Finch was flat on his back and counted out. Four months later, Turpin added the European title with a forty-eight seconds knockout over Dutchman Luc Van Dam.

Despite his high standing with British fans, few gave Turpin much of a chance when Sugar Ray Robinson stopped off in London at the end of a busy fighting tour of Europe to defend his world title against 'the Leamington Licker' at Earls Court on 10 July 1951. Turpin, as cool as ice, discarded his normal attacking style to thoroughly outscore the American with his lunging left jab and clubbing rights. Turpin also proved much the stronger at close quarters. Robinson, badly cut over the left eye in the seventh round, knew he was a loser for only the second time in 132 contests before referee Eugene Henderson raised the Englishman's hand after fifteen rounds. It was the signal for the 18,000 capacity attendance to join voices in 'For He's a Jolly Good Fellow'.

A more experienced manager than George Middleton would have stalled Robinson when he demanded an immediate rematch. But he felt obliged to meet his commitment and the return went on at New York's Polo Grounds on 12 September, sixty-four days after the London encounter. Turpin was happy with his $200,000 purse. Besides, he felt confident he could beat Robinson again, even without the volume of support he had enjoyed at home. After nine rounds, referee Ruby Goldstein had the fighters even, while the two judges had Robinson slightly ahead.

In the tenth round, Robinson's left eyebrow was split open. Realising that the fight might be stopped, he unleashed a terrific right that caught the champion on the temple and sent him crashing on his back. Turpin rose at nine, but was sent into the ropes by the fury of Sugar Ray's attack. He ducked and swayed to avoid most of the blows, but enough were getting through to cause Goldstein to call a halt. Protests by the British camp that the round had only eight seconds left and that Turpin would have recovered with the benefit of a minute's rest fell on deaf ears. It was also suggested that the referee had been influenced by the death eleven days earlier of a boxer in a New York ring and was afraid to take any chances.

Back on the domestic scene, Turpin stepped up a division to lift Don Cockell's British light-heavyweight title on an eleventh round stoppage. But he still had his sights set on regaining the world middleweight crown. This looked a good prospect when Robinson announced his retirement. Randolph beat the rugged Frenchman Charles Humez to retain his European title, but was disappointed to hear the London crowd booing his wide points win. They had expected more fire from 'Licker', not the restrained boxer who relied on his long left to dominate the tedious fifteen rounds.

It was back to New York in October 1953 to face Carl 'Bobo' Olson, winner of an American elimination series, for the vacant world middleweight title. It was to prove a disaster for the Englishman and the hopes of his loyal fans. From the time he arrived in the States, it was clear that he was unsettled. He neglected his training, which led to a blazing row with Dick, refused to talk to the press and several times threatened to pack up and go home. The reappearance of a woman, Adele Daniels, he had met on the Robinson trip, didn't help. Although Randolph told her his divorce was final and he planned to marry Welsh girl Gwenneth Price, the American woman refused to accept the brush-off. She caused several scenes.

All of this was widely reported and it was no surprise that he entered the ring a 3/1 underdog. Yet, for the first three rounds, he made nonsense of the odds as he tore into Olson, ripping in punches and making the American cover up to avoid the onslaught. It was Turpin's desperate attempt to score a knockout before he ran out of energy. From the fourth round onwards, he was never really in the fight. Floored twice and his left eye cut and swollen, he did exceptionally well to last the fifteen rounds. The verdict for Olson was unanimous. The day before he was due to return to England, Adele Daniels accused him of rape and assault. The case was later settled out of court, with Daniels accepting a paltry $3,500. Turpin's costs were considerably higher.

His boxing career hit rock bottom in May 1954 when he lost his European title on a first round knockout in Rome to Tiberio Mitri, who was not noted as a puncher. Turpin complained afterwards of suffering from double vision. He got back on the winning trail by knocking out Alex Buxton to reclaim the British and Empire light-heavyweight titles he had relinquished years earlier to stay in the middleweight division. He won a Lonsdale Belt outright by beating Buxton again, but was lucky to survive in his final title defence against Arthur Howard. Randolph was down five times, yet fought his way to a clear points victory.

He notched up six more wins before Yolande Pompey brought the curtain down on his career by knocking him out in the second round in September 1958. He scored a couple of knockouts on unlicensed shows, tried his hand at wrestling and even engaged in degrading boxer-vs-wrestler farces. The estimated $300,000 fortune he had earned from boxing long gone, he ended up as a cook in a back-street transport café run by his wife. It was called Gwen's Café, as he didn't want to be pestered by customers asking him about his boxing days and how it all went wrong.

Turpin had never taken care of his taxes and, when he said he couldn't pay a £17,126 demand from the Inland Revenue, he was declared bankrupt. In 1964, a compulsory purchase order was served on the café, which was to be converted to a car park. Two years later, the Inland Revenue were on his back again, for a percentage of his wrestling earnings.

In May 1966, a final tax demand arrived. Turpin took his young daughter, Carmen, to an attic bedroom. Some time later, Gwen found her husband's body slumped by the side of the bed. Carmen had also been shot, but she survived. In a suicide note pinned to the bedroom door, Turpin, aged thirty-eight, had written about his tax problems, but insisted his mind was not disturbed. There was no explanation as to why he shot his daughter.

MIKE TYSON

Nickname: Iron Mike.

WBC heavyweight champion 1986-87. WBA heavyweight champion 1987. World heavyweight champion 1987-90. WBC and WBA heavyweight champion 1996.

Born in Brooklyn, New York, USA, 30 June 1966.

Career: 1985–present.

Total contests: 49. Won: 46 (40 KOs). Lost: 3.

When wild man Mike Tyson made his Dracula-like swoop on Evander Holyfield, biting chunks out of both of the WBA heavyweight champion's ears, he earned the revulsion of the world at large. To boxing fans, who had honoured him as a great fighter, he suddenly became the most reviled champion in history.

Despite its basic savagery, the sport has a generally accepted code of conduct. If you step way over the line, as did Tyson on 28 June 1997, you lose the sympathy and support of the people whose admiration you had gained. What Tyson did was the action of a vicious thug. Like all bullies, he couldn't take it, and resorted to the tactics of the gutter. Boxing would be glad to see the back of him.

In many eyes, Tyson's unforgivable act has served to diminish his standing in boxing history. This would be ignoring the facts, however. It takes more than one night of madness to erase the memory of a man who was one of the most feared fighters of all time. With his tight haircut, no robe, plain black shorts and boots without socks, he looked like a throwback to the champions of old. That's exactly what he was. Old-timers imagined they were seeing a black reincarnation of Jack Dempsey. In the modern era, with massive heavyweights all the rage, the five feet, eleven inches Tyson might appear an unlikely menacing force. But into that squat frame, with its bulging muscles and a nineteen-inch neck that seemed to be part of his back, he packed tremendous power. At his peak, there was no more destructive force in heavyweight history.

While he won widespread admiration for his fistic prowess, he frequently upset many people by his tasteless remarks. Admitting he prolonged his battering of Tyrell Biggs, who was stopped in seven rounds, Tyson said: 'I could have knocked him out any time after the first round, but he talked too much. He didn't show any class or respect. I wanted to make him pay with his health.' His most infamous comment came after his sixth round knockout of Jesse Ferguson: 'I wanted to catch him right on the tip of his nose and push the bone into his brain.'

Trouble was never far away from Tyson. Street fights, car crashes, lawsuits, disputes with trainers and a long catalogue of misbehaviour towards women combined to suggest he was on a determined self-destruct course. While boxing gave him a focus, the real fear was what would happen to him when his ring career was over.

Life was never easy for Mike. The product of a broken home, he roamed the tough streets of Brownsville, New York, as a boy and almost inevitably drifted into crime. By the time he was twelve, he had been arrested thirty times for offences ranging from pickpocketing to armed robbery. Sent to the Tryon School, a correction centre, he came to the notice of Bobby Stewart, a former professional boxer and the school's athletic coach. Stewart soon realised the youngster had the natural ability to make it as a fighter.

He introduced him to Cus D'Amato, the seventy-year-old manager and trainer, who had guided Floyd Patterson and Jose Torres to world titles.

D'Amato not only taught Tyson to box, but he instilled in him a love of ring history by showing him fight films and books and in long talks about the sport. Cus became Mike's legal guardian after Tyson's mother died, but he didn't live to see his protégé become what the old man had no doubt he would be – heavyweight champion of the world. Tyson's management was taken over by Jim Jacobs and Bill Cayton, long-time friends of D'Amato, and owners of Big Fights Inc., a huge library of fight films.

Though he had an impressive amateur career, Tyson failed to make the 1984 Olympics team when he was twice outpointed in the final trials by Henry Tillman, who went on to win the gold medal in Los Angeles. So angry and frustrated was he at his second loss to Tillman that he went outside the arena and used a tree as a punchbag. D'Amato decided Mike was ready for the professional ranks and, with Kevin Rooney brought in as trainer, Tyson dispatched Hector Mercedes inside a round on his debut in March 1985.

Three days after Tyson's eleventh straight win – eight in the first round – D'Amato died of pneumonia. Nine days later, Mike flattened opponent number twelve in seventy-seven seconds. Not only had he shown he was an explosive hitter, but the speed of his punches and his skilful lateral movement impressed everyone. This was one guy who couldn't miss!

At the age of twenty years, four months and two days, he became the youngest heavyweight champion in history when he knocked out WBC titleholder Trevor Berbick in the second round on 22 November 1986. 'I saw the fear in his eyes and I knew I could go for a quick knockout,' said the new champion. Berbick wasn't the first – or the last – to experience that fear. Not since Sonny Liston had turned on his menacing look two decades earlier had opponents felt such intimidation before a punch was thrown. Within a year Tyson had won universal recognition as world champion by defeating WBA titleholder James 'Bonecrusher' Smith and IBF claimant Tony Tucker, although both men took him the distance.

At this stage, Iron Mike looked unstoppable. He was awesome in demolishing Larry Holmes, an outstanding heavyweight king in his time, inside four rounds, and in sending the previously unbeaten Michael Spinks crashing for the count in the opening round. Britain's Frank Bruno gave him a brief scare when he shook him with a left hook, before Tyson brought down the curtain on the pantomime favourite in the fifth round.

While it was plain sailing in his ring career, Tyson's private life was in turmoil. The two men who had meant most to him, D'Amato and Jim Jacobs, had died within three years of each other and he lacked someone close who could keep him in line. A stormy marriage to actress Robin Givens lasted just six months. He got into a street fight with Mitch Green, a former opponent. He crashed his car into a tree, an incident seen by some as a suicide attempt. Bill Cayton, the only surviving member of his original management team, was ditched in favour of flamboyant Don King.

Hardly surprisingly, all this largely self-inflicted pressure affected his preparation for a title defence against James 'Buster' Douglas in Tokyo in February 1990. Yet there wasn't an expert who thought Douglas, a good but unremarkable contender, would cause an upset. In fact, the odds against him winning were 42/1.

From the opening bell, it was obvious Tyson wasn't throwing his usual explosive combinations with 'bad intentions' and was trying to put his challenger away with single blows that lacked timing and accuracy. Only once, in the eighth round, did Tyson produce a vintage punch, a terrific right uppercut that sent Douglas crashing to the floor. The referee, Octavio Meyran, had trouble picking up the timekeeper's count and Douglas was actually down longer than the count of nine he was given.

It was Iron Mike's final fling. He was under fire from a rampant Douglas in the ninth round and, in the tenth, he crumbled under a furious barrage. As the dazed champion fumbled on the canvas for his gumshield, the referee counted him out for his first loss in thirty-eight fights. Don King made a shameful attempt to change the result by claiming Douglas had been given the benefit of a long count, but the decision stood. Tyson commented: 'Losing is no big deal. I'll be back.'

It seemed like the old Tyson when he returned to action after four months to knock out Henry Tillman, who had twice beaten him in the Olympic trials, in the first round. A petrified Alex Stewart also succumbed inside the opening three minutes, but Tyson was unimpressive against Donovan 'Razor' Ruddock, whose stoppage in the seventh round was booed as being premature. Tyson's unanimous points win in a return with Ruddock didn't excite the fans either.

The following month Tyson attended the Miss Black America beauty pageant in Indianapolis. He was accused of raping one of the contestants, Desiree Washington, in his hotel room and stood trial in the spring of 1992. He was found guilty and sentenced to six years in prison. It gave him time to think about the many detours he had made in his life and also to try to work out how his $50 million fortune had dwindled to $15 million. During one court case, he had admitted he didn't know how much money he owned.

Released after three years for good behaviour, he began his comeback with an easy first round defeat of Peter McNeeley on a technical disqualification, when McNeeley's manager, Vinny Vecchione, dived into the ring to save his man from further punishment. A third round knockout of Buster Mathis Junior set up Mike for the chance to get a championship belt strapped around his waist once again.

WBC heavyweight champion Frank Bruno had the look of a condemned man as he strode towards the ring in the MGM Grand Garden, Las Vegas, in March 1996. Tyson performed the part of the executioner to perfection. The finish, in the third round, was cold and clinical. Next victim, Bruce Seldon, conceded his WBA belt when he felt the wind of Tyson's punches sailing over his head. No one saw the 'knockout blow' that downed Seldon in 109 seconds.

Maybe it was complacency, or perhaps a sign of his dwindling powers, but Tyson suffered a sensational loss to Evander Holyfield in November 1996. Holyfield, though never considered more than a 'beefed up' cruiserweight, had twice won and lost versions of the heavyweight title. He had looked 'shot', however, when being stopped by Riddick Bowe and there were genuine fears for his health when the Tyson fight was arranged. But Holyfield 'shocked the world' by standing up to the bully, constantly beating him to the punch, and battering him to an eleventh round stoppage. Tyson, discouraged by the fired-up challenger's refusal to buckle like the others in his comeback, showed little of the upper body movement or punching combinations that were so much part of his earlier winning style. He seemed to think all he had to do was land one big punch and it was all over. Holyfield, however, refused to play his game.

The hugely hyped return match, with Tyson disqualified in the third round after his infamous ear-biting lunges, proved that he would never be the same force he was before his enforced lay-off. Nobody realised that more than Mike himself. That was why the man who had wrecked opponents with his dynamite fists now felt the need to resort to vicious thuggery. Perhaps Tyson, with his great love of boxing history, secretly longed to be back in the early bare-knuckle days, when a couple of ear-bites would be par for the course, along with hair-pulling, eye-gouging and the odd knee between the legs.

Banned from boxing for a year and fined $3 million by the Nevada State Athletic Commission for the Holyfield attack, it was January 1999 before Tyson was back in the ring. His timing affected by his nineteen-months lay-off, he lunged and missed as his South African opponent, Frans Botha, piled up a points lead. But, once again, Mike's big punch came to the rescue. A single right hand to the head sent Botha crashing for the full count in round five.

Within two months, Tyson was back in jail. He was sentenced to a year for punching and kicking two motorists following a minor traffic accident. The Indiana authorities added sixty days to his term for violating his probation for the 1992 rape conviction. His future in boxing was, at best, uncertain.

PANCHO VILLA

Real name: Francisco Guilledo.

World flyweight champion 1923-25.

Born in Illoilo, Philippines, 1 August 1901. Died in San Francisco, California, USA, 14 July 1925.

Career: 1919-25.

Total contests: 105. Won: 73 (22 KOs). Lost: 5. Drew: 4. No decision: 23.

Pancho Villa's life was dramatically cut short when, not yet twenty-four, he failed to recover from an infection following the removal of a wisdom tooth. A relentless attacking fighter with a solid punch for one who stood just over five feet and never weighed more than 115 pounds, Villa is considered by many experts to be the greatest ever Asian ringman. In a career that lasted only six years, the busy little Filipino managed a grand total of 105 fights. He often entered the ring with just a week between contests.

Born Francisco Guilledo, he was given the ring name Pancho Villa by his manager, Frank Churchill, after the famous Mexican revolutionary. He was taught to box by American military personnel based in the Philippines. Most of his early fights were against bigger men, but he had only suffered two defeats and had won two Filipino titles by the time Churchill took him to the United States in 1922.

Within three months of his arrival, Villa was American flyweight champion after knocking out Johnny Buff in eleven rounds. Though he lost the title on a controversial decision to Frankie Genaro, he was built into a major attraction by promoter Tex Rickard.

Rickard offered Welshman Jimmy Wilde a record $65,000 to defend his world flyweight title against the Filipino at New York's Polo Grounds on 18 June 1923. Wilde, though he had been inactive for two years, couldn't refuse what was an enormous sum for that time. The thirty-one-year-old champion was unable to stem Villa's relentless attack. He took a severe beating before the referee came to his rescue in the seventh round.

Villa made four successful defences before taking a non-title fight with Jimmy McLarnin in Oakland, California, in July 1924. Weakened by the extraction of a wisdom tooth the day before the contest, and conceding weight advantage to the future world welterweight champion, Villa took considerable punishment in losing a ten-round decision. He had taken the fight against the advice of his doctor, who saw that his jaw was still swollen following the dental surgery. But the purse of $12,500 was too good to turn down.

Still suffering from his aching jaw, he made another visit to the dentist, who discovered an infection, as well as removing three more teeth. Villa was told by his doctor to take things easy, but that wasn't his nature. He lived it up for a week, until his trainer, Whitey Ekwert, noticed his distress and rushed him to hospital. It was too late. He died in the hospital of Ludwig's Angina, an infection of the throat cavity.

JOE WALCOTT

Nickname: the Barbados Demon.

World welterweight champion 1901-06.

Born in Barbados, British West Indies, 13 March 1873. Died in Massillon, Ohio, USA, 4 October 1935.

Career: 1890-1911.

Total contests: 134. Won: 69 (44 KOs). Lost: 23. Drew: 18. No decision: 21. No contest: 3.

Nat Fleischer, in his book *Fifty Years at the Ringside*, published in 1958, listed his all-time top ten greats in every weight division. His choice as best welterweight was Joe Walcott, known as 'the Barbados Demon', who earned his place ahead of legendary champions like Jack Britton, Ted 'Kid' Lewis, Henry Armstrong, Barney Ross and Jimmy McLarnin. Even allowing for *The Ring* editor's bias towards the fighters from the early part of the century, it is obvious that Walcott was something special.

The West Indian was just under five feet, two inches tall, but he had a powerfully developed body and a long reach. He thought nothing of giving away weight to middleweights – even heavyweights. In 1900, he scored a seven-round win over Joe Choynski, who was over two stone heavier and nine inches taller. Choynski went on to knock out Jack Johnson in three rounds the following year, which gives an indication of the merit of Walcott's performance. Walcott also beat world light-heavyweight champion George Gardner and drew with another of that division's titleholders, Philadelphia Jack O'Brien.

Walcott's family moved from Barbados to Boston, Massachusetts, when Joe was a boy. He boxed and wrestled as an amateur before signing up with professional manager Tom O'Rourke. After thirty-six wins in forty-nine fights, he was offered a crack at George 'Kid' Lavigne's American title in December 1895. The trouble was that it was at lightweight, and Joe was a natural welterweight. Nevertheless, he accepted that opportunities such as this didn't come along too often, especially for black fighters.

According to the *New York Herald*, both men weighed just over 130 pounds. The articles of agreement stipulated that Walcott had to score a knockout to win. In a tremendous battle, Walcott overcame an early beating to hand out savage punishment and almost tear off Lavigne's ear with the strength of his assault. At the end of the twelve rounds, Lavigne got the decision. Fleischer felt that Walcott had won. They met again two years later. Lavigne had beaten Britain's Dick Burge to win recognition as world lightweight champion. In another terrific scrap, Lavigne was floored in the tenth round, but stormed back to force Walcott to quit in the thirteenth.

In 1898, Walcott got a world title chance at welterweight, for which he was better suited, but he lost on points to Mysterious Billy Smith over twenty rounds. This was the only one of their six meetings in which a title was at stake, but they were all vicious brawls. Before one, Smith was required to lodge a bond of $250 guaranteeing his good behaviour. The score for the series was three wins for Walcott, one win for Smith and two draws.

Walcott made no mistake in his second crack at the welterweight crown, knocking out Rube Ferns in five rounds in December 1901. Skulduggery was rife in boxing around the period, and Walcott was adjudged to have lost his title to Dixie Kid on a disqualification, though no one could figure the reason for the referee's action. Later it was discovered that the official had placed a bet on Dixie Kid to win, so Walcott continued to be recognised as champion. Black fighters often were forced to take part in rigged matches. Before he won the title, Walcott was forced to 'throw' a fight against Tommy West because his manager's life had been threatened if he won.

Walcott, who gave boxing tuition to Jack Johnson, drew in non-title fights with fellow blacks Sam Langford and Joe Gans. Then, in a bizarre accident, he shot himself in the hand with the same bullet that killed his friend Nelson Hall.

Joe announced his retirement in 1905, but a year later he was back defending his world title against the quaintly named Honey Mellody. Walcott lost on a fifteen-round decision, and was stopped in twelve rounds in a bid to reclaim the championship from Mellody a month later.

He fought on for another five years, finally hanging up his gloves at thirty-eight. Jobs as a fireman and a porter on a freighter didn't last and he was a down-and-out when his plight was brought to the attention of New York's Lord Mayor Jimmy Walker. The mayor, a long-time fight fan, used his influence to get the ex-champ a job as a handyman at Madison Square Garden.

In 1935, Walcott was killed when struck by a car near Massillon, Ohio. He was buried in nearby Dayton.

JERSEY JOE WALCOTT

Real name: Arnold Raymond Cream.

World heavyweight champion 1951-52.

Born in Merchantville, New Jersey, USA, 31 January 1914. Died in Camden, New Jersey, 26 February 1994.

Career: 1930-53.

Total contests: 72. Won: 53 (33 KOs). Lost: 18. Drew: 1.

If anyone ever needed an inspirational figure to show how patience and self-belief can triumph over adversity, he should look no further than Jersey Joe Walcott. For the first seventeen years of his career, he was beating good heavyweights, losing to a few, and was hovering on the fringes of the top-ten ratings. When he finally got recognition as a genuine contender, it took him five tries at the world heavyweight title before he emerged as champion at the age of thirty-seven years and six months.

On his overall record, Walcott may not seem to deserve ranking among the greats of the century. But who knows what he might have achieved had he got his big chance during his prime years? As it was, he was desperately unlucky not to get the decision in his first challenge to Joe Louis. He took the title from Ezzard Charles in one of the best one-punch knockouts of all time. And had his championship defence against Rocky Marciano taken place today, with title fights limited to twelve rounds, he would have been the first man to beat the Rock. He was way ahead when Marciano finished him in the thirteenth round.

Walcott's real name was Arnold Cream. When he started boxing at sixteen, he didn't relish the prospect of funny newspaper headlines about 'whipped Cream'. He called himself after the old welterweight champion Joe Walcott, 'the Barbados Demon', and added the name of his home state to become Jersey Joe Walcott.

A deeply religious man, with a wife who would produce six children, Walcott's faith in the Lord and in his own fighting ability was put severely to the test many times. So badly treated was he by a succession of unscrupulous managers and promoters that he retired seven times. He laboured on construction sites, drove a truck and worked as a garbage collector. He even joined the dole queue when work was scarce. But he always believed boxing was the way to a better life – if only someone would give him the chance.

That someone was Felix Bocchicchio, a boxing manager who had seen him fight and recognised his talent. When Bocchicchio visited Walcott at his New Jersey home in 1945, Joe pointed to an empty coal-bin in the corner of the living room and said: 'Mister, if you can keep that bin full for me, I will fight for you.' It was filled to the brim from that day on.

In his first three years under Bocchicchio's management, Walcott lost just three times in twenty-one fights and avenged each defeat. Among his victims were top-notch contenders Jimmy Bivins, Joe Baksi, Lee Oma, Curtis Sheppard and Joey Maxim. Still, when he was offered a title tilt at long-reigning Joe Louis in December 1947, the bookmakers thought so little of his chances that they offered even money he wouldn't last five rounds. It was originally planned as a ten-round exhibition bout, but when the New York Commission insisted that exhibitions must be limited to six rounds, promoter Mike Jacobs upgraded it to a title fight.

Louis had been champion for ten years and was making his twenty-fourth defence, yet he was four months younger than the man getting his first title chance. Walcott's style gave the fading 'Brown Bomber' all sorts of problems. A crafty counter-puncher, he confused Louis by frequently stopping boxing and 'going walkabout'. He twice floored Louis with sneak right-handers and almost closed the champion's left eye. At the end of fifteen rounds, referee Ruby Goldstein's scorecard showed Walcott as the winner, but the two judges thought otherwise and enabled Louis to stay champion on a split decision. The crowd reacted with a chorus of boos and jeers.

Walcott got another chance a year later and, though he again put 'the Brown Bomber' down for a count, he was knocked out in eleven rounds in Louis' last title defence. When Louis retired in 1949, Walcott was matched with Ezzard Charles for the NBA version of the title, but was decisively beaten on points. He stayed in contention with two trips to Europe to beat Sweden's Olle Tandberg and German Hein Ten Hoff. A particularly impressive performance was his third round knockout of Harold Johnson, a future world light-heavyweight champion, in Philadelphia. This bout often crops up in boxing quizzes for an odd coincidence. Fourteen years before his 1950 win over Johnson, Walcott had knocked out Phil Johnson, Harold's father, also in the third round – and also in Philadelphia.

After being outpointed by Ezzard Charles for a second time, though it was much closer than their initial encounter, Walcott seemed unlikely to get another try. But Bocchicchio, claiming the last verdict was a robbery, mounted a successful publicity campaign. Together with his two challenges to Louis, Jersey Joe's bid for Charles' title in Pittsburgh on 18 July 1951 was his fifth attempt to lift the world crown. He knew this was his last chance – and he took it in style.

An inspired Walcott belied his years by outboxing and frequently hurting the champion, then finishing him off with a magnificent left hook to the chin in the seventh round. Twenty-one years of failure and disappointment were wiped out with that one memorable punch. The bookmakers again made Charles the favourite in the return match a year later, but Walcott kept his title on a close decision. Waiting in the wings was the menacing figure of one Rocky Marciano.

When the fight with Marciano was arranged for Philadelphia on 23 September 1952, Walcott showed contempt for the heavy-hitting, unbeaten challenger. 'This will be one of the easiest fights I have had,' he said. 'Marciano is an amateur. He wouldn't have qualified for Joe Louis' Bum of the Month Club.' Jersey Joe's confidence seemed to be justified when, midway through the first round, he put Marciano on the floor with a left hook. Rocky was up at three to continue his ceaseless advance, but the champion constantly beat him to the punch and gave him a boxing lesson. By the start of the thirteenth round, Walcott was ahead on the judges' scorecards by eight rounds to four, by seven to five, and by seven to four with one even. Even if he lost the last three rounds, the worst he would have got was a majority draw.

One thunderous right hand to the jaw – a punch that matched Walcott's left hook knockout of Charles for perfect delivery and dramatic effect – wiped out all of the champion's early good work. He never had a hope of beating the count. Recalling the event many years later, Walcott said: 'I felt the great, deep hurt of losing a fight that was so one-sided. In no fight that I ever fought did I ever feel better or more confident.'

Clearly, Walcott had no real heart for another long bruising battle with the irrepressible Marciano. He took the count after just two minutes and twenty-five seconds of the first round at Chicago in April 1953. He pocketed his $250,000 cheque and never fought again.

Joe worked as a parole officer for juvenile offenders and maintained his connection with boxing by becoming a respected referee, although his reputation was badly sullied by his poor handling of the second Muhammad Ali vs Sonny Liston affair.

He served as sheriff of Camden, became chairman of the New Jersey State Athletic Commission and was a director of special projects for New Jersey Governor Brendan Byrne. He also played a part in *The Harder They Fall,* the boxing movie based on Budd Schulberg's novel.

The man regarded by esteemed trainer Eddie Futch as 'one of the finest technicians in heavyweight boxing history' died a month after his eightieth birthday in 1994.

MICKEY WALKER

Real name: Edward Patrick Walker.

Nickname: the Toy Bulldog.

World welterweight champion 1922-26. World middleweight champion 1926-31.

Born in Elizabeth, New Jersey, USA, 13 July 1901. Died in Freehold, New Jersey, 28 April 1981.

Career: 1919-35.

Total contests: 163. Won: 93 (60 KOs). Lost: 19. Drew: 4. No decision: 46. No contest: 1.

Some fighters' nicknames are contrived or downright silly, but Mickey Walker's tag, 'the Toy Bulldog', was entirely appropriate. He got the name for his grim determination not to let go once he had an opponent on the hook. He wasn't a one-punch knockout artist, but he overwhelmed his rivals with the speed and ferocity of his attacks. He also used a clever bob-and-weave style to avoid punishment as he made his way forward.

Though he stood only five feet, seven inches and never weighed more than 170 pounds, he frequently took on light-heavyweights – even heavyweights – and beat them. One of his finest achievements was to hold Jack Sharkey to a draw, eleven months before Sharkey won the world heavyweight title. Most of the ringside reporters thought Walker should have got the decision. In a sixteen-year career, he fought fifteen world champions.

Outside the ropes, Walker was equally adventurous. A notorious womaniser, he had a long list of girlfriends and married seven times. Three of these were to women he had married before, prompting the wisecrack that he not only had return fights, but return marriages. There were numerous stories of how he would leave the bed of a latest girlfriend, go to the arena to fight, then take off on an all-night drinking session with his friends and hangers-on.

Brought up in the Irish district of Elizabeth, New Jersey, Walker was a professional fighter at seventeen. Within three years, he was world welterweight champion after easily outpointing veteran Jack Britton. He defended the title four times before being dethroned by Pete Latzo. Legend suggests he had been on a drinking spree beforehand and just about sobered up in time to realise the referee was raising Latzo's hand.

During his spell as welterweight champion, Walker had tried for Harry Greb's middleweight belt. After a terrific fifteen-rounder, Greb was declared the winner on points. When they met up later at a night-club, it is said, the two fighters started joking about the fight, but then got serious. Walker said to Greb: 'If you hadn't stuck your thumb in my eye, I'd have knocked you out.' Greb retorted: 'Come on out in the street and we'll see who knocks who out.' The unofficial 'rematch' was quickly broken up by the police. After losing his welterweight championship to Latzo, Walker made a second bid for the middleweight title, now in the hands of Tiger Flowers, in December 1926. Mickey dropped Flowers twice without a count, but he suffered a cut eye and seemed to be outscored over ten rounds. Nat Fleischer described the decision for Walker as 'one of the worst ever handed down in a ring'.

For his first defence, 'the Toy Bulldog' took his belt to London.

Challenger was the talented Scot Tommy Milligan. Walker and his flamboyant manager, Jack 'Doc' Kearns, were fearful of a raw deal and insisted on nominating their own referee. They put forward Georges Carpentier as candidate, but the challenger wanted Eugene Corri to officiate. The Americans then brought the negotiations to a point of absurdity by proposing the Prince of Wales for the job. That was too much for promoter C.B. Cochrane, who said he would cancel the show if Corri wasn't acceptable. Walker and Kearns then backed down.

Their caution was understandable. They had bet Walker's entire £20,000 purse on his winning, at odds of 3/1 in favour of the British champion. Milligan put up a game show, but was no real match for Walker and was stopped in ten rounds.

Walker and his entourage nipped over to Paris for a riotous few weeks until the money was gone.

Now struggling even to make middleweight, Walker proved he could more than hold his own among the light-heavyweights by beating two former champions in that division, Mike McTigue and Paul Berlenbach. An attempt to capture his third world title at different weights failed, however, when he was outscored by master craftsman Tommy Loughran in a light-heavyweight championship bout. After two successful defences of his middleweight crown against Ace Hudkins, Walker decided it was too much trouble getting off the poundage and relinquished the title. His real ambition was to capture the heavyweight championship and he was good enough to beat much bigger men, including Paolino Uzcudun, King Levinsky, Johnny Risko, Jim Mahoney and Bearcat Wright, who outweighed him by one hundred pounds and was almost a foot taller.

Despite his meritorious draw with Jack Sharkey, Walker proved no match for another former heavyweight champion, Max Schmeling, in Long Island City, New York, in September 1932. The German gave him a frightful beating before Mickey retired after eight rounds. Writer Paul Gallico reported: 'Walker was a study in pain in the last round. Can you imagine how he must have hurt? His mouth was cut. Both eyes were shut. One of them was cut. His lips were mashed. He had nothing but a smear on his face and into that smear Schmeling kept driving his fists...'

Mickey wisely abandoned his heavyweight hopes after that and got his second crack at the light-heavyweight title in November 1933. Though outpointed by Maxie Rosenbloom, he beat 'Slapsie Maxie' in a non-title bout the following year. He also drew twice with Bob Godwin, the former NBA light-heavyweight claimant, before retiring in 1935.

He opened the Toy Bulldog Tavern, a successful restaurant and bar on New York's Eighth Avenue, which was a popular meeting spot for sports writers and fans. He wrote a boxing column for the *Police Gazette* and even trained women boxers. His variety of other jobs included acting and salesman for a distillery. Later he developed his hobby of painting and his primitive art won critical acclaim. He beat a drink problem and, for a short spell, did a night-club comedy routine.

By the mid-1970s, his money – and his women – had gone. Suffering from Parkinson's disease, he was found unconscious on the street, having fallen and struck his head. Admitted to hospital, he was diagnosed as suffering from amnesia and anaemia. A charity fund was set up to look after him. The one-time 'Toy Bulldog' was seventy-nine when he died in 1981.

PERNELL WHITAKER

Nickname: Sweet Pea.

IBF lightweight champion 1989-92. WBC lightweight champion 1989-92. WBA lightweight . champion 1990-92. IBF light-welterweight champion 1992-93. WBC welterweight champion 1993-97. WBA light-middleweight champion 1995.

Born in Norfolk, Virginia, USA, 2 January 1964.

Career: 1984–present.

Total contests: 45. Won: 41 (17 KOs). Lost: 3. Drew: 1.

Slick southpaw Pernell Whitaker picked up titles in four weight divisions with the ease and cunning of the Artful Dodger picking pockets. Hailed as a Willie Pep of the 'nineties, he is an expert at making opponents miss with clever feints and subtle shifts of direction. Although not a powerful hitter, he puts together impressive combinations which have a cumulative destructive effect, enabling him to compile a fair percentage of short-route wins.

Until August 1996, *The Ring* rated Whitaker as best current pound-for-pound fighter in the world. It then conceded that his best days were probably over and gave the spot to Roy Jones. Despite its long-term support for Whitaker's status, the magazine was less impressed by the fighter's attitude. In its October 1996 issue, *The Ring* stated: 'The guy's a great fighter and a future hall-of-famer, but on the personality meter he registers somewhere below zero. Forget that he's cocky. No harm there. But we've found him to be rude and inconsiderate. Let's face it: boxing doesn't have many stars. How many like Whitaker can we afford?'

His ring antics didn't please the purists either. When he fought Alfredo Layne, he jumped in the air, spun around and hit him on the jaw. Against Roger Mayweather, he pulled his opponent's trunks down to his knees. His favourite move was to slip a punch, duck down, step around and slap his rival on the butt. 'People pay good money to see me fight,' he said. 'I feel I owe it to them to put on a show. One thing they know for sure: they come to see Sweet Pea, they get their money's worth.'

Pernell, one of a family of three brothers and four sisters, grew up close to the Scope, a sports arena in Norfolk, Virginia, and his boyhood dream was that some day he would top the bill there. He climaxed a brilliant amateur career of over 200 contests by winning the 1984 Olympic Games lightweight gold medal. Turning professional that year, he made such rapid progress that his manager, Lou Duva, decided to put him to the test against experienced Roger Mayweather in only his twelfth fight. Whitaker was knocked down early on, but gained a convincing points win over the future WBC light-welterweight champion.

The victory took him into contention for a title shot and, in March 1988, he challenged Jose Luis Ramirez for the WBC lightweight belt in Paris. Whitaker was favoured to beat the French-based Mexican in a battle of southpaws. It looked as if he had justified the odds by outscoring Ramirez over twelve rounds, but the split decision went to the local hero. Whitaker dropped to the floor in disbelief as the verdict was announced.

Though upset at the loss of his unbeaten record in such controversial circumstances, he knew his chance would come again – and next time he would make certain. It was 18 February 1989, when Whitaker climbed into the ring before an enthusiastic crowd of his supporters in Hampton, Virginia, to bid for Greg Haugen's IBF lightweight title. Whitaker performed brilliantly to totally outbox the dour, rugged champion. He floored Haugen for the first time in his career and seemed to get better and better as the fight progressed. The decision was unanimous, with two of the judges awarding Whitaker every one of the twelve rounds. Life grew even sweeter for 'Sweet Pea' six months later when he gained revenge over Ramirez. This time Whitaker was the complete master and gained a unanimous decision. The win also added the WBC belt to his IBF prize.

Further praise was heaped on the Virginian when he unanimously outpointed the legendary Azumah Nelson in defence of his two titles. He wiped out any doubts about his right to recognition as world lightweight champion by knocking out WBA titleholder Juan Nazario in the first round in August 1990. This proved he had power to go with his sweet skills.

Whitaker forsook the lightweight division in 1992 to take the IBF light-welterweight title from Rafael Pineda, then took another step up to beat Buddy McGirt for the WBC welterweight belt. There was only one man the experts said could match him – the magnificent Mexican Julio Cesar Chavez. The showdown everyone wanted to see was arranged for Mexico City's San Antonio Alamodrome on 9 October 1993.

Chavez had won all of his eighty-two fights, seventy inside the distance. Whitaker had only that questionable loss to Ramirez, against his twenty-nine wins, thirteen by the short route. More than 56,000 people paid to see the fight live, making it the tenth greatest drawing card in history. Millions more watched it on worldwide TV. If the fight generated great interest in the build-up, the result stirred up more prolonged debate. Chavez took the early rounds with his ceaseless aggression, but he found difficulty coping with Whitaker's jab-and-move tactics when the champion stepped up a gear. So confident in the later stages was Whitaker that he took the fight to the Mexican and even forced him to retreat. *Boxing Illustrated*'s Bert Randolph Sugar got a bit carried away with his report that Whitaker 'did for boxing what Degas did for ballerinas, what Van Gogh did for sunflowers, what Warhol did for soup cans ... He laid layer after layer of his masterpiece on the canvas.' But the thrust of his words was fair enough. Whitaker had outshone the master.

In the final analysis, of course, it was how the judges saw the fight that mattered. One gave it to Whitaker by 115 points to 113. The two other officials had them dead even at 115-115. The result was a majority draw. It meant that Whitaker kept his WBC welterweight title, but that didn't ease the pain of being robbed of outright victory.

Just to prove how far he could stretch his capabilities, Whitaker outscored Argentinian hard man Julio Cesar Vasquez in March 1995 to capture the WBA light-middleweight championship, but immediately gave it up to concentrate on his welterweight title.

As he entered his thirties, Whitaker lost some of his speed, but compensated to some extent by punching with greater authority. He dropped rugged Wilfredo Rivera, and put Scotland's Gary Jacobs down twice – and almost out – in the last round, but had to be content with a points win each time. He beat Rivera twice in 1996, the first time on a split decision, but he dominated the return match.

There were disquieting reports of Whitaker's lack of discipline in his private life and his fondness for drinking. His deterioration seemed to be emphasised by having to come from behind to halt Diobelys Hurtado in the eleventh round of his eighth defence of the WBC welterweight title. Not surprisingly, Whitaker was a 7/2 underdog when he put his belt up for grabs against the sport's newest superstar, Oscar De La Hoya, at the Thomas and Mack Center, Las Vegas, on 12 April 1997. De La Hoya, the reigning WBC light-welterweight king, was moving up to try for the welterweight crown. The Californian, aged twenty-four, had won all of his previous twenty-three fights, all but three inside schedule.

Once again, a Whitaker decision was dogged by controversy. Although the three judges made De La Hoya the winner by margins of 116-110, 116-110 again and 115-111, most of the ringside media had Whitaker ahead at the finish. Pernell scored the only knockdown of the fight, although it looked more of a slip, and scored well with his right jab against a man five inches taller. De La Hoya did most of the chasing and shook the champion at times, but Whitaker was always ready to trade with him. After the fight, De La Hoya said: 'Whitaker's style is the most difficult I'll ever have to face because he does things that no other fighter does. But I felt I did enough to win the fight with no problem.'

Whitaker said: 'That was the Pernell Whitaker of old. You can't hit what you can't see. I showed I still have the legs of a twenty-one-year-old. I'm not whining. Oscar's a good fighter, but he never came close to hurting me. I'm the best fighter in the world pound-for-pound and there's a whole lot left in Pernell Whitaker.'

But his deterioration was painfully evident when he returned to the ring after an enforced absence of sixteen months, during which he had been in drug rehabilitation and was arrested for drunk driving. Challenging for Felix Trinidad's IBF welterweight title in February 1999, Whitaker was hit more often than in any of his previous fights. Though he lasted the distance against the unbeaten champion, he was outscored on the judges' cards by 118-109, 117-110 and 118-109. It was the first time Whitaker, who afterwards went to hospital with a broken jaw, could have no argument with the verdict.

JIMMY WILDE

Nicknames: The Ghost with the Hammer in his Hands, the Mighty Atom.

World flyweight champion 1916-23.

Born in Tylorstown, Glamorganshire, Wales, 15 May 1892. Died in Cardiff, Wales, 10 March 1969.

Career: 1910-23.

Total contests: 145. Won: 130 (99 KOs). Lost: 3. Drew: 1. No decision: 11.

No one can seriously dispute that Jimmy Wilde was the greatest British fighter of them all. Though only five feet, two inches tall and never weighing more than the present light-flyweight limit of seven stone, ten pounds (108 pounds), he cleaned up the flyweight division and frequently beat bantamweights and even featherweights.

The little Welshman had a phenomenally successful record. He was only beaten three times and held to a draw once in 145 fights. Wilde claimed he actually had 854 contests, but it is impossible to substantiate this. He included hundreds of appearances in boxing booths, which were unrecorded. On one occasion, it is said, he took on all-comers for three and a half hours, scoring nineteen knockouts. Then he rested for thirty minutes and won four more times before heading home with a 'fortune' of £40 in his pocket. Nat Fleischer once mistakenly listed Jimmy in his *Ring Record Book* as two and a half inches tall. When informed of his slip-up, Nat remarked: 'I'm not surprised. He didn't look any bigger than that.'

Wilde was the only man named as the greatest fighter in his division's history by Fleischer who still retained his number one spot when *The Ring*'s editorial team drew up a new list in 1994. It rated him the best-ever flyweight, ahead of Miguel Canto, Pascual Perez, Frankie Genaro and Benny Lynch. Watching old ring legends on film can often be a disillusioning experience, but Wilde, seen against Joe Symonds in 1914, is revealed as a quick-footed, clever boxer with tremendous accuracy and power in his fists. He fought from a wide-legged stance, his hands resting on his thighs, as he sought openings to launch his furious barrages. His career total of inside-the-distance wins was only one short of a hundred.

Like so many Welsh fighters, Wilde got his first boxing instruction while working in the mines. One of his workmates was Dai Davies, a former prizefighter, who became his landlord and sparred with the eager youngster in the only room available, his bedroom. Because the space was so confined, Jimmy learned the body shifts and defensive skills that were to stand him in such good stead in later years.

His landlord's daughter, Elizabeth, accepted his marriage proposal, but only on the understanding that he would quit the ring. He obeyed his vow – for a while. Pretty soon he was drifting back to the booths, making sure he didn't pick up any cuts or bruises to give a clue to his wife what he was up to. He found the best way to keep his secret was to knock out his opponents before they could do any damage. This was how his terrific hitting power was developed. When there was a pit strike, Elizabeth was convinced by her husband that he could earn more than enough with his fists to pay the bills. His professional boxing career then began in earnest.

Though Teddy Lewis became his manager of record, Elizabeth controlled his finances and even acted as his sparring partner, wearing a protector made from an old corset, when required.

Although Wilde was unbeaten in twenty-eight fights when he arrived at the Blackfriars Ring for his London debut in 1910, the wife of promoter Dick Burge protested about allowing 'a mere boy' into the ring. Jimmy told her he was a married man with a child and proceeded to knock out his opponent in forty-five seconds. Still he found it difficult to get London bookings. Promoters were afraid that, because he was so puny, they would be accused of bad match-making. Only when a Frenchman was found who was even smaller than himself was he able to perform at the prestigious National Sporting Club. He put up such a classy showing in stopping his opponent in six rounds that it was clear no one need worry about his welfare.

His career moved ahead from then on and, in January 1915, he was matched with Tancy Lee for the British and European flyweight titles. Wilde contracted influenza a few days before the fight and his manager, Teddy Lewis, along with wife Elizabeth, advised a postponement. Jimmy, however, had waited so long for his big opportunity that he didn't want to let it slip. Severely weakened, he took a fierce bombardment from the tough Scot. Though floored several times, he refused to quit. His cornermen took the decision for him, throwing in the towel in the seventeenth round.

Just over a year later, Wilde stopped Joe Symonds in twelve rounds to win the British title in a bout also billed as for the world championship. He gained revenge over Tancy Lee and knocked out Johnny Hughes in contests advertised as world title fights, but only earned worldwide acclaim as a true champion when he flattened Young Zulu Kid, a New York-based Italian whose real name was Giuseppe di Mefi, in the eleventh round in December 1916.

Wilde served as a British Army physical education instructor during World War One. During this period, he took part in numerous exhibitions that kept him fit. He could get leave for an actual fight, but was not allowed to accept monetary payment. He was still in uniform at the end of the war, when he was asked to appear in a charity contest against featherweight Joe Conn. The Welshman's canny wife got around the fee stipulation by accepting a bag of diamonds worth £3,000 on Jimmy's behalf. Wilde, though outweighed by twenty-one pounds, put Conn away in twelve rounds.

Jimmy suffered only his second career loss when outpointed by Memphis Pal Moore over three rounds in the bantamweight final of the Inter-Allied King's Trophy Competition in London in December 1918. He beat Moore over twenty rounds a year later and also notched up a fine points win over Joe Lynch, who would go on to capture the world bantamweight title the following year.

In 1920, Wilde toured the United States and was unbeaten in his twelve fights. Back home, he took an ill-advised match with Pete Herman, who had only lost his world bantamweight title three weeks earlier. Money, however, was always the prime consideration with the Welshman and the £8,000 purse was too good to turn down. Wilde, knowing he would be conceding more than a stone if the American came in at his normal weight, insisted on there being two weigh-ins, one on the day before the contest and the other at the ringside just before the bout. When fight time arrived, Herman, who was over the agreed poundage, refused to go on the scales again. Wilde insisted on the terms of the contract being met and it looked like there might be a riot as the crowd realised there wouldn't be a fight. Only after a personal plea from the Prince of Wales, who visited him in his dressing room, did the Welshman announce that he would go ahead with the contest. Wilde fought gallantly against the younger, stronger and much heavier American until, in the seventeenth round, he was rescued from further punishment by the referee.

It was two years before Wilde got back in the ring. Generally thought to have retired, he accepted a £13,000 offer to defend his world flyweight title against Pancho Villa at the Polo Grounds in New York on 18 June 1923. A month past his thirty-first birthday and ring-rusty after his lay-off, Wilde took a severe beating from the faster, nine years younger Filipino. Knocked flat on his face by a sizzling right that landed just as the bell rang to end the sixth round, he insisted on coming out for the next round. Elizabeth buried her face in her hands as her husband was battered to the canvas for the full count.

The badly concussed ex-champion spent four hours on the rubbing-table being treated by a doctor. It was fully three weeks before he was able to recognise his wife. The first thing he told her was that he would never fight again. He kept his word.

For many years, Wilde wrote a newspaper column, often antagonising readers with his dismissive comments about current fighters in comparison to those of his era. He was seventy-two when he was beaten up by a gang of thugs at Cardiff railway station. He never fully recovered and, for the last four years of his life, he was unaware of who he was or what a great champion he had been.

IKE WILLIAMS

Real name: Isiah Williams.

NBA lightweight champion 1945-47. World lightweight champion 1947-51.

Born in Brunswick, Georgia, USA, 2 August 1923. Died in Los Angeles, California, USA, 5 September 1994.

Career: 1940-55.

Total contests: 154. Won: 125 (60 KOs). Lost: 24. Drew: 5.

One of the outstanding world champions in the period immediately after World War Two, Ike Williams used short, jolting punches to score many knockouts. He also showed versatility with his grace and finesse. He beat most of the leading lightweights in an era when talent was plentiful and was good enough to defeat welterweight champions Kid Gavilan and Johnny Bratton (three times) in non-title bouts.

Born in Brunswick, Georgia, Williams moved to Trenton, New Jersey, with his family when he was a boy. He started boxing as an amateur in 1938 and made his professional debut at the age of sixteen. Although he fought often, he found progress slow and was badly set back by a heavy defeat by Bob Montgomery in January 1944. He took an unmerciful pounding until, in the twelfth round, he slid to the floor to be counted out.

Wins over top-ten rated fighters Joey Peralta, Willie Joyce and former world champion Sammy Angott saw him soar in the rankings and he captured the NBA version of the world lightweight title by blasting out Mexican veteran Juan Zurita in the second round in April 1945. The fight took place in Mexico City and the result almost caused a riot. Williams held his championship belt for five minutes before it was taken from him. He never saw it again.

After halting Enrique Bolanos in eight rounds in his first defence, he gave Welshman Ronnie James a glimpse of his championship belt at Ninian Park, Cardiff, on 4 September 1946. That was all it was – a quick look. Whatever notions the British champion had of snatching the trophy were ruthlessly dismissed. Williams scored six knockdowns before applying the *coup de grâce* in the sixth round. The British fans marvelled at the knockout blow, a right-hand bolo punch, which they had never seen before. *Boxing News* described Williams as a 'truly great' champion, whose body punches were so powerful that the Welshman's 'gasps for breath and cries of pain as they landed could be plainly heard'.

Ike got himself into trouble with the all-powerful Managers' Guild when he split with his manager, Connie McCarthy, to go out on his own. The guild made it difficult for him to get meaningful fights, until he signed up with a new manager, Frankie 'Blinky' Palermo. The well-connected Palermo succeeded in getting him a match with Bob Montgomery, the New York-recognised champion, for the undisputed world lightweight title in August 1947. He well and truly avenged his knockout defeat by Montgomery, hammering him to defeat in six rounds. The win gave him extra satisfaction, because he alleged Montgomery had 'fought me very dirty' the first time.

In 1951, Williams testified to the US Senate's investigation of organised crime's ties to boxing that Palermo often suggested to him to throw fights. He insisted that he never took a dive, but admitted that he often 'carried' opponents. Sometimes he never saw a penny of his purses, he told the Kefauver Committee.

Ike kept his strong hold on the world title by thwarting the hopes of

Enrique Bolanos (twice), Beau Jack, Jesse Flores and Freddie Dawson. When he wasn't risking his championship belt, he mixed with top welterweights like Kid Gavilan, who outpointed him twice, Johnny Bratton, whom he stopped in eight rounds, and Joe Miceli, who won two of their three clashes.

Clearly no longer a lightweight, he was forced to shed twenty-one pounds to make the limit for a title defence against Jimmy Carter in May 1951. The effort proved too much and he was stopped in the fourteenth round by the unsung challenger. So little chance had Carter been given that only 3,594 fans paid into Madison Square Garden. It was the smallest crowd ever to attend a championship fight there.

Williams concentrated on the welterweight division from then on, but his best days were behind him. He was halted in ten rounds by Gil Turner, lasted less than five rounds against Chuck Davey and was outscored by Carmen Basilio. He only won two of his last six fights, finally calling it quits in 1956 after drawing with fellow veteran and former rival Beau Jack, then stopping Jack in nine rounds in his farewell appearance.

Interviewed in retirement for *In This Corner*, Williams told author Peter Heller: 'I had so many fights. I made so much money. Like, in 1948 I made almost a quarter of a million dollars, just that one year alone ... I did a first class job of managing my money real bad. Gambling heavy on golf, playing golf ... I gave an awful lot away too. I felt if you was going to help someone, give it to them, don't lend it to them, because if you lend it to them you're going to lose friendship because they're not going to pay you back. At least if you give it to them, you're not looking for it.'

Ring historian Hank Kaplan told *Boxing Monthly*'s Graham Houston in 1994, just after Ike's death at the age of seventy-one: 'Williams had to be on anybody's list of all-time great lightweights – a great, great lightweight. He was a 'payday' puncher who didn't waste anything, and a clever, cool kind of boxer too. He would have been a greater fighter had he not been handled by the Mob guys. He was a mild-mannered guy and they paid him what they wanted to pay him, not always what he was entitled to.'

AD WOLGAST

Real name: Adolphus Wolgust.

Nickname: the Michigan Wildcat.

World lightweight champion 1910-12.

Born in Cadillac, Michigan, USA, 8 February 1888. Died in Camarillo, California, USA, 14 April 1955.

Career: 1906-20.

Total contests: 133. Won: 59 (38 KOs). Lost: 11. Drew: 13. No decision: 50.

Including Ad Wolgast among the ring greats might seem to be stretching credulity a bit too far. The German-American was acclaimed as much for his extraordinary ability to absorb punches as he was for handing them out. But few fighters in history matched his raw courage and adamant refusal to admit defeat. Unfortunately, Wolgast paid a terrible price for his hit-or-be-hit style of fighting. He took so many savage beatings in 133 battles stretched over fourteen years that he wound up in a sanatorium for the mentally ill.

As his nickname 'the Michigan Wildcat' signifies, his tactics were simply to wade in and keep punching until the other fellow dropped. He was a terrific hitter, especially to the body, although he wasn't too fussy if his blows landed above or below the belt. Referees were either remarkably tolerant, or they knew what to expect when Wolgast was in action and turned a blind eye to his indiscretions. He was disqualified only four times.

Wolgast had his first fight in 1906, at the age of eighteen. He had lost only once in sixty-nine contests when he challenged Battling Nelson for the world lightweight title at Port Richmond, California, in February 1910. In a brutal marathon contest, with both men giving and taking sickening punishment, Wolgast had his blood-soaked right glove raised in the fortieth round as the referee, Eddie Smith, belatedly responded to the crowd's calls for a stoppage.

Five challengers over the next two years were thwarted by Wolgast. One of his victims was Englishman Owen Moran, who had caused a sensation by knocking out Battling Nelson in eleven rounds. Against Wolgast, Moran collapsed in the thirteenth round, his face contorted in agony as he clutched his groin. The referee, Jack Welch, saw no foul and awarded the fight to Wolgast on a knockout.

It was not unusual in those days for world champions to pick their own referees, and it was no surprise that Welch showed up for Wolgast's next defence, against Mexican Joe Rivers. What happened was one of the most blatant incidents of biased officiating in boxing history. In the thirteenth round of another bloody brawl, Wolgast sank a low blow into the challenger's body. At the same moment, Rivers connected with a left hook to the jaw. Both men crashed to the canvas, with the champion on top. It looked like one of boxing's rarest happenings – a double knockout. But as Wolgast struggled to get to his feet, the referee gave him a helping hand, while continuing to count over Rivers. The bell rang before he got to ten. As both boxers staggered to their corners, Welch signalled that Wolgast had won on a knockout. The official ran for safety as the challenger's fans fought to get their hands on him. Welch later justified his action by alleging that Wolgast's punch had landed first.

Justice was done in Wolgast's sixth defence, in November 1912, when he was disqualified for fouling Willie Ritchie. The challenger had insisted upon an independent referee. Jim Griffin got the job. Wolgast's crude swings failed to disturb the cool, crafty challenger. A tiring and frustrated titleholder was knocked down twice in the sixteenth round. While on the canvas, he struck out and hit Ritchie below the belt, earning his instant dismissal.

Two years later, Wolgast was matched with Freddie Welsh, the Welshman who had beaten Ritchie for the world title. Although the Welch-Wolgast bout was billed as a title fight, historian Barry Hugman, author of the *British Boxing Board of Control Yearbook*, insists it could not have been, as both men were over the 135-pound weight limit. Wolgast broke a bone in his arm in the eighth round and could not continue. The two men met again on 4 July 1916, in a legitimate title fight. Wolgast was disqualified in the eleventh round. The terrible effects of his long, gruelling career were becoming apparent. He quit after being knocked out in two rounds by Young Francis, only the second time he had lost inside the distance, but came back for one more fight – a four-round draw with Lee Morrissey – three years later.

By 1927, his irrational behaviour had caused him to be committed to a sanatorium in Camarillo, California. He would spend the last thirty-eight years of his life there. In his dementia, he worked out regularly so that he would be ready for another crack at the world title when the offer came.

CARLOS ZARATE

WBC bantamweight champion 1976-79.

Born in Tepito, Mexico, 23 May 1951.

Career: 1970-88.

Total contests: 65. Won: 61 (58 KOs). Lost: 4.

The bantamweight division has produced many outstanding champions, but it's hard to argue with *The Ring*'s choice of Carlos Zarate as the pick of the bunch. In its list of the top five bantamweights, he made the top spot ahead of Eder Jofre, Ruben Olivares, Manuel Ortiz and Panama Al Brown.

Zarate, tall for his weight at five feet, eight inches, used his reach to advantage, but his typical approach was to stalk his opponent relentlessly until he found the right moment to unleash his crushing blows. The Mexican was one of the hardest hitters, pound-for-pound, in history. Of his sixty-one victims, only three were around to hear the final bell. Three of his four losses occurred when he stepped out of his normal division to try for the super-bantamweight title. The other was a hotly disputed decision which cost him his WBC bantamweight belt.

A professional at eighteen, Zarate never ventured outside his homeland for the first four years of his career. He built up an impressive knockout record, most of his victories completed inside three rounds. In May 1976, he fought for only the second time outside Mexico to challenge fellow-countryman Rodolfo Martinez for the WBC bantamweight title at the Inglewood Forum in Los Angeles. Zarate floored the champion in the fifth round and finished him off in the ninth. It was his thirty-ninth win by the short route in forty fights.

The best performance of Zarate's career was his savage destruction of another big-hitting Mexican, Alfonso Zamora, the WBA titleholder, at Inglewood in 1977. Unfortunately for Zarate, it was a non-title affair. Zamora, a1972 Olympic silver medallist, had compiled an impressive twenty-nine consecutive wins inside the distance, including five world title defences. Zarate dominated the fight, knocking down his rival three times.

Zarate's great winning sequence finally came to a halt in October 1978. He got a trifle too ambitious in attempting to relieve the brilliant Wilfredo Gomez of his WBC super-bantamweight championship. Suffering from the effects of influenza, Carlos was stopped in five rounds.

In his own division, he reigned supreme. He defended his title nine times against challengers from four continents – proving a world champion in the true sense. His grip on the WBC belt was finally prised loose by his stablemate, Lupe Pintor, in June 1979. The points decision was highly controversial. Two judges made Pintor the winner by a single point (143 to 142) while the third had Zarate ahead by a massive 145-133 margin. The Associated Press reporter gave it to Zarate by nine points. Carlos pleaded with the WBC to reverse the verdict, but the organisation's president, Jose Sulaiman, while agreeing the decision appeared to be incorrect, refused to change it.

Disgusted with his treatment, Zarate announced his retirement. He made a comeback seven years later and seemed to have lost none of his old power as he racked up another twelve quick wins. His last two fights, however, resulted in defeat. Challenging for Jeff Fenech's

WBC super-bantamweight title in Sydney, Australia, in October 1987, the Mexican lost on a technical decision in four rounds. Fenech suffered a bad cut under the right eye, which American referee Hank Elespuru ruled had been caused by an accidental butt. He ordered the judges' scorecards to be added up. Fenech led by forty to thirty-four points on all cards.

Zarate tried again for the same title four months later, but was stopped in the tenth round by fellow-countryman Daniel Zaragoza. Aged thirty-six, he looked an old, tired fighter as he failed to keep pace with the faster, busier southpaw champion. Though he wasn't floored, Zarate took a pounding and was rescued by the referee after being badly shaken by a left to the chin. He realised he no longer had it and hung up his gloves for good.

Author's Top Ten

Okay, it's head-on-the-block time. Having opened the debate with my choice of the best hundred boxers of the century, I'm probably inviting the wrath of fight fans everywhere by narrowing it down to a top ten. For what it's worth, here is my choice (with apologies to those who nearly made it):

1. Sugar Ray Robinson
2. Muhammad Ali
3. Joe Louis
4. Henry Armstrong
5. Willie Pep
6. Roberto Duran
7. Archie Moore
8. Sugar Ray Leonard
9. Jimmy Wilde
10. Benny Leonard

Acknowledgements and Bibliography

My trip down boxing's memory lane, and my re-acquaintance with so many ring legends, has been, for me, a fascinating and rewarding journey. It was only made possible through the enterprise, skill and diligence of many authors and historians. For anyone wishing to pick up the trail, I can do no better than recommend they consult the following excellent works:

Arnold, Peter, *History of Boxing*, Deans International Publishing, London, 1985.

Blewett, Bert, *The A-Z of World Boxing*, Robson Books, London, 1996.

Butler, Frank, *A History of Boxing in Britain*, Arthur Barker, London, 1972.

Collins, Nigel, *Boxing Babylon*, Robson Books, London, 1991.

Fleischer, Nat, *The Heavyweight Championship*, Sportsmans Book Club edition, London, 1954.

Fleischer, Nat, *Fifty Years at the Ringside*, Corgi Books, London, 1960.

Frazier, Joe, with Phil Berger, *Smokin' Joe: the Autobiography*, Robson Books, London, 1996.

Giller, Norman, and Neil Duncanson, *Crown of Thorns*, Boxtree, London, 1992.

Golesworthy, Maurice, *The Encyclopaedia of Boxing*, Robert Hale, London, 1971.

Grombach, John V., *The Saga of the Fist*, A.S. Barnes, New Jersey, 1977.

Gutteridge, Reg, *The Big Punchers*, Stanley Paul, London, 1983.

Harding, John, *Lonsdale's Belt*, Robson Books, London, 1994.

Heller, Peter, *In This Corner*, Dell Publishing Company, New York, 1973.

Hugman, Barry J., *The British Boxing Board of Control Yearbook*, 1985 to 1997.

Lewis, Morton, *Ted 'Kid' Lewis: His Life and Times*, Robson Books, London, 1990.

Morrison, Ian, *Boxing, the Records*, Guinness Superlatives, Middlesex, 1986.

Mullan, Harry, *The Illustrated History of Boxing*, Hamlyn, London, 1987.

Mullan, Harry, *The Ultimate Encyclopaedia of Boxing*, Hodder and Stoughton, London, 1996.

Odd, Gilbert, *Encyclopaedia of Boxing*, Hamlyn, London, 1983.

Roberts, James B., and Alexander G. Skutt, *The Boxing Register*, McBooks Press, New York, 1997.

Roberts, Randy, *Papa Jack: Jack Johnson and the Era of White Hopes*, Robson Books, London, 1986.

Schulman, Arlene, *The Prizefighters*, Virgin Books, London, 1995.

Sugar, Bert Randolph, and Nat Fleischer, *The Ring Record Book*, The Ring Publishing Corp., New York, 1980.

Suster, Gerald, *Champions of the Ring*, Robson Books, London, 1992.

Suster, Gerald, *Lightning Strikes*, Robson Books, London, 1994.

Walsh, Peter, *Men of Steel*, Robson Books, London, 1993.

Magazines: *Boxing Monthly, Boxing News, International Boxing Digest* (formerly *Boxing Illustrated*), *The Ring*.

Videotape series: *Boxers*, Marshall Cavendish Collection. *The World's Great Fights*, Rank Home Video. *Boxing's Greatest Champions*, Pickwick Videos.

Photographs in this book are from the author's private collection and from Derek O'Dell.